ADVISOR LIFE

A Business Coach's Collection of

Short Stories

With

Tools, Techniques, and Transformational Moments

DANIEL C. FINLEY

Copyright © 2023 Daniel C. Finley
Edited by Melissa M. Denham
All rights reserved. No part of this book may be reproduced, stored, or transmitted by any means—whether auditory, graphic, mechanical, or electronic—without written permission of both publisher and author, except in the case of brief excerpts used in articles and reviews. Unauthorized reproduction of any part of this work is illegal and is punishable by law.
ISBN: 9798853988224

DEDICATION

This book is dedicated to my loving parents David H. Finley and Janice Kathleen Finley who not only gave me life, but unconditional love, which in turn makes life worth living. It's amazing how a parent's love can fuel a child's dream; thus, my tank is forever full.

Their constant and never-ending encouragement during my early years in this business was the driving force behind my success. Without my parents, my will to succeed in the financial services industry would have been short-lived; thus this book would have gone unwritten.

The memory of my father, his faith, and the words that he lived by still hold true today,

"GOD is good, all the time!"

Table of Contents

Preface xiii
    An Advisor's Journey xiii

Introduction xix
    Living the Advisor Life xix

Chapter 1   **The Advisor's Evolution:** *Mastering Tools & Techniques to Create Transformational Moments* 1

Chapter 2   **Advisor Solutions Tools:** *Equipping You with Instruments for Success* 11

Story #1	Building a Balanced Business	14
Story #2	The Bottom Line List	17
Story #3	Being Passionately Productive	20
Story #4	How to Keep Score of Your Success	23
Story #5	Realizing the Advisor's Rejection Spectrum	26
Story #6	The One Minute Business Coach	29
Story #7	Conquering Self-Talk	32
Story #8	Finding Your Flow	36
Story #9	The New Business Strategy List	39
Story #10	Beyond the Gatekeeper	42
Story #11	Monologue vs. Dialogue	46
Story #12	Great Questions Create Great Connections	50
Story #13	Realizing the Importance of the Filler Formula	53
Story #14	The Empathetic Advisor	57
Story #15	Five Elements of the Agreement Close	60
Story #16	Doing the Mood Dance	63
Story #17	Sell the Sizzle	68
Story #18	Understanding the Reconnection Strategy	71
Story #19	The Power of Pause	74
Story #20	The Flipside of Foolish	76
Story #21	The First Appointment F.O.R.M	78

Story #22	The Power of Preparation	82
Story #23	The Client-Centered Referral Dialogue	88
Story #24	Strategically Segmenting Your Client-Base	92
Story #25	Being Proactive in a Reactive Environment	96
Story #26	What It Takes to Shine	98
Story #27	How to G.R.O.W. the Business from Within	101
Chapter 3	**Advisor Solutions Techniques:** *Equipping You with the Skillsets for Success*	**104**
Story #28	Protecting Your Inner Peace	107
Story #29	Do You Know How to Read Your Gauges?	110
Story #30	How Coachable Am I?	113
Story #31	Beyond the Silver Bullet Mentality	117
Story #32	The Emotionally Intelligent Advisor	120
Story #33	The Snowball Effect of Solutions	124
Story #34	Keep Swinging For the Fences	127
Story #35	Understanding the Standards Circle	130
Story #36	Embracing Change	133
Story #37	Lug It or Leave It!	136
Story #38	Five Strategies for Connecting During the Process	139
Story #39	What's in Your Whitespace?	142
Story #40	The Focused Advisor	146
Story #41	The First Step	149
Story #42	Ascending Into Greatness	151
Story #43	The Flipside of Failure	156
Story #44	The Art of Rejection Perception	158
Story #45	The Top 5 Myths of Prospecting Procrastination	161
Story #46	Creating a Positive Prospecting Attitude	164
Story #47	Building Rapport	166
Story #48	Beyond the Band-Aid	169
Story #49	The Subtle Art of Helping Prospects Understand	174
Story #50	Properly Preparing for a Closing Appointment	177
Story #51	The Science of Service	179
Story #52	Pushing Past the Upper Limit	182
Story #53	Managing Uncertainty	185

Story #54	The Solutions Formula	187
Story #55	The Elephant in the Room	190
Story #56	Establishing Constructive Connections	193
Story #57	Practicing the Principle of Strategic Replacement	195
Story #58	Crafting Your Desired Outcomes	198
Story #59	Sowing the Seeds of Significance	201
Story #60	The Value of Vulnerability	203
Story #61	Opening the Door to Opportunity	206
Story #62	Leveraging the Power of LinkedIn	209
Story #63	Connecting the Room	212
Story #64	Getting Comfortable with Being Uncomfortable	215
Story #65	The Mind Space Exercise	218
Story #66	Creating an Effective Email System	221
Story #67	The Science of Systems	224
Story #68	The Power of Belief	227
Story #69	Striving for Excellence	230
Story #70	The Significance of Self-Leadership	233
Story #71	Strategies for Measuring Success	238
Story #72	Turning Busyness into Business	241
Story #73	Just Get Out There and Do It!	243
Story #74	Redefining Your Reference Point	246
Story #75	What Every Genius Knows	249
Story #76	Mastering the Art of Excellence	252
Story #77	Stretching Beyond Your Business Limitations	255
Story #78	Creating an Attitude of Gratitude	258
Story #79	The Science of Success	261
Story #80	What Is Your Focus?	264
Story #81	Action is the Antidote to Anxiety	267
Story #82	Listening to Your Wake-Up Call	270
Story #83	No More Excuses	273
Story #84	Taking Action is THE Key Ingredient	276
Story #85	Where There is A Will, There is a Way	279
Story #86	Building Your Business in a Bear Market	282
Story #87	Beyond the Blame Game	286
Story #88	Building Healthy Business Habits	289

Chapter 4	**Advisor Solutions Transformational Moments:**	
	The Evolution of Success	292
Story #89	Writing the Next Chapter	295
Story #90	Do What You Love and Love What You Do	297
Story #91	The Will to Succeed	300
Story #92	The Paradox of Pain in Your Practice	303
Story #93	Are You Only Tuned into Station W.I.I.F.M.?	305
Story #94	Reaching Beyond Your Limiting Belief System	307
Story #95	Heroes to the Rescue	310
Story #96	You Are Not Alone	314
Story #97	What is Your Why, What, When, Where and How?	317
Story #98	Lasting Lessons	320
Story #99	Groomed for Greatness	322
Story #100	The Seriousness of Success	325
Story #101	Put Me In, Coach!	329
Story #102	Winning the Inner Game of Business	332
Story #103	Creating a Childlike Curiosity	336
Story #104	The Reality of Creating a Record Setting Year	338
Story #105	The The Client's Evolution	342
Story #106	Is There Passion In Your Practice?	345
Story #107	Watching Where You Step	347
Story #108	The Advisor's Guide to Perseverance	350
Story #109	It Is All About Perception	352
Story #110	To Give is To Get	355
Story #111	Learning From the Lessons of Failure	358
Story #112	The Picasso Factor	361
Story #113	Beyond "Yeah But..." and "What If..."	364
Story #114	Maintaining the Momentum	368
Chapter 5	**Putting the Last Puzzle Piece into Place:**	
	Summary	372
Afterword		376
	Leaving The Advisor's Legacy	*376*
Acknowledgements		379

References 384

About Advisor Solutions 385

About the Author 388

"Living the life of an advisor is not an easy one. It takes honesty, integrity, and expertise at all times!"

Dan Finley

Business Development Consultant/Business Coach

2023

PREFACE
An Advisor's Journey

In the fall of 1993, I was a twenty-six-year-old unemployed young man looking for a job in Milwaukee, Wisconsin, a city in which I knew less than a dozen people. Just a week earlier, I had lived in Summit County, Colorado, the home of six major ski resorts! I had been living an easy life in a beautiful place, enjoying my position as a group sales coordinator for the largest lodging company in Summit County. I had moved there the previous year with a girlfriend who was willing to leave the Midwest behind and start a new life in the mountains, and for that, I will forever be grateful.

It was agreed upon that we would live in the mountains for one year and then move back to be closer to her family by moving to Milwaukee, which was just a few miles from the small town in which she was born and raised.

When I arrived in Milwaukee, I was faced with the reality that I had no family close by, no friends and no job! Immediately, I secured what I refer to as "transitional employment" by becoming a waiter at Olive Garden.

Then, I tracked down an old friend whom I had lost contact with that I knew lived in the area. Later, he would become my next roommate. In the short term, having some type of income and finding an old friend gave me a sense of comfort. But, I had no idea what would happen in the long-term and the transformational moment that was about to occur!

It was in the journey of trying to find employment that would yet again take an unexpected turn. That it would become more about finding my career or my own advisor's journey.

The unemployment rate was high in Milwaukee at the time and finding the right type of job was not easy. I had mailed over one hundred resumes looking for any type of sales or marketing position available. I didn't much care where I worked but rather that I found some type of employment that would have unlimited potential, so I could stop living off of my credit card!

One day I opened up the want ads (since we didn't have the internet back then) and read a job posting that would forever change my life. It read, *"Registered Investment Advisor position available. Must be personable. For more information, call."* While I had no idea what a Registered Investment Advisor did, I did know that I liked the title and I was curious to find out more. So, I called the next day and got an interview.

I arrived early to meet with the portfolio manager and was greeted at the door by the receptionist. Mary was a forty-three-year-old wife and mother of two teenage boys who had worked for the firm since it began. The portfolio manager was running late and by the time he was available, I had already felt like I had known her all of my life.

She wished me good luck as I nervously walked back to the portfolio manager's office to have an interview about a job that I knew nothing about, in an industry that I knew even less about! Somehow, that interview went well enough to get a phone call from Mary the following day letting me know that the portfolio manager would like me to come in for a second interview and to meet the other two principal partners.

The second interview went just as well as the first. And, again, Mary called the following day asking if I would come in again to speak with the principal partners once last time.

I'm sure by now you have realized that they offered me the position, but what you don't know is the reason why. It wasn't my experience, knowledge of the stock market, or the financial services industry. In fact, I must have had a look of shock on my face when they extended the job offer to me because after accepting, the portfolio manager asked, *"Do you know why we are offering you this position?"* I admittedly replied, *"No....I have no idea!"* All three principal partners laughed and the portfolio manager said in a matter-of-fact voice, *"Mary told us to hire you!"*

What I didn't know at the time was that she was married to one of the principal partners and that everyone respected her. If it weren't for her I would not have begun in the financial services industry thirty years ago as of this writing. And, you would not be reading this book today!

After passing the Series 65 exam, I officially became a Registered Investment Advisor. I was hired with the sole purpose of cold calling business owners and comptrollers to discuss how our hedged equity portfolio or our model mutual fund portfolio might work for a portion of their pension or profit-sharing dollars. This might seem like a relatively simple task, but at the time, I was completely ignorant about either of these types of portfolios.

Now, I was forced with the reality that I pretty much knew next to nothing about the market, investing, sales, prospecting, and above all, handling rejection. I did know that I liked meeting with business owners more than I liked cold-calling them! Thus, I tried to develop my appointment-setting skills as quickly as I could, so I searched for any tools and techniques that could help me.

After a year, I realized that it was time to move on to a bigger firm, so I could get additional training as well as be able to build my own business instead of working for others to build theirs. In full disclosure and with the blessings of the three principal partners, they understood my position and even allowed me to use their phone, computer and fax machine. They each gave me a letter of recommendation as I looked for the next stop in my journey.

Within a week, I had seven interviews as well as two job offers! It was the culture of a small regional firm called A.G. Edwards & Sons,

Inc., as well as the gut feeling I had about the branch manager in the downtown Milwaukee office, that made me feel like this would be my new home. For the next four years, I built a business from scratch and managed to open up over 500 accounts!

During that time, the branch manager had hired several rookies and oftentimes he would send them to me for the second interview, not because I was in management, but because he wanted me to let him know if I thought they would make it in business.

One day he asked me if I would stay late that evening for Pizza Night, in which he would order pizzas, and I would teach the rookies how to cold call and handle objections. I replied, *"Sure, I'm here every night cold calling until 8:00 p.m. anyway, so I'm happy to help!"* Neither of us knew it at the time, but by the mid-1990s, I was already taking on the role of coach.

In the summer of 1999, I realized that it was time to move closer to my hometown of Prescott, Wisconsin. My niece had been born six months earlier and I didn't want to see another one of my nieces and nephews grow up without me being around.

So, I transferred to the A.G. Edwards & Sons. Inc. office in downtown Minneapolis and kept my entire client base. It didn't take long before my new branch manager learned about my coach role and he asked me to help the six rookies in his office. Once again, I began teaching the tools and techniques that were working for me to help others so they could see lasting change!

In January 2004, I realized that it was time to make coaching advisors and agents a full-time business instead of just helping the rookies in my office. So, I created **Advisor Solutions,** a business development consulting and coaching service for financial advisors and insurance agents.

Since launching **Advisor Solutions**, I have coached thousands of financial advisors and insurance agents, logging an estimated 25,000+ coaching hours in individual and group coaching sessions.

My coach role has morphed into several additional roles over the years, such as consultant, professional speaker, facilitator, course creator, blogger, host of The **Advisor Solutions** Podcast, a contributing author as well as a published author of (now) two books!

However, the thing I am most proud of is that I have created countless tools and techniques, which in turn have created numerous transformational moments for my clients! The amount of success that my clients have had throughout the years is overwhelming. When a client says, *"I would be out of the business if it weren't for you?"* it reinforces that I have taken and still am taking the right steps forward on my journey.

That is why I wrote this book. I wanted to make sure that my readers could take a step in the right direction by having the tools and techniques that they need to be successful in this industry! My story is just one of the countless **Advisor Solutions** success stories that you will soon read.

My wish is that you digest the stories in the pages of this book to become inspired to take action, so that you can live your best **Advisor Life!**

Daniel C. Finley

November 3, 2022

Introduction
Living the Advisor Life

Living the life of an advisor is not an easy one. Whether you are a financial advisor, insurance agent or wholesaler your business consists of providing knowledgeable advice and exceptional service to those who have entrusted their financial futures to you.

You have decided that this is your calling and as you know, the professional life that you have chosen is not a fit for everyone. *"If it were easy, everybody would do it!"* is a phrase that I've heard time and time again over the course of my thirty years in the financial services industry.

The reason why it is not easy and not a fit for everyone is because each day brings with it new challenges and unless you learn from your mistakes, you are destined to repeat them. Those that don't learn from errors tend to wash out of the business early on, or if they do make it past the survival stage tend to remain stuck on a production plateau.

And, that's what this book is all about, understanding and applying the tools, techniques and transformational moments that are the solutions to your challenges, so that you can live your best life as an advisor (or agent or wholesaler).

But, let me digress a bit since this isn't my first book.

On the morning of December 24, 2011, I set my alarm because I wanted to wake up early and see if the one present that I had wanted to give myself for two and half years had arrived. I quickly ran to my home office, logged on to my computer and went to the UPS website to track the package.

Apparently, during the course of the night it had shipped from a UPS hub in Minneapolis, and traveled to my front doorstep. I rushed down the stairs, retrieved the package and carefully opened up the box to make sure that I didn't damage the fragile contents inside.

And there it was, my inaugural book...**101 Advisor Solutions:** *A Financial Advisor's Guide to Strategies that Educate, Motivate and Inspire!* This 473-page book had taken two years to write, and another six months to format. I couldn't believe my eyes, what was once just a thought had now come to fruition and was sitting on my dining room table!

I started in the financial services industry in 1993 as a Registered Investment Advisor. In 2004, I co-founded **Advisor Solutions** with my great friend Gene Lawrence who unfortunately unexpectedly passed away two years later. After five years of coaching financial advisors, insurance agents, wholesalers, branch managers and agency managers I had accumulated a plethora of challenges that my clients had experienced.

But, unlike most who don't make it in the business or stay stuck on a production plateau, I took it upon myself to find the solutions and begin to coach others on how to look at every obstacle as an opportunity. As a result, in May 2009, it was time to put these challenges and solutions together in a book.

The Process Begins Again

The interesting thing about writing a book is that it never seems to turn out the way you think it will. You may have all the planning, rough drafts, rewrites and edits that you expected, but somewhere along the way it inevitably, organically evolves into a finished product that varies from the original framework.

When I announced the idea of writing the book to Melissa Denham, my editor (www.thewordmuse.com), she had a number of questions regarding how the book would be mapped out. My thought was simple, we accumulate at least 101 common challenges that advisors and agents had shared with me over the previous five years of coaching, followed by the solutions that I had provided to them.

Then, we separate out the topics based on different facets of the business, such as motivation, time management, prospecting and sales, so that the reader could easily see how the combination of these solutions could help them. That was the original plan.

The reality was that the original plan morphed into including a toolbox at the back of the book because we knew we had referenced several tools within my solutions and we needed to expound on what those were in greater detail.

We also decided to add an Advisor Success Story section between all of the challenges and solutions chapters and tools to help with readability. And, the next thing I knew, two and half years went by and the book had exponentially grown to 473 pages!

As I stared at the first copy of my inaugural book, I thought to myself that I would never write another word again because I had shared all of my coaching wisdom. I had no idea of knowing at the time how dead wrong I was. And, over the course of the last decade, it became clearer and clearer there was much more for me to share because as much as I was coaching my "clients", they were teaching me and pushing for different solutions to new challenges.

In 2014, The National Association of Insurance & Financial Advisors (NAIFA) was kind enough to allow me to do a series of free group coaching sessions twice a month for their members. These group sessions were so popular that we continued doing them for six years!

What I remember most about those sessions was that it was a lot like my inaugural book, but in real time. In other words, advisors and agents would attend the session and answer this question, *"What is your #1 challenge?"* I would call on a group member, hear their challenge and coach them with the solution(s).

I rarely knew what challenges they were going to discuss. Oftentimes, others would say, when I would ask what their single takeaway was from being in the group coaching session that they had experienced the same challenge that someone who I had called upon had. As a result, they would get just as much out of listening to their peers being coached as they did when they were speaking.

I took this same concept and format all across the U.S., professionally speaking to local NAIFA and FPA chapters. It turned into my signature presentation and no two presentations were alike because I never knew what challenges the audience would bring up during the presentation, but I had an arsenal of solutions from years of coaching!

What Does This All Have to Do With the Book You Are Holding Right Now?

This book is a deeper dive into the daily struggles that my clients had experienced before they received coaching. I am assuming many of those struggles are what you most likely are experiencing today. In fact, over the course of almost two decades of coaching advisors and agents and over a decade since my last book was published, I am absolutely confident that there are a number of stories in this book that will resonate with you.

If there is one thing that I hope that you glean from this book it's this: whatever challenges you have gone through, whatever challenges you are going through right now and whatever challenges you will go through in the future, just know…there is always, always, always a solution!

Dale Carnegie has a great quote that sums up this point best, *"The past is where you learned the lesson. The future is where you apply the lesson. Don't give up in the middle!"*

My hope for you is that you not only can relate to these stories, but can embrace them as well, so that you do not give up somewhere in the middle! Instead, you learn from not only your own past challenges, but the past challenges of the advisors and agents in this book and live a life full of understanding and applying the tools, techniques and transformational momentum that are the solutions to your challenges, so that you can live your best life as an advisor-**The Advisor Life!**

How to Read and Apply this Book

As you read through this book you will quickly notice that it is split up into three sections: tools, techniques and transformational moments. All of these are important for any advisor and/or agent to utilize to get to the next level with their business.

Your business is like a puzzle. Let's say that you have a 1000-piece puzzle sitting in the box and you've never put a puzzle together before. You might be tempted to dump out all the pieces onto the table and start quickly sifting through them to find two pieces that fit together.

However, since I have put countless puzzles together I would be the first to tell you that there is a right and a wrong way to do it.

I would suggest that you start by turning all of the pieces picture-side-up and determine the method for putting this puzzle together that will work the best. I would suggest that you first look for the corner pieces. It might seem like a small step, but if you can find all of the corner pieces and put them together then you have a framework for the entire puzzle.

Next, you need to group all of the remaining pieces by color; thus, creating piles of grouped colored puzzle pieces. In other words, if you have a section in the lower left-hand corner that is blue you will start placing all of the blue pieces together in that area.

Finally, you begin to see the picture on the box take shape when you have all of the corner pieces and enough similar colored sections nestled together. Eventually, you fill in any missing pieces and you are finished!

What Does Putting a Puzzle Together Have to Do With This Book?

As I had said earlier, your business is like a puzzle. Ironically, each day that you are working "IN" your business and not working "ON" your business is like having one half-done puzzle taking up space on your table. All of your current and future business challenges most likely seem overwhelming. And, if you don't ever find the solutions to your challenges you might feel like you have missing puzzle pieces!

In addition, now that you understand my suggested process for putting a puzzle together you will also understand how the analogy makes sense with the following descriptions as it pertains to this book:

Tools are like the corner pieces of the puzzle. They create the architecture for taking your business to the next level. In my inaugural book, I included an entire section called The **Advisor Solutions** Toolbox: *Equipping You with Strategies for Success,* in which I explained twenty-six of my coaching tools. However, I did not give real-world examples of how my clients or I have applied the tools. In this book, you will read how this is done by the accompanying story that is applicable to each tool!

Techniques are like the non-corner pieces of the puzzle or in this case the heart of the business that make up the details of what to do and how to do it. Typically, techniques are the step-by-step processes that will help you to make effortless connections with prospects and clients alike. Take for instance learning several prospecting techniques, those would be like the aforementioned example of taking a pile of blue puzzle pieces, noticing that the picture on the box has a lot of blue in the lower left-hand corner, putting those pieces together and finishing that part of the puzzle!

Transformational Moments are moments that transform your business. The more you apply the Tools and Techniques to become habits the more you will have Transformational Moments where you realize that your business is now taking shape and it's starting to look like your business vision (aka a completed puzzle).

I have found that most people read a book in one of two ways: either cover to cover or as a reference guide, seeking out specific topics found in the table of contents and going to the appropriate pages and reading only those passages.

This book is designed to help you do both!

I recommend that you first read it cover to cover. Take your time…digest each tool, then each technique and lastly each transformational moment. The reason is this book is not meant to be devoured in one sitting. Rather, read ten stories or so and absorb the concepts before you move on to your next helping.

As you read, ask yourself this question—*"Is this something that I have gone through, am going through or could possibly go through?"* Since I'm a big believer in you getting the most out of this book, please grab a highlighter, magic marker or red pen and circle what stands out most to you. Then take your newfound knowledge and apply it.

Why? Well, I've seen too many people get information, but then don't want to do what it takes to make lasting transformation!

As you read the stories you may also notice that it seems conversational, as if you are eavesdropping on a session between a financial advisor or insurance agent and myself—the advisor's business coach. This book was intended to be read this way so that you would truly live the experience of how the interaction happened.

Finally, if you are a fan of the **Chicken Soup for the Soul** book series, which consists of inspirational true stories about ordinary people's lives, you will love **Advisor Life:** *A Business Coach's Collection of Short Stories With Tools, Techniques and Transformational Moments.*

I am taking you into the lives of ordinary people who have done extraordinary things by turning obstacles into opportunities to build a better business…one solution at a time!

Now, let's begin…

Chapter 1
The Advisor's Evolution:
Mastering Tools & Techniques to Create Transformational Moments

Your business is typically in one of three states, either trending up, down or resting on a production plateau. If your business is trending up, that's great! Keep doing what you are doing and you will keep seeing continued success. If your business is going down, something must happen to turn the boat around because it can only go in that direction for so long before you are out of the business.

So, the question is ...*what can you do right now to make sure that you row in the right direction?*

If your business is not where you want it to be then it's time to learn about and master the tools and techniques in this book to create the types of transformational moments for yourself that you will soon read about that come from your peers.

But, before we do that let's first learn some lessons from our past so we can move towards a better future as well as how the evolution of the **Advisor Solutions** Tools, Techniques and Transformational Moments came to be.

A History of Tools

The creation of tools has shaped the course of history. They are the most important items that humans have used for protection, gathering food and survival. The earliest evidence of humans using tools was from the Stone Age, which was more than 2.6 million years ago.

During this time, humans experienced harsh climate conditions because the Earth was in an Ice Age. As a result, our ancestors survived by inventing the right types of tools that were based out of necessity rather than any sense of luxury.

When you think about the tools of the Stone Age period you might think that every tool was made of stone. However, during the later era period other raw materials such as bone, ivory and antlers were used.

When you think about the tools they used during that era you may picture spears, hand axes or scrapers. But, one of the most important tools that were invented at that time was the needle! It allowed our ancestors to sow animal hides together and stay warm when they weren't able to be near a fire.

So, what does all of this talk about tools have to do with you and your business?

Well, as Abraham Maslow, the American psychologist said it best, *"If the only tool you have is a hammer, you tend to see every problem as a nail."* In other words, if you don't have the right tools you may not survive or you may be able to survive, but certainly not thrive!

Have you ever wondered what your business would be like if you didn't have any tools? Would you or even could you be successful?

The Evolution of Advisor Solutions Tools

When I began in the business in 1993 I shared a computer and an office with a colleague. Although the computer had a CRM tool, I did not have access to the Internet. So, I essentially used it to keep track of new or current prospects and when to follow up with them.

Today, most advisors and agents not only have access to an elaborate CRM system, but have a whole host of information, software and hardware to assist them in managing client communications and tasks. However, a CRM has its limitations and as such, I was finding from coaching clients over the years that additional tools were an absolute necessity.

In January 2004, Anney F. a rookie independent financial advisor was my first coaching client. She had a charismatic nature, strong work ethic and a true desire to succeed. I had been coaching her on a weekly basis around challenges and solutions that would help her get past her survival stage. During my early days of coaching, I only had one tool to give my clients. My clients would fill out what I call "The Pre-Session Questions" which was a seven-question questionnaire that helped me to better understand the details around that week's obstacles before we met for coaching.

It remains a part of my coaching process to read a client's Pre-Session Questions and know exactly what tools, techniques, strategies and solutions that we should review that week.

But, back then I had not created any additional tools except for that questionnaire and that was just a variation of what a business coach had sent to me years earlier.

"Anney, did you apply what I taught you last week?" I excitedly asked when we began our coaching session. *"I did but I have forgotten a lot of what we talked about."* There was a strange silence on the phone as if she was trying to choose her next words carefully, *"Do you ever write this stuff down? That way I could read it or at least have the tools we talked about in our coaching sessions and I could reference them when I try to apply the solutions each week."* she hesitantly replied.

My stomach sank when I realized that I was making her life harder. *"No."* I paused, *"I just explain what works and then you go and do it. I guess I should write down what we talk about or at least map out the tools I'm explaining, so that you can apply them better."* There it was, the cold hard truth. Having a conversation about the solutions wasn't enough. What clients needed most were tool templates.

3

And, just like that the evolution of **Advisor Solutions** Toolbox was born. Every time I had a solution I created a tool or template so that clients could have something to reference.

Over the course of the next few years, I realized that most financial advisors, insurance agents, wholesalers, branch managers and agency managers have similar challenges. When I would run into a challenge that I didn't have the solution for I would research the subject, find the solution, try and find a tool to implement the solution, learn the tool and then teach my client how to apply it.

If I couldn't find the tool I would create one. Eventually, I had over forty different tools and resources that I had ended up creating while looking for tool and template solutions. As a result, I have created an extensive toolbox of **Advisor Solutions** Tools to help advisors and agents!

A History of Techniques

Just as the creation of tools has shaped the course of history, so has the advancement of techniques. And, one of the most important examples of this is our ancestor creating techniques to control fire. There is some debate over the approximate time of when this first began but campfire remains found in South African caves suggest that controlled fire could have begun approximately 1 million years ago.

Since this evidence was found deep inside the caves, scientists suggest that it was a protected environment less prone to spontaneous natural fires. One thing is for sure, the evolution from a non-controlled fire (such as from lightning strikes) to controlled fire that our ancestors could create on their own had a lasting impact of them.

The evolution of fire starting techniques range from using pieces of flint stone hit together to create sparks to rubbing sticks together to create enough friction to start a small blaze. Contrast those techniques to today's methods of using a match or lighter and you've got the makings of an entirely different technique, one that is almost effortless!

So, what does all of this talk about techniques have to do with you and your business? Well, as Zig Ziglar, an American author, salesman and motivational speaker said, *"The young athlete who aspires to greatness, generally speaking, learns a number of things from several different coaches. The first one taught him the fundamentals; the second one instilled discipline in him and taught him more of the techniques that must be mastered to excel."*

If you want to find success you have to move past the fundamentals and put theory into practice.

The Evolution of Advisor Solutions Techniques

In May 2011, I began writing the preface for my inaugural book **101 Advisor Solutions:** *A Financial Advisor's Guide to Strategies that Educate, Motivate and Inspire!* The book had taken two years to write. I knew that I wanted to tell a story of a defining moment that happened in the fall of 1993 when I was a rookie Registered Investment Advisor faced with the daily struggle of constant rejection and how I overcame it by enjoying the journey.

Here is the shortened version of the story:

I was hired with the sole purpose of cold calling business owners and comptrollers to discuss how our hedged equity portfolio or our model mutual fund portfolio might work for a portion of their pension or profit sharing dollars.

One day, one of the principal partners was on his way out of the building when he noticed I was frustrated while getting off the phone after being rejected for the double digit time that day. He walked towards the back door without saying a word and then stopped dead in his tracks. It was one of those defining moments and thus for me that moment is as clear today as it was almost thirty years ago. He turned and walked with purpose back towards my office, poked his head in the doorway and said in a matter-of-fact voice, *"Enjoy the journey."*

What was that supposed to mean!? I was getting rejected all day long and those were his parting words of wisdom! I replied, *"What?"* Again, he said, *"Enjoy the journey."* But, this time he paused and followed his statement with, *"This journey will be over before you know it. Enjoy the journey while you can because you will wake up one day and be surprised at how fast time has gone by."* Then, as purposefully as he had walked back towards my office he turned and walked away.

There, in my small office with my phone directory and tally sheet in front of me, I made a decision that I would indeed enjoy the journey, regardless of the destination. What followed was an amazing set of events. Soon after, I began enjoying the conversations that I was having with prospects regardless of whether or not they wanted to meet with me. I began to notice that because I chose to not take their responses personally, I was not carrying any negativity into my next call.

As a result, I set and went on 60 appointments that October! I was averaging 3 appointments a day as well as setting 3 additional appointments a day! There was so much activity that I could not believe how much fun I was having! I was in fact enjoying the journey because I was choosing to enjoy the journey.

What I didn't know at the time was that fall I had in fact created my first technique, a strategy for enjoying the journey!

Since that time, I have created plenty of techniques on a wide range of topics because most advisors and agents want to get from Point-A to Point-B and it takes the right steps and/or strategies. That's why you will notice that the largest section of this book is on techniques.

Over the years, I have crafted fifty different techniques that I have used while coaching clients.

A History of Transformational Moments

The creation of tools and techniques has shaped the course of history and both of those served as pre-cursors for huge transformational moments. A great example of this is what happened after our ancestors developed the tools and techniques to create controlled fire.

Scientists believe that cooking food not only makes it easier to chew and digest, but also releases more calories into the body. And, as a result the cooking of food could very well have been one of the reasons for the expansion of brain size in early humans.

In addition, our ancestors were able to preserve their food longer by cooking it. And the time spent nightly around controlled fires may have also increased their communication skills. As you can see, the combination of tools and techniques to create controlled fire had transformational moments that caused humans to evolve!

So, what does all of this talk have to do with you and your business?

Rick Warren the author of the book **The Purpose Driven Life:** *What on Earth Am I Here For* says, *"Transformation is a process, and as life happens there are tons of ups and downs. It's a journey of discovery-there are moments on mountaintops and moments in deep valleys of despair."*

Have you ever wondered what transformational moments you are missing out on in your business? Would you or even could you be more successful if you were more aware of what you wanted to improve on?

The Evolution of Advisor Solutions Transformational Moments

In the fall of 2006, I noticed a pattern with my individual coaching clients who were financial advisors and insurance agents. During our individual coaching sessions I used the same coaching format for everyone. My client would discuss a current challenge, I would explain the solution/s, teach them a tool or technique to help them overcome the challenge, they were to go apply it and report back their results in the following session.

The pattern was that if they applied the solution, tool or technique on a continual basis they would eventually experience a transformational moment. If they did not apply the resource consistently, they would remain stuck on the same challenge.

What I also realized was that since none of my clients had ever met each other, they felt like they were the only one to experience the challenge they were discussing. Unfortunately, it was like having a number of people isolated on individual islands where they thought they were the only ones experiencing these challenges. However, since I was working with all of them, I knew who had a similar challenge and had applied the solutions to create lasting results and who had not.

Around this time, I had been asked to facilitate a message board for **The Horsesmouth**, which at the time was a popular online business development site that helped financial professionals educate their clients and grow their businesses. The concept was simple, they would advertise a topic of my choosing and at a specific time they would open it up for an online discussion on a message board.

The topic that I suggested was *"What's Your Challenge, Here Are the Solutions"*. While they loved the concept they hated the title so they retitled it, *"What's Your 500 Pound Gorilla?"*

The message board launched at 12:00 pm ET and for the following five hours I was flooded with challenges from financial advisors and insurance agents! It's difficult to remember all of the challenges that they had that day, but one specific challenge stands out among all of the rest.

Laura was rookie financial advisor who had been an assistant in the same office for seven years. Her challenge was that although she had known all of the other financial advisors before she had transitioned from an assistant to a financial advisor, none of them had any interest in helping her succeed.

To make matters worse she was the only female financial advisor in the office, which just added to her feeling of isolation. Her challenge was simple; she wanted to know where she could go to connect with other female financial advisors that had similar challenges in growing their business.

I didn't hesitate to respond when I replied, *"Why don't you join the* **Advisor Solutions** *Women's Only Group Coaching Program?"* The only problem was that I didn't have this group coaching program! And that's when I added an additional comment, *"If anyone else feels the same way please email me at* dan@advisorsolutionsinc.com *and let's talk."* Within minutes I was receiving emails from women requesting information and scheduling an appointment to hear more about this group coaching program.

The next day I mapped out the outline for a program. The next few days were a blur as a dozen women joined it. I contacted all of my individual clients and asked them if they felt isolated as well. Each one of them were interested in joining a group coaching program so I launched a men's group with current clients too!

Over the course of the following six months I created 24 weekly group coaching topics covering eight facets of the business. This became the **Advisor Solutions** flagship group coaching program. Hundreds of advisors and agents went through this program, which was a springboard for a half dozen other group coaching programs that I have created since then.

What I didn't know at the time was that in the fall of 2006, I had created a platform where continuous transformational moments evolved for my clients. It became a place where advisors and agents could learn tools and techniques together as well as share their challenges and solutions! And, just like that the evolution of **Advisor Solutions** Transformational Moments was born because now advisors and agents had a place where they didn't have to feel isolated!

What I've learned from many of my clients over the years is that they get as much out of the ancillary learning from their peers during group sessions as they do from the material that I am teaching. It never ceases to amaze me that there comes a time when each group becomes a tribe. It's the moment where these clients who were once strangers to each other turn into friends.

Since that first group, I have worked with clients in both group and individual coaching programs. With many years of coaching in my rear view mirror, I could write an entire book on my clients Transformational Moments, many of which you will read about in this very book. It is my hope that one day I add your success story to this experience as well!

CHAPTER 2
Advisor Solutions Tools
Equipping You with Instruments for Success

The financial services industry utilizes several tools that are designed around hard skills. A basic definition of hard skills is a skill set that is steeped in job-related knowledge or the abilities that an employee needs to know to effectively perform their job. Hard skills are essentially those you would list on your resume.

During my three-week rookie financial advisory training class, I was exposed to a number of hard skill tools. Although each student had already passed the Series 7, Series 63, life and health insurance exams, the company I worked for wanted us to understand the processes for buying stocks, bonds, mutual funds, insurance and annuities.

If a client wanted information about a stock, we had a process to look up what our analyst had to say about it. If the client was interested in a bond, we had a process to look up our bond inventories. All of these examples and many more were important to learn to grow and maintain an advisory business, but none of them helped me, or any of the other students with our soft skills.

A basic definition of soft skills is the personal qualities that help an employee thrive in the workplace by increasing their interpersonal skill sets to help them get along with others. They are the skill sets needed to make connections with not only colleagues, but with prospects and clients alike. Unfortunately, these skill sets are harder to define and more challenging to hone.

In an industry where your income depends on making connections with people to turn strangers into client and eventually clients into friends I was faced with the reality that after three weeks of training I had virtually NO soft skill tools.

As a result, I came back from training, got a copy of both the Yellow and White pages so I could call business owners during the day and homeowners in the evening, found a script out of a book and started cold calling with no real solid soft skills!

When I think back to those early days, it's like asking a caveman to rub two sticks together to create fire when all I really needed was somebody to hand me a match and take the time to teach me how to use it! In other words, I needed tools to connect with people, to know what to say, how to say it, how to handle objections, tell stories and to let people know that I was listening.

Ironically, I survived! In fact, as I'm writing this I can't for the life of me tell you how I did it. In my first year I opened 100 accounts. In my second year I opened another 100 accounts. But, in my third year I actually tripled my income! And, all the while I had no idea that there was such a thing as soft skills. It was over a decade later that I heard the term when Mike P. a financial advisory client announced to his team of six advisors during a group coaching call, *"We are learning the **Advisor Solutions** Soft Skills!"*

Soon after Mike's statement, I came to my own realization that somehow I must have organically increased my soft skills each year without ever consciously being aware of it because each year I had increased my level of success.

When I think back to those early years I do remember that there were times when I would surprise myself. I would put down the phone after overcoming an objection and set the appointment or I would get in my car stunned that I closed the sale only to ask myself, *"How did that happen?"*

Then, I would dissect the event to understand what I did differently from the countless times that I had failed before. Eventually, I would develop a tool out of the experience and try to repeat the same success. If I was continuously successfully, I would create a habit out of using the tool.

This trial and error process had increased my soft skills. And, until Mike put a label on it calling it "soft skills" I never realized that these tools were helping my clients increase theirs as well. From then on, I knew I needed to be more overt and create these types of soft skill templates in the form of additional tools.

The evolution of **Advisor Solutions** Tools has quite a history. For the purpose of this book, I wanted you to understand the stories and descriptions of the tools that follow should be viewed as puzzle pieces that fit nicely together to form the picture of what a successful business could look like.

As you read this section please note that the tools aren't listed in a particular order, as they all work as standalones, however, when utilized in conjunction with one another, they can collectively strengthen and streamline your processes and systems.

It is my hope that as you read through this book's Tools Section that the stories resonate with you. They can all be customized to fit the specifics of your business, so that you can create your own unique finished image (puzzle) of what success could be for you.

Story #1
Building a Balanced Business

Most advisors/agents struggle with building balance into their business. They excel at only a few business facets such as client servicing or portfolio management at the expense of other business facets such as prospecting and sales.

It's interesting to note that balance in your business is not something you magically find, but it is something that you strategically create. How do you know if your business is balanced in the first place? How do you know if you have a challenge you might not be aware of?

I suggest you utilize a tool that I created called **The Advisor's Business Wheel** which is a simple, but effective exercise in understanding how you rank your current level of satisfaction in each of the eight fundamental facets of your business: time management, prospecting, sales, relationship building, client servicing, marketing, product knowledge and managing accounts.

Here is how it works.

Draw a Pie Chart With 8 Pieces

The first step is the easiest. Draw a pie chart with eight pieces of the pie assigning one of the facets for each piece. Make sure that you write your labels outside of the crust of the pie. You will understand in a minute.

Tom W. was a thirty-five-year veteran financial advisor who was not happy with the level of success that he was having in his business, but he couldn't articulate what his specific challenges were much less what facet of the business he needed to improve upon. So, I had him create a pie chart and label it *Tom's Business Wheel*.

Rate Yourself in Each Facet

The second step is to rate yourself for each facet of the business. The best way to do this is to write each facet out below the pie chart.

Next, record on a scale of 1-10, (1 being not satisfied to 10 being very satisfied) your level of satisfaction for each facet of your business. Remember, each ranking is independent of the others.

Once Tom had his business wheel created I explained the rating system and had him do the exercise. It was starting to become apparent to him that his business was not balanced because his highest rankings were in client servicing, product knowledge and managing accounts while his lowest rankings were on prospecting, sales and relationship building.

Plot Your Ratings Points

The third step is to look at the pie chart you created with a horizontal line, a vertical line and an "X" line. Again, your pie chart should have 8 lines that intersect into the middle point. Take the middle point and move upward on the vertical line to the crust of the pie. If the middle point was a 0 and the crust of the pie was a 10, plot your number accordingly on that line. Outside of the pie chart, you would have labeled that line *Time Management* and continue this process for each of the 8 facets of your business.

I explained to Tom how to plot his ratings points and I asked him what he liked and disliked about the business. He said, *"I like talking to my clients and helping them."* Then he paused and sheepishly admitted, *"What I don't like is trying to find additional clients after all of these years."*

Connect the Dots

The fourth step is to connect the points! This is what your **Advisor's Business Wheel** looks like. Is your business balanced or round like a wheel? Is it shaped like a star? If it is a star, your business is out of balance!!!

Tom connected the dots and looked at his **Advisor's Business Wheel** in silence. *"Tom"*, I curiously said, *"If we walked out to the parking ramp at the end of the day and we looked at your driver-side wheel what would you do if it looked like your **Advisor's Business Wheel**?"*

15

He quickly lifted his head and said, *"I'd change it. When do we begin?"*

Why the Advisor's Business Wheel Works

As you can see from this story, the **Advisor's Business Wheel** works because it gives you a bird's eye view of what your entire business looks like, in terms of your level of satisfaction with each facet of the business, while increasing your awareness of what areas you need to work on. It also could help you get motivated to make changes, just like Tom!

Story #2
The Bottom Line List

Do you control your time during the day or do unforeseen events, interruptions and lack of structure control you? If it's the latter, don't worry you are not alone. Mike Ditka said, *"Success isn't measured by money or power or social rank. Success is measured by your discipline and inner peace."*

Typically, advisors and agents have the best of intentions as their day begins, but just don't have the tools and resources to help them with their daily tasks. That's why I created this exercise for my advisor/agent clients called **The Bottom Line List.**

The Bottom Line List is a time management tool for building structure into the day. It is designed to map out your top 5 Bottom-Line Activities each day and then compartmentalize those activities into 45-minute time blocks with a 15-minute break between each block.

Understanding The Bottom Line List

This tool is essentially a game that you can play. If you accomplish at least 4 out of 5 activities you win the game. If not, you lose. And, when you assign a reward to a daily win and a consequence to a daily loss you have extra incentive to stick to your mapped out activities.

To better understand this tool you may want to create your own **Bottom Line List** as you read and digest what follows.

Column #1: Priorities

This column has five rows, numbered 1 to 5. The reason you are titling this column "Priorities" is because there is essentially an order of importance. Stay tuned.

David V., a forty-year veteran financial advisor and branch manager client wanted my help taking his personal production to the next level. I had him create a **Bottom Line List** and label his "Priorities" column.

Column #2: Time Blocking

In this column, you are determining when you will do each 45-minute activity. The reason we leave a 15-minute buffer is in case you start late or need a break.

After explaining this column, David knew that it would work. He had used time blocking when he was a rookie and he had created productive habits that helped to grow his business. He filled in each of the 5 blocks starting at 8:00 a.m.

Column #3: The Bottom Line Activity

In this column, you are briefly describing what it is that you will do during a particular time block. Order in the following priority (hence the 5 priority columns): prospecting, client servicing, prospect follow-up, appointment (or appointment preparation) and miscellaneous.

After explaining this to David he admitted that his least favorite thing to do was to prospect. He had gotten out of the habit and frankly had created a fear of rejection for himself. I reminded David that he hired me to help him get to the next level and that prospecting is the only way to fill up the pipeline.

Column #4: The Bottom Line Value

This column is designed to reinforce why you are doing the activity in the first place. Each row in this column will have the same type of sentence, "*What is important to me about* _____ *today is* _____*.*" The advisor/agent fills in the blanks each day to reinforce why they are doing the activity.

I explained this to David and he didn't fully understand so I gave him an example. "*What is important about prospecting today is that if I don't prospect today my business won't grow tomorrow.*"

Column #5: Done

In this column, you issue a check mark every time that you complete a **Bottom Line List** Activity. Again, if you complete 4 out of 5 you win the game and get a reward. Anything less is a loss and a consequence should be associated with it.

It didn't take David long to realize that by sticking to this exercise he was getting more done in the same amount of time because he was in control of what he was doing and when he was doing it! Over a short time frame, he began to work quickly towards reaching the next level with his business.

Why the Bottom Line List Works

The Bottom Line List works because it architects a form of structure for your daily activities. If you find yourself busy, but not productive, try using this tool to build discipline and time management into your day!

Story #3
Being Passionately Productive

Many advisors and agents run their day-to-day activities around which fire they need to put out at any one particular moment. Their passion is focused on appeasing the most current client request, which is usually not a time-sensitive issue and thus an unproductive use of valuable time.

Henry David Thoreau said, *"Success usually comes to those who are too busy to be looking for it."*

Have you ever taken the time to think about the level of success you could have if you spent your time being passionately productive, prioritizing on efficient and effective activities?

If so, utilize the following steps to help guide you through that process.

Prioritize Tasks & Interruptions

The first step is to prioritize tasks and interruptions into one of four categories-*now, today, this week* or *whenever.* Using a tool that I created for my coaching clients, **The Time Matrix To-Do List,** can help you do this.

Mike S., a twenty-year veteran financial advisor client couldn't keep up with putting out the constant fires that his clients contacted him with each day.

Unfortunately, he had lost his assistant a few weeks earlier and was feeling the full effect of juggling everything on his own. I had him fill out **The Time Matrix To-Do List** so we could organize his activities and client asks.

Manage Time-Sensitive Items First

The second step is to tackle only the urgent (*now*) and important (*today*) activities.

Once Mike had his **Time Matrix To-Do List** tool filled out, I recommended that he manage the time-sensitive items, the urgent (*now*) ones first. He began working on all of those tasks until they were completed. Next he moved onto any important (*today*) items, which needed to be addressed by the end of the day.

Handle Weekly Deadlines

The third step is to schedule a time during the week to do anything that is tagged as *this week* moving any items that need to be done by the end of the week into the important (*today*) category as the week wears on.

One of the most common mistakes that advisors/agents make when they start to get caught up is to forget managing moving deadlines, as those tasks that were not urgent (*now*) or important (*today*) a few days ago or when they originally surfaced, but as the week wears on they become last minute items that now require attention.

To avoid this I suggested that Mike schedule 30 minutes at the end of each day to work on any items that needed to be accomplished by the end of the week, so that a backup wasn't created. He did this and found that it decreased the stress that procrastinating was generating for him.

Take Care of Loose Ends

The fourth step is to parse out and time block for your *whenever* activities so that a dedicated time is assigned and they don't continue to get pushed on your calendar.

Mike took care of loose ends on Friday afternoons, a time to work on any ongoing projects or items that didn't have a due date. That way he could go into the weekend with peace of mind with nothing having slipped through the cracks.

Why Being Passionately Productive Works

Following this stepwise approach you view each task and interruption as merely an opportunity to check off each one based on true priority and not by being immediately reactive. The reason why being passionately productive works so well is because it puts you in the driver's seat, it's that simple.

After a month of using this system Mike not only felt more in control of his time and to-do list, but found himself more productive (and thus successful) than he could ever remember.

Story #4
How to Keep Score of Your Success

Have you ever wondered why most sports teams use a scoreboard during a game? The answer is obvious; they want to know who won and who lost. What if you looked at your daily activities the same way? What if at the end of the day you could sum up whether it had been a productive day or a non-productive day, would you want to know? If so, then it's time for you to learn how to keep score of your success!

John C. Maxwell said, *"The secret of your success is determined by your daily agenda."* I believe this quote to be true and that's why I created the **Daily Scorecard** to do just that.

A **Daily Scorecard** is merely a system of measuring your productive activities throughout the day, so that you can reach daily goals. This is a tool designed to help keep track of daily activities and it allows you to time block, assign point values to activities, keep track of total daily points and give yourself daily and weekly rewards! Without a systematic way of monitoring the activities required to obtain your daily goals, you will never reach them. This has a domino effect in that if you do not reach your daily goals, you will not reach your weekly, monthly, quarterly and yearly goals either. Thus, the **Daily Scorecard** is designed to keep you in line and accountable with doing the activities you need to achieve success.

Not all **Daily Scorecards** are alike. The main difference is that each is designed with various degrees of detail. While some financial advisors may wish to keep score of a number of details during the day, others find it more effective to keep score of less. Let's take a look at three common types. The following describes each type of **Daily Scorecard**.

Example 1: The Detailed Daily Scorecard

This scorecard is a detailed account of the tasks that you would do in any given time blocking period. Each task has a point value system, which is recorded, at the end of the time block. There is a daily targeted point number, which is the score to beat each day. If this is accomplished, you reward yourself, if not you establish a punishment of some kind.

John C. was a five-year veteran financial advisor who had been a CPA before making a career change. He was a detailed oriented person. When he started individual coaching with me he said that he needed help with time management and staying motivated. So, I showed him a sample of **The Detailed Daily Scorecard** and he immediately took to the process. Within a few months he was more productive, less stressed and felt in control of his day!

Example 2: The Activity Daily Scorecard

This scorecard is similar to the **Detailed Daily Scorecard** in that it records point values for each activity accomplished, but it is less detailed in when to accomplish each activity. One example in this scorecard is that you record dials all day long, but in the previous scorecard you would only record dials during the Prospecting Time Block.

Bill J. was a fifteen-year veteran financial advisor who was very results driven. He had built his business the old-fashioned way by cold calling. His method for measuring success was to record how many dials, contacts, appointments set, appointments held and new accounts established each day.

When I asked why he stopped using this process just a few short years into starting his business he said he had built up, so many clients that he found himself servicing clients more than prospecting. However, since he had converted his book from a transactional business to a fee-based business he had freed up some of his time and wanted to get back to prospecting. I showed him **The Activity Daily Scorecard** and he agreed that this would work for him. Within a few weeks he had more prospects in the pipeline than he could remember having in years!

Example 3: The Transactional Daily Scorecard

This scorecard is much less detailed in nature and is geared towards daily commissions or setting appointments. The goal is to have 25 contacts a day with the belief that with enough contacts brings success! This is a perfect scorecard for the financial advisor who runs a transactional business, but it can also be tailored to the financial advisor who is trying to build their business with face-to-face appointments.

Tom G. was a thirty plus year veteran financial advisor who said that he wanted to grow his business back to where it was before he moved to his current brokerage firm. In the move he had lost some clients who were not willing to transfer their accounts over to the new firm. After a few individual coaching sessions, he explained to me that he had a large natural market of professionals that worked downtown within walking distance of his office.

We mapped out a campaign that I call The Social Marketing Campaign, so that we could convert his natural market into new clients. The campaign hinges on contacting his natural market and setting appointments, so that he can find out about what they are doing and offer a free financial plan. I showed him **The Transactional Daily Scorecard** and we modified, so he had two ways to win the game by either making 25 contacts in a day or by setting one lunch appointment daily. As a result, he gathered six million in new assets in six months and had fun doing it!

Why Using a Daily Scorecard Works

It is important to understand why the **Daily Scorecard** system works so well. The reason is because it allows you to focus on daily activities and be accountable via reward or punishment depending on your outcomes. In addition, when used on a consistent basis it fosters a new productive habit, which in turn generates a greater degree of success!

Story #5
Realizing the Advisor's Rejection Spectrum

During one of my specialty coaching sessions on The 25 Most Effective Ways to Conquer Rejection, I came to an amazing realization. Although we had marketed this two part series to thousands of advisors and agents only <u>two</u> actually registered.

Was it because advisors and agents don't have a fear of rejection? No, I don't believe so. In fact, the fear of rejection is just as much a challenge today as it was thirty years ago when I started in the financial services industry as an advisor. Perhaps I may never know why we had such a low turnout, but what is more important is the a-ha moment that I had during the first session.

We had two advisors that could not have had more polar opposite experiences in their careers; one was a veteran advisor with 33 years of experience who was in his sixties while the other was a woman with less than four years in the industry (who was ironically 33 years old).

What I realized was that although they had vastly different ages, product knowledge, communication skill sets and years in the business they had one very important thing in common, they had a fear of rejection. Following my initial session with them, I coined what I now call **The Advisor's Rejection Spectrum,** which states that no matter where you are in your career path you may be subject to this type of fear however you may have it for a very different reason and consequently you may need a very different solution to overcome it.

The following illustrates what I mean:

Spectrum #1: The Rookie Advisor

I wasn't surprised when my more rookie advisor explained that she was taking rejection personally. She had spent many hours cold calling and had come up against rejection numerous times. That is what her perception was until I explained what she had really experienced. The solution was for her to realize that rejection is not the same as handling objections, which are a natural part of the sales process.

Since prospects didn't know her personally they weren't personally rejecting her. Instead, they were rejecting the value that they thought she could bring them and they did this by using excuses in the form of objections such as, *"I am all set, I'm busy* and *Let me think about it."* Once she understood this difference, I shared with her three strategies to better manage objections and that's when she had a paradigm shift, *"I can't wait to try these strategies out!"* In other words, she now had far less a fear of rejection.

She now understands the difference between working harder by doing more of what she was doing and working smarter by having a system for when objections arise.

Spectrum #2: The Veteran Advisor

I was surprised to hear my veteran advisor tell me that although he has acquired 33 years in financial services he had not prospected in the last five years. I was not surprised by the reason why, he liked talking to clients rather than speaking with prospects. He went on to explain that when he would prospect his natural market they rarely wanted to do business with him. He said he found it discouraging to have longtime friends and acquaintances reject him.

The solution was for him to also understand that these people were not rejecting him personally, but instead rejecting the value they perceived taking his advice would bring them. He was too busy telling them what they should do instead of asking the right questions to help them come to the conclusion on why they should do it. In other words, he was trying to sell them his recommendations instead of helping them understand why they should accept his recommendations! *"Wow! All I have to do is to learn how to ask better questions so they understand how I can help. Why didn't I think of that?"* he said.

Why Finding Your Rejection Spectrum Works

As you can see, both advisors were taking rejection personally, but each had a different solution for overcoming their fear of it. Can you relate? At some point in every advisor's career they develop some degree of the fear of rejection. Don't wait to realize why you have it and what to do about it, find your rejection spectrum today and get going at building a better business tomorrow!

Story #6
The One Minute Business Coach

Do you ever feel like you are on an emotional roller coaster ride? One minute you are emotionally up and the next minute emotionally down. In times like those, wouldn't it be great to be able to coach yourself in a minute or less to handle life's highs and lows?

I created an exercise I call **The One Minute Business Coach** that I use when working with advisors/agents. Connor McGregor, a former Ultimate Fighting Championship said, *"Life is a roller coaster. You're up one minute, you're down one minute. But who doesn't like roller coasters?"*

To some extent I believe that is true. However, if you aren't able to get off the emotional roller coaster then the antidote is to learn a better way to manage your emotions!

Learning how to be your own **One Minute Business Coach** is an art, not a science. The most effective way to determine if a high or low could benefit from this exercise is to increase your level of awareness by using questions. However, the first step is in determining when to ask yourself the questions and know what questions you should be asking.

Typically, individuals know when they are experiencing a win or loss. It surfaces internally when you get that feeling of accomplishment or disappointment. Recognizing those emotions are the catalyst for when you need to incorporate a **One Minute Business Coach** session. If things are status quo and you find that you are not feeling up or down then you probably do not need a session. On the other hand, when you experience an activity that leaves you feeling those bigger emotions then it is time for a session.

It is important to understand the elements of the **One Minute Business Coach** session model so that you can be fully effective when applying the process. The following is a brief description and example steps in this case for coaching a loss.

Identify an Activity That Creates An Emotional Trigger

What activities have caused you an emotional high or low? An example would be, *"I did not close a presentation."* This outcome doesn't feel good. So, figuring out your triggers is a good place to start.

Identify the Associated Feeling(s)

You need to identify the associated feeling (s) that correspond with the activity that is causing a high or low. Some examples would be, *"I feel angry, concerned, and/or depressed."* The reason you want to define the feeling(s) is so you can actively recognize patterns on how many good feelings versus bad feelings you experience over the course of a day or a week.

Ask Great Questions

Asking the right questions helps you to identify desired outcomes, causes and new behaviors. Remember, it's important to ask questions that get to the heart of things. Not asking detailed questions that require responses will keep you spinning your wheels. Let's take a look at an example of some solid questions you should ask yourself.

What was the desired outcome? *I wanted to close the presentation.*

What was the cause? *I did not prepare for objections; thus, I did not close.*

What can I do differently next time? *I will prepare for a minimum of 5 objections for every presentation I have.*

One thing to note is that the last question helps you create a new behavior pattern. In other words, in this example the next time you are getting ready for an appointment you would prepare for a minimum of five common objections and be ready to close the sale.

Why The One Minute Business Coach Works

This is an exercise in self-awareness and learning how to manage your emotions throughout the day. The reason why it works is because it reinforces wins/highs, so you continue doing what is working and helps you to learn from losses/lows by creating new and more rewarding patterns, so you can smooth out your emotional roller coaster and better enjoy the ride!

Story #7
Conquering Self-Talk

After over a decade in production 20+ years coaching financial advisors and insurance agents I have found one thing to be absolutely true for each and every advisor/agent I have ever worked with, we all have an inner voice speaking to us dictating our thoughts, behaviors, actions and results regardless of the voice issuing good or bad thoughts.

Steve Jobs said, *"Your time is limited, so don't waste it living someone else's life. Don't be trapped by dogma - which is living with the results of other people's thinking. Don't let the noise of others' opinions drown out your own inner voice. And most important, have the courage to follow your heart and intuition."*

While I agree with the previous quote, the big question is what do you do when our own inner voice is constantly negative?

Conquering negative self-talk is not a matter of just stopping the negative dialogue. You cannot separate easily from the little voice inside your head. It might possibly be that you have been listening to your negative inner advisor for years, even as far back as early childhood. So, how is it possible to just turn it off? Unfortunately, you can't. However, you can conquer negative self-talk by doing several things: countering it with positive self-talk, using relief statements and supportive counterstatements to support building a new positive belief system.

I have had my advisor clients' use a tool I designed called **The Negative Self-Talk Worksheet,** which is the three-step process that follows.

Identify Your Negative Self-Talk

Typically, negative self-talk comes in one of the four common types of negative self-talk, which are *worried, critical, victimized* and *perfectionist*. I refer to these inner voices as negative inner advisors.

The first step in managing each of these dialogues is to identify when you have experienced them. Here are a few examples:

The Worried Advisor: *"What if I lose everything trying to build my business?"*

The Critical Advisor: *"I will not close this account because they always need to think about it."*

The Victimized Advisor: *"I can't cold call because it doesn't work in this environment."*

The Perfectionist Advisor: *"I have to hit my gross goals this month!"*

Create Relief Questions

One way to weaken the power of negative belief systems is to use Socratic questions. Socratic questions are a form of questioning in which Socrates used to create a negative argument to rational investigation. By subjecting your negative self-talk or your negative belief systems to rational scrutiny, you break down the belief systems validity. The following are a few examples:

"What is the evidence that I will lose everything?"

"Is this always true? Have I ever closed an account before with any prospect?"

"Has this always been true in the past?"

"What's the worst thing that can happen?"

These questions can also be viewed as relief questions, which are questions designed to relieve you of anxiety by questioning the severity of your perception of the situation.

The Positive Counterstatement

The final step is to substitute your negative self-talk with positive counterstatements. Remember; you cannot eliminate a belief system, but you can replace negative belief systems with positive ones. The amount of effectiveness that you have on this process will be determined by how valid your new positive counterstatement can stand up to any and all objective scrutiny. In other words the stronger you can make a case for your new positive counterstatement the less likely that the old negative self-talk will continue.

The Negative Self-Talk Worksheet

The following is an example of how **The Negative Self-Talk Worksheet** can be applied when using all three steps for The Worried Advisor dialogue:

The Worried Advisor: *"What if I lose everything trying to build my business?"*

The Relief Question: *"What is the evidence that I will lose everything?"*

The Positive Counterstatement: *"A bad month or bad quarter while financially uncomfortable is not the end of my financial security. I am on a salary for another year, I have equity in my home and I am consistently adding new assets, new accounts and new gross commissions to my business every day. I have never lost everything before and will work smart to never be in that type of financial situation."*

This is not a quick fix for years of negative self-talk, but it is a process that with practice can transform your way of thinking!

Why Conquering Negative Self-Talk Works

Anyone can build an investment advisory business. The greatest obstacle that you face is creating a positive daily mental attitude. You may have come into this business with years of emotional baggage.

The reason why **The Negative Self-Talk Worksheet** works is because it gives you a process for identifying negative dialogue, questioning negative beliefs and backing up a new belief system with positive counterstatements.

In other words, it's a process for shifting the negative dialogue to positive dialogue and having an opportunity to leave your emotional baggage behind.

Story #8
Finding Your Flow

Recently, during one of my group coaching sessions we were discussing the topic of turning strangers into clients with what I refer to as, **The 9-Step Client Acquisition Process.**

The following is a brief overview of each step:

1. Initial Contact—is managed by following a tool called **Framing the Conversation**

2. Needs Assessment— is managed by following a tool called **S.P.I.N Selling.**

3. Getting the Appointment— is done when you have overcome all objections and close.

4. Reconfirming the Appointment—done by **Framing the Conversation**.

5. 1st Appointment—is done by using a tool called **The First Appointment F.O.R.M.**

6. Reconfirming the 2nd Appointment—is done by using **Framing the Conversation**.

7. 2nd Appointment—is done by using a tool called **The 2nd Appointment Template**.

8. Referrals—is done by using a tool called **The Client-Centered Referral Dialogue.**

9. Client Servicing—is done by having an **Effective Client Servicing System**.

Each of the aforementioned steps and tools take time to learn to effortlessly turn strangers into clients and eventually clients into raving fans. All of which are discussed in this book.

After I explained the details of each of the nine steps, we role played them. One of the advisors after our initial role play session said,

"You made is sound so natural." He paused and added, *"I need to find my flow."*

What he was referring to is being able to seamlessly respond to anything that a prospect/client may say to take them down a path in helping them understand why they would want to accept his recommendations and ultimately buy them. When you can do this, after much practice, you will naturally find your flow.

Let's take a closer look at how you can find yours.

Finding the Clog

We all have a clog (or two) in our pipeline. It may be getting a first appointment or securing a second appointment or closing the sale. To find your flow you have to be honest with yourself and find your clog(s).

The best way to do this is to ask yourself, *"What would need to happen in order for me to find new business?"* The easy answer might be, *"I need to prospect."* For the sake of argument let's assume that you are prospecting. Then you need to figure out what exactly your clog is whether it be in your prospecting technique or otherwise.

Unclogging the Pipeline

At this stage, it's important to figure out specific solutions for your specific challenges. An example would be if your clog is not getting the first appointment then possibly your solution is to learn how to handle objections better.

However, if your clog is not being able to explain your recommendations in easy to understand terms and you seem to confuse the prospect then your solution is to learn **Story-Based Selling**, the art of using metaphors, analogies or stories to help make a better connection with your prospects/clients.

The point is, you may need dedicated direction at figuring out your weaknesses and doing what it takes (training, coaching, finding a mentor) to assist you in mapping out a plan to turn those weaknesses into strengths and thus clear out those clogs.

Perfecting the Process

When my client pointed out that I sounded natural, I quickly assured him that I didn't always sound that way. It had taken years of perfecting the process. Learn what has worked for so many other advisors and agents, customize the process to make it sound like your own then practice and role play with a trusted peer or colleague and ask for feedback, so you can make additional tweaks to smooth things out.

Why Finding Your Flow Works

Most advisors/agents know that winging it doesn't work. That's why it's so important to use these steps to unclog your pipeline and build a better connection with prospects and clients.

When you take the time to understand what is not working, how you can work smarter and apply what you learn you not only help yourself, but you help the prospects and clients feel more relaxed and confident because you are more relaxed and confident.

Story #9
The New Business Strategy List

Do you have a prospecting pipeline? If so, is it more than just a list of people who might do business with you? Many advisors and agents do have a prospecting pipeline but very few have a step-by-step strategy to move prospects into and through it! That's why I created one for my coaching clients, **The New Business Strategy List.**

Jack Canfield said, *"I believe that people make their own luck by great preparation and good strategy."*

The New Business Strategy List is a pipeline-monitoring tool. It is designed to not only keep track of who is in your pipeline, but where each person is in the client acquisition process of converting prospects to clients! The following is a brief illustration of a recent conversation I had with a client to help him fill out this tool and fully understand it.

Understanding The New Business Strategy List

The New Business Strategy List is designed best on an Excel spreadsheet with seventeen columns that make up three separate sections of the tool. Each section has a specific purpose to help the advisor/agent understand the prospect better as well as strategize to move them to the next step.

To better understand this tool you may want to create your own **New Business Strategy List** as you read and digest the following.

Section #1: The Prospect's Information

Section #1 is made of the first five column headings to offer a clear picture on the prospect's information. They are as follow: *date, name, dollar amount found in investable assets, insurance policy type* and *policy face amount.*

John T. a ten-year veteran financial advisor client of mine needed help creating a prospecting pipeline. Unfortunately, he had spent his entire career using what he thought was the best way to manage his pipeline. He had written down the names of people who were in his pipeline and left it at that!

So, I recommended he start using **The New Business Strategy List** by filling in the first five columns of the tool to get the prospect information all in one place.

Section #2: Understanding What Stage of the Pipeline Each Prospect is in

Section #2 is made of the next four column headings to get a clear picture on the prospect's stage in the pipeline. They are as follows: *Stage #1-Initial Contact, Stage #2-First Appointment (Discovery Meeting), Stage #3-Second Appointment (Closing Meeting) and Stage #4-Referrals or Prospect Call Back-* (because you didn't close initially).

After I explained this section, John and I discussed each prospect in his pipeline to determine what stage they were in and put the number "1" in the appropriate box. I had designed the stage columns to automatically total every time a new entry was made, so we could see the total number of people in each stage.

Section #3: Understanding the Strategy for Each Prospect

Section #3 is made up of the next four column headings to create a strategy for each prospect. They are as follows: *Notes, Challenges, Solutions* and *Actions Steps*. It's interesting that in this section you typically run into the same challenges time-and-time again, which requires the same solutions and action steps.

In John's case, we had already identified that his clog was in Stage 2, the discovery meeting. His biggest challenge was to get prospects to meet with him again to hear his recommendations. The solution was to ask better question to uncover the prospect's problems, implication of not fixing the problem/s and the value of utilizing solution/s. This helped the prospects see the value in moving to the next step with John as their guide.

Section #4: Recording the Outcome

Section #4 is made up of the final four column headings to record the outcome once the sale is closed. They are as follows: *Assets Gathered, Fees/Commissions from assets, Fees/Commissions from insurance* and *Done*.

John started using these strategies to unclog his pipeline and was able to close a lot of the prospects that previously had been stuck. Since these columns are automatically tallied as well, we knew exactly how many assets were gathered and the fees/commissions from both investments and insurance at any given time!

Why the New Business Strategy List Works

The **New Business Strategy List** works for several reasons. This resource allows you to be able to forecast any potential pipeline problems such as not having enough assets in the pipeline, not having enough people flowing through to the next step or finding bottleneck activities to help ensure a steady stream of people at each step of the process.

So, the next time you are wondering why your current prospecting pipeline process is not producing the results you need, try using a better tool to unclog your pipeline!

Story #10
Beyond the Gatekeeper

During coaching sessions, I often listen to financial advisors/agents discuss their frustrations about how long it takes to get their foot in the door while trying to build up their pipeline.

Take for instance, my client Darrell, a financial advisor, who had recently started prospecting business owners. During our coaching check-in, I asked Darrell how prospecting to his new target market was going.

He replied with *"Well, I have become frustrated at not being able to get through to these potential clients. The person answering the phone seems to think they know what my contact wants and answers for them with a reply of "No, thank you he/she would not be interested" which is very aggravating! I keep hitting a wall which is holding me back from growing my business!"*

This is a common challenge when prospecting business owners. I informed Darrell that it was the job of the gatekeeper to screen the calls, so not to take any rejection personally. And, that it was important to play the game of giving the gatekeeper enough information, but NOT too much information.

So, I coached Darrell to do the following:

- Be sure to ask for the prospect using their first name, it promotes the assumption that you have a relationship with them already.
- Announce who you are, what firm you are with and your reason for calling; and do this without a pause. Offering this information leaves few questions for the gatekeeper to ask and they are more likely to put the call through as a result.

I also referred him to a white paper I had written called **Creating Your Own Great Scripts,** which maps out a three step-by-step process of using tools for cold calling:

1. **Frame the Conversation**
2. **The Smoke Screen Technique**
3. **The Objection Resolution Model**

I knew that it would not only help Darrell gather the additional information he needed once he got through to business owners, but it would help him get beyond that initial gatekeeper as knowing what to say to the target market is irrelevant if you never get to speak to him/her.

We also talked about the specifics of each tool starting with **Framing the Conversation**, a process to create structure into the initial conversation. This is a four-step process:

1. **Introduction**—who you are and where you are from.
2. **Reason**—explaining the reason for your call.
3. **Three Benefits**—explaining the three biggest benefits of why they should meet.
4. **Close**—asking for the appointment.

We then mapped out the **Smoke Screen Technique**, a process for finding the real objection. This is a three-step process:

1. **Empathy or Acknowledgement**—so that you make a connection.
2. **Open-Ended Question**—so that that you get the prospect to open up about the real objection.
3. **Closed-Ended Question**—so that you finalize the point and confirm that we found the real objection.

Finally, we mapped out some **Objection Resolution Model** so that he could prepare for any possible objections that he might hear. This is a four-step process:

1. **Empathy/Acknowledgement**—so that you make a connection.
2. **Best Question**—so that you get the prospect to question their own objection.
3. **Three Benefits**—explaining the three biggest benefits of why they should meet.
4. **Close**—asking for the order.

By the end of the session, he felt more prepared with these outlined steps and confident that he could utilize them successfully.

The following week, I couldn't help, but be curious about what had happened. *"So, how did it work? Did you get beyond the gatekeeper?"* I asked waiting in anticipation. *"The strangest thing happened..."* Darrell paused in deep thought *"I did exactly what we scripted and role played from the* **Creating Your Own Great Script**. *And, I was shocked at how pleasant these gatekeepers were!"* I could feel him grinning from ear to ear as he continued. *"They just thanked me and said "one moment please". Then they would usually put me through to the business owner."*

"Congratulations!" I exclaimed. *"Did you set any appointments?"* *"Yes, I actually did."* he proudly announced.

I could tell that the anxiety and frustration Darrell had had the previous week was gone. He went on to tell me that the first couple of times were a little shaky. He stumbled with his pace, but then remembered to be conversational and not to pause.

"So, what do you think did it for you?" I asked in anticipation. *"Why did it work so well?"*

"I think it was a combination of a lot of things; I had a system for what I was going to say, giving them just enough information. I think

they seemed to believe they had enough information to give to their boss.

And, it must have been intriguing enough to make the business owner want to speak with me as well" he stated, *"But, the one thing that really made the difference was putting it all together by thinking of this as a game. That to me was the key to getting beyond the gatekeeper; and, just playing the game over-and-over again."*

Why Getting Past the Gatekeeper Works

Gatekeepers are people too. In fact, they are people whose job (or at least part of their job) is to make sure they filter incoming calls and visitors. The reason why using this process to get past the gatekeeper works so well is because you are helping the gatekeeper do their job by volunteering the information that they need. Darrell was successful because he was treating them with respect and helping make their job easier.

Story #11
Monologue vs. Dialogue

For almost two decades, I've been coaching financial advisors and insurance agents in a wide variety of facets of their business. One of the most important of those is sales as without the ability to sell, you would not have a client base.

A common theme that I have heard from individuals during coaching sessions is that selling is telling, if you just tell them what they need, they will buy. However, telling prospects what they "should do" could be a recipe for disaster. The alternative is a well-thought out strategy of asking prospects what they think they "should do" to create success for themselves.

Creating Connections Using the Right Types of Questions

You may be surprised to learn that not all questions you ask necessarily create a connection though. For example, take Jake, a financial advisor client of mine whose boss hired me to help him increase his sales skills. During an individual coaching session we role played the first appointment process.

Knowing that questions are important, Jake did his best to uncover my character's situation and make a good connection, but instead he ended up merely pushing me away. After five minutes of me grunting replies such as *"yes"," no", "I guess", "I don't know"* and *"maybe,* I knew Jake didn't fully understand what he was doing that was hurting him during the conversation; he was in a monologue-only delivery whereas he needed to be in a dialogue with me instead.

How Open-Ended Questions Open up the Conversation

"Do you think I was connected?" I cautiously asked. *"No, but I asked a lot of questions. I guess they weren't the right ones,"* he said with shame in his voice. *"Jake, it's not that your questions were wrong, but instead it was that you were using the wrong types of questions,"* I replied. *"Most of the questions you were asking were*

closed-ended questions, which typically elicit a 'yes' or 'no' response."

"If most of my responses are words like, "yes, no, I don't know" and so on, are we in a dialogue or are you in a monologue?" He paused and excitedly said, *"So, in order to connect I need to get you to open up by using opened-ended questions? Let's go over those!"*

The Evolution of the Question Exercise

At that moment I knew it was time to create a simple exercise to increase his questions selling skill sets so I had him draw a vertical line on a piece of paper and label the left side Monologue and on the right side Dialogue.

"Jake, underneath the Monologue heading I want you to write "closed-ended" questions and underneath the Dialogue heading I want you to write "open-ended" questions, one question for each line." I said. I gave him a list of each and he wrote them down. *"Next, I will do a five minute role play in which I am the advisor and you are the prospect. My goal is to get you do open up. How do you think I will do that?" "Well,"* he paused, *"By asking me open-ended questions."*

After five minutes I asked him, *"Did you feel connected?" "Absolutely, I did all the talking and your questions got me to open up more than I thought I would!"* he said in surprise. *"That's exactly why open-ended questions work so well because they get the listener to open up and that creates a dialogue which creates a better connection."* I explained. *"Now, it's your turn."*

The next role play was amazing! Jake got me to open up as this simple exercise opened his eyes to understanding how important it is to use the right types of questions.

Since then, I've added elements to the exercise to turn it into a game and I have played that game in several individual and group coaching sessions; time-after-time it has improved the communication process!

The Monologue vs. Dialogue Exercise

The following is a step-by-step process to create the **Monologue vs. Dialogue Exercise** so you can increase your skill sets at asking Open-Ended Questions.

Step 1: Understand Close-Ended vs. Open-Ended Questions

The two common types of questions are Closed-Ended Questions and Open-Ended Questions. A Closed-Ended Question is a question that limits the type of responses that someone could make.

They are typically used to finalize a point. An Open-Ended Question is a question that encourages the type and amount of responses that someone could make. They are typically used to deepen conversations.

Step 2: Create the Monologue vs. Dialogue Scorecard

Once you understand Closed-Ended vs. Open-Ended Questions make a vertical line on a piece of paper to create two columns. Label the left column Closed-Ended Questions and the right column Open-Ended Questions.

Next, write the following words in the left column under Closed-Ended Questions: *is, are, am, do, did, does, would, could* and *should*. Then, write the following words in the right column under Open-Ended Questions: *who, what, why, when, where,* and *how*.

Step 3: Play the Monologue vs. Dialogue Exercise

The advisor would role play a first appointment meeting with a prospect asking only Open-Ended Questions checking off each question on the right column when asked. The goal is to try and ask all Open-Ended Questions during the role play to make a great connection.

If this is accomplished the advisor won the game, if not the advisor lost the game! Keep score of the Closed-Ended Questions to determine which type of questions are being asked most.

Why Knowing How to Create Dialogue vs. Monologue Works

The reason using open-ended questions works so well is because it gets the listener to open up, which in turn creates the connection. The reason why Jake could easily make a connection in our role play was because his questions were doing just that, allowing me to do all of the talking. So, the next time you feel disconnected just know that it most likely is because you are stuck in a monologue. When this happens, ask open questions to create a dialogue and watch how quickly they open up.

Story #12
Great Questions Create Great Connections

Most advisors/agents eventually get to the point in their careers where they become very knowledgeable about the products and services they recommend. It's just a natural progression. Unfortunately, so is what I call "veteran-itis", which is the tendency to tell people what to do.

As a result, many veterans can sever their connection with prospects/clients or never create one at all. The challenge is not in knowing what to sell but in helping the prospect and/or client know what they need to buy.

How do we do this? We do this by asking questions! Claude Levi-Strauss said, *"The wise man doesn't give the right answers, he poses the right questions."* And, when we craft great questions we create great connections because we aren't telling people what they need to do. Instead, they are coming to their own conclusions.

The 4 Types of Questions-Based Selling Questions

Questions-Based Selling is a term used for asking a series of questions to guide a sales discussion down a clear path to help the prospect and/or client understand their current situation, the problems that they have, the implication of not fixing the problems and the value of having the right solutions.

In addition, it is not so much about "what" questions to ask, but "how" to ask the right ones. The "how to" can be applied in any situation to get the positive results you desire because you are applying the tools/techniques that actually help the prospect bridge the gap between needs and solutions.

The following are the 4 Types of **Questions-Based Selling** Questions also known as **S.P.I.N Selling** because of the acronym that these types of questions spell out.

1. **Situational-Based (S) Questions**

   Situational-Based Questions uncover what the prospect or client's situation is. These are fact-based questions such as, *"How old are you? Do you have a company plan? When was the last time you reviewed it?"*

   Unfortunately, many advisors/agents are stuck on only asking Situational-Based Questions and as a result they don't help the prospect/client get to a deeper level of understanding. Take Dana M. a thirty-year veteran bank financial advisor that I've worked with, who is consistently given referrals by the personal bankers she knows. She explained that when she meets with the referred prospects they seem satisfied with their current investments and typically don't want to meet again. In other words, she wasn't uncovering problems. She was merely telling them what she does and asking them about their current situation.

2. **Problem-Based (P) Questions**

   Problem-Based Questions are questions that uncover the problem with a current situation such as, *"Does it concern you that you are 55 and you haven't put enough money away for retirement? What concerns you most about not having a comfortable retirement?"* Or, *"What keeps you up at night when you think about not having enough in retirement?"*

   After Dana and I designed specific **Situational-Based Questions** (which could lead to uncovering possible problems), she started asking them in her initial meetings. Her follow-up Problem-Based Questions helped the prospects understand that they actually could have problems. This deepened the conversations because the prospects were starting to see the value in getting a second opinion on their investments.

3. **Implication-Based (I) Questions**

   Implication-Based Questions are questions that uncover the implications of not having a solution to the problem such as, *"What are the consequences of not putting enough money away for retirement?* Or, *"What do you think would happen if you didn't have enough money in retirement? Would you sell your house?"*

   As Dana applied **Implication-Based Questions**, she realized that when the prospect was the one telling her the severity of not fixing the problem and what could happen over time; the prospect then understood the urgency that they might need some help now before it was too late.

4. **Needs/Pay-Off (N) Questions**

   Needs/Pay-Off Questions are questions that uncover the value of your solution such as, *"How would it benefit you most if I put together a complete financial plan that showed you how much money you will need in retirement, what kind of income you will have and what would happen to your spouse if anything happened to you?"*

   After role-playing the entire process, Dana started adding **Needs/Pay-Off Questions** to her dialogue and realized that the prospects were now telling her how valuable her services were. As a result, she easily got the second appointment!

Why Asking Great Questions Works

The reason Dana was having so much success was because she wasn't just telling people what she does and what they needed to do. Instead, she asked them the right types of questions to help them understand how she could help them. If you can do the same/similar you will be making much better connections and getting your prospects and clients to realize their situation and how your solutions can be a benefit to them both short and long-term.

Story #13
Realizing the Importance of the Filler Formula

I've noticed a common challenge over the years that I have coached advisors/agents that they typically are unaware of. It seems that rookies and veterans alike tend to want to rush a conversation by either making too many statements or asking too many questions without offering enough of a pause in between for the client/prospect to feel connected. I call this realizing the importance of **The Filler Formula**.

Picture a brick wall. Your questions and statements are the bricks and "The Filler" is the mortar.

If you just make statements, you are probably in monologue mode and not having much of a two-way dialogue.

If you just ask questions, it may seem to a client/prospect more like an interview or interrogation. In either case this can result in a disconnection between you and them which makes closing the loop and getting a sale all the more difficult!

There are five Forms of Filler, which are great strategies that can and should be, used anytime a prospect or client answers your questions. They are as follows:

Strategy #1: Acknowledgment Statements

Acknowledgement Statements are quick statements that let the prospect or client know that you are listening. Typically, this is the easiest Filler to use and should be used often. Here are some examples:

- *"Okay. All right. Sure."*
- *"I can see what you mean."*
- *"That makes sense."*

Strategy #2: The Connection Story

Stories are a great way to help prospects or clients know that you understand what they are saying. It adds an additional layer to the conversation because they understand what your experience is with the subject matter.

Typically, this is Filler that needs a little pre-appointment planning because you want to have a few stories ready at a moment's notice so that you can tell them.

Here is the best way to set up the story:

That sounds like a client I had years ago... (Insert story)

I can relate to that because... (Insert story)

That's actually pretty common, one of my clients... (Insert story)

Knowing your story phrasing is a great way to transition from what they said to your story. Once you start the story, remember to ask questions while telling it to make sure that you pull them in.

Strategy #3: The Sound Bite

One of the best ways to make a connection is to give the prospect or client a sound bite that could be a famous quote or phrase.

This allows you to change the focus of the conversation to what someone else said so you are not directly telling them what to do and yet show the prospect or client that you were listening. It also helps them comprehend your point without you having to repeat it.

Here are a few examples:

- Albert Einstein said, *"The definition of insanity is doing the same thing over and over again and trying to get a different result."*
- Warren Buffet is right when he said, *"Risk comes from not knowing what you are doing."*

I recommend that you pick a topic such as market volatility, price, risk, value, procrastination or other things that you have heard prospects and clients state they are concerned about and design your sound bites around them.

Strategy #4: The Curiosity Question

Oftentimes, prospects and clients may make a statement or answer a question that leaves you wondering what they mean.

In addition, you may hear something that you believe to be inaccurate. Instead of assuming what they meant or making a statement defending your position, simple try the following Curiosity Questions:

- *"That's interesting, tell me more about that? Why is that?"*
- *"Why do you think _____ is happening right now?"*
- *"So, why do you think that is?"*

Strategy #5: The 4 Levels of Empathetic Listening

Unfortunately, listening can be one of the hardest things for an advisor or agent to do because they are too busy talking. That's why it is so important to slow down and let the prospect or client know that they are truly being heard. The following are the **4 Levels of Empathetic Listening:**

- Mimic saying exactly what the prospect or client said (not suggested)
- Rephrasing—*"It sounds like (explain what you heard)."*
- Feelings—*"That sounds (insert feeling), is it?"*
- Feelings and Rephrasing—*"That sounds _____, because of _____."*

Why The Filler Formula Works

It is important to understand why **The Filler Formula** works in general rather than to know how to use multiple examples. The reason it works is because it allows the individual to take a breather from your questions and statements requiring them to instantly reply and instead listen to a story from you while coming to a conclusion on their own.

At the very least they know that they have been heard, which helps them to open up even further and allows them to feel connected. Remember, people don't care how much you know until they know how much you care. So, it's your job to make them feel that way.

Story #14
The Empathetic Advisor

It never ceases to amaze me that after thirty years in the financial services industry, both as an advisor and as a coach, there is still so much that I learn as I work with individuals on better ways to increase their overall communication skills.

A recent example of this would be when one of my advisor clients, who had recently played the role of a prospect during our ten-minute role play session, said afterwards, *"I felt the most connected when I knew the advisor was listening."*

A lengthy dialogue followed this brief statement with others in the group about the value of listening. Another advisor suggested that we take a page out of Stephen R. Covey's book **The 7 Habits of Highly Effective People** in which he describes the four developmental stages of empathetic listening.

The following is an interpretive summary of each of those stages and an example of how it could be utilized when prospects state, *"I've had it with advisors. They all promise great returns, but never deliver."* These stages are not consecutive, but independent possibilities when having a conversation and should be scattered throughout your dialogue.

Stage #1: Mimicking Content

In this stage you as the listener are merely repeating what you have heard. It is the most basic of all listening skills although be careful as this method can seem a little insulting if used too often during the same discussion. However, it does force you to listen so that you can repeat what has been said. Example: *"So, you've had it with advisors, they promise great returns, but never deliver?"*

Stage #2: Rephrasing Content

In this stage you as the listener merely put the content you have heard from the prospect into your own words. Example: *"With your experiences, you don't believe what advisors have to say anymore?"*

Stage #3: Reflecting Feelings

In this stage you as the listener interpret what he/she believes the other person is feeling. It is much more effective because you are focusing on both what is being said as well as the way you believe the speaker feels about what they are saying. Example: *"That sounds extremely frustrating."*

Stage #4: Reflecting Feelings and Rephrasing Content

In this stage you as the listener combine stage #2 and #3 to make an authentic connection so that the speaker is feeling understood. Example: *"It sounds like you are really wary of all advisors because many of them have over-promised and under-performed?"*

After spending five group coaching sessions with one of my teams, I created the **4 Levels of Empathetic Listening Exercise**, an exercise where we role play using a combination of the stages previously discussed. I have found that each advisor is making a much better connection with their prospects because they have increased not only their listening skills, but also their ability to gain trust leading them towards becoming (in the eyes of their prospects) a much more empathetic advisor.

Why Empathetic Listening Works

I think it's safe to say that most people want to be heard. The reason why **Empathetic Listening** works is because it gives the advisor/agent a process to let the listener know that they are doing just that, being listened to. Once you know how to apply the four stages of **Empathetic Listening** and can toggle between each stage the process becomes relatively easy.

The flow of the conversations is no longer just question and answer, much like an interview, but rather question, answer then **Empathetic Listening**, much more like two old friends that can relate to one another. So, if you want to help the listener feel heard apply this tool and watch how quickly you become an empathetic advisor!

Story #15
Five Elements of the Agreement Close

Have you ever noticed that one of the most amazing moments is when one of your prospects comes to the conclusion that they want to buy? What a terrific feeling to know that they are in agreement that your recommendations are the solutions to their financial challenges.

Did you know that you can actually use a method I call, **The Agreement Close**, to close a sale or secure setting an appointment? All it takes is you knowing the steps to help "walk" a prospect to that place.

At some point in your career you will realize that prospects and clients alike enjoy talking about themselves. And, why not? It's a subject that they are very familiar with.

During these moments of revelation you may make a realization that they have a real challenge and that YOU have the solution. However, just telling them this is not an effective strategy to forming a good connection.

Rather, help them come to this conclusion by using the following elements:

1. The Prospect's Key Closing Phrase

One of the most important things to remember when using **The Agreement Close** is to know when to begin. Ironically, the prospect will unknowingly tell you when that is by making a statement or using a phrase that indicates they are a little lost, frustrated or unsure about something you know you can help them with. The following is an example:

Prospect: *"I'm not really sure how I'm doing with my portfolio."*

2. Empathy/ Acknowledgement

At this point, just taking the time to empathize or even acknowledge what they said can go a long way in building a connection because it helps the prospect know that you truly and genuinely understand. Try something as simple as this:

Advisor: *"I completely understand, most people don't know how their portfolio is doing."*

3. The Agreement Close

Next, we need to strengthen the connection by agreeing with them. This is a very important step because the prospect will find it very difficult to disagree with you for agreeing with them. The following is an example:

Advisor: *"And, that's exactly why we should get together."*

4. Benefit Statements

At this point, you need to add to the statement above and clarify why you said what you said (aka **The Agreement Close**) so that the prospect understands what the benefits are to them. Once you do, they will soon be agreeing with you! Here is a brief example:

"You don't want to realize that you are taking too much risk after the market goes down and you lose a lot of money."

5. Final Close

All you need to do now is ask for the order! Try this alternative close:

Advisor: *"Do you have time to meet Tuesday at 3:00 or Wednesday at 4:00, which time works better for you?"*

Prospect: *"Tuesday at 3:00."*

Why The Agreement Close Works

As you read through the dialogue, did you understand how the prospect might feel during this conversation? If so, you already understand why this works.

If not, let me explain that the reason why **The Agreement Close** works is because you are agreeing with the prospect (their Key Closing Phrase) and explaining to them how moving forward with you will help them most. In other words, you are acknowledging their challenge, agreeing that it is a valid challenge and that is exactly why they need your solutions.

Story #16
Doing the Mood Dance

Have you ever been in an appointment and realized the mood has shifted, from good to not so good? Things seemed to be going along pretty well because the prospect or client was receptive to what you had been saying and then all of the sudden their demeanor turned defensive or even aloof.

This is what I call Doing the Mood Dance; in every interaction there is someone who is leading the mood of the conversation and someone who is mirroring the mood of the conversation. In this scenario, the prospect/client took the lead!

Unfortunately, most advisors & agents who encounter a negative shift in the mood of a client or prospect have no idea why the mood changed much less what to do about it. When this happens, you need to be ready and that is why I've created an emotional management system so you will be prepared.

Understanding the Five Step Emotional Management System

In a recent group coaching session with a very successful team, I noticed one of the junior advisors getting completely distracted during role play when his colleague (who was playing the role of the prospect) became very distant. The junior advisor had absolutely no idea how to draw the "prospect" back into the conversation.

Let's take a look at each of the five steps in the **Advisor Solutions** Emotional Management System to illustrate what he should have done.

Step 1: The Emotional Barometer

When the conversation seems to start to go "cold" it's time to use an emotional barometer to find out how the prospect is feeling. Here is an example dialogue:

Advisor: *"It's important to have a truly balanced portfolio at your stage in life so you don't experience another 2008."*

Prospect: *"My portfolio was fine in 2008 because it was balanced."*

At this point the conversation seems to be going south. Now is the time to take the prospect's emotional temperature.

Advisor: *"True! You are ahead of most investors, but did you still lose money? And, if so how did it feel?"*

As you can see, we are trying to emotionally warm back up the prospect with hopes that he will be honest about whether he lost money and remind him that it was not a pleasant experience.

Step 2: Getting the Emotional Buy-In

At this point the emotional climate might be changing for the better, but it's important to get emotional buy-in by getting a sense that your prospect is indeed starting to warm up and change their feeling (mood) about the subject. Here is an example:

Prospect: *"Yes, I lost money that year. Nobody likes it lose money."*

Advisor: *"You are right, nobody likes to lose money. And when the market dropped 50% from peak-to-trough even if you lost half it still wouldn't be pleasant, right?"*

As you can see, we are trying to turn up the "emotional heat" by helping the client understand how they actually felt at that time.

Prospect: *"No, it really wasn't fun at all. I just quit looking at my statements."*

Step 3: Leading the Mood Dance

At this point in the conversation we are starting to Lead the Mood Dance because we now shifted the prospect's mood from one on the defensive to one where he is at least admitting that he lost money and that it wasn't fun. Now is the time to continue taking the lead.

Advisor: *"We feel the same way too and that's why we searched for what we call a "Truly Balanced Portfolio"-one that can make money in good times and bad. But, before I explain it let me ask you, does that sound like something that you might be interested in learning more about?"*

Prospect: *"Yes, I guess."*

As you can see, a brief statement such as this can qualify the prospect's emotional state as well as continue to help you lead the Mood Dance.

Step 4: The Reverse Experience Story

Now, it's time to help the prospect become even more a part of the dialogue by hearing more about their own story, I call it The Reverse Experience, getting the prospect or client to explain what happened to them.

Most advisors/agents that tell stories do so from their own experience. However, when you get a prospect or client to tell you their own story and they realize what went wrong they are more open to your recommendations if they are in fact the solution to their problem.

Advisor: *"What type of portfolio did you have back then, was it U.S. stock and bond mutual funds like you have now?"*

Prospect: *"Yes, it's pretty much what we have now-all in the U.S. That way if the stock market doesn't do well hopefully the bond market will."*

Advisor: *"But, where are both of those markets in, and what has to happen?"*

Prospect: *"They are both U.S. markets and one of them has to do well."*

By now the prospect may start to understand where you are going with your line of questions. And, they may start to see the light. However, let's move to the next step.

Step 5: The Agreement Close

This is the final step in **The Agreement Close**, agreeing with the prospect and possibly even using their verbiage to close the sale. It's a three-step process:

1. **Agree-** allows you to diffuse the situation.
2. **State the Benefit-** So that they understand the why behind what you want them to do.
3. **Close**- Ask for the order so that you close the sale.

Here is an example:

Advisor: *"And, that's exactly why most U.S. balanced portfolios don't do well in down markets, because one market has to go up farther than the other goes down. Besides, nobody seems to factor in a 25% loss in their investment strategy, but they seem to accept it after that happens. Do you know what an alternative strategy would be?"*

Prospect: *"To not be completely tethered to the U.S. markets?"*

Advisor: *"Yes! Now you are getting it. And, that's exactly what our strategy does? Does that make sense?"*

Prospect: *"Yes, it actually does."*

When you get this point in the conversation, you have already closed the business even if you haven't explained all of the details yet. The reason is because people hate to be sold, but they love to buy.

And, the way to get someone to buy is to help them come to their own conclusion that they need or want to buy your product/s or service/s. In the preceding dialogue the prospect got to what I call **The Pivotal Moment**—where the prospect truly understands now when he replied with the answer, *"To not be completely tethered to the U.S. markets."* He just realized the reason why he had lost money even with a balanced portfolio.

Why Doing the Mood Dance Works

For illustrative purposes this conversation was mapped out using a perfect world scenario. And, it was used as an example and not my own personal investment strategy. But, we don't live in a perfect world. Instead, we do live in a world that has somewhat predictable patterns.

What I mean by that is that you have probably been in an appointment and had some part of the discussion misinterpreted. If so, use these steps to map out the conversation beforehand so that you can lead the mood dance!

Story #17
Sell the Sizzle

Have you ever wondered how top advisors/agents sell? Do they just have a natural ability to connect with prospects and clients or is "it" something that can be learned by everyone? Well, stop wondering! Top advisors/agents who sell their sizzle use great stories.

Clients and prospects connect with a great story because they understand your products and services better when they can relate it to something that is familiar to them.

The key is to use an analogy that is easily understood and tie it to a product that is not easy to understand. Successful **Story-Based Selling** connects concepts that the prospect or client understands to explain concepts they do not understand! The simpler the concepts are the better the story turns out.

Preparation is vital to **Story-Based Selling**, but very few financial advisors/agents take the time to write out a story for each product or service that they have. They truly are rarely prepared for the one moment when inserting a great story could make all the difference!

How to Craft a Great Story

Creating a great story starts with the end in mind. First, find a familiar object that your client(s) could relate to. If your client is a farmer make the object or story about something farm-related, such as growing corn. If the client is an executive that likes to sail, make the story about something sailing-related.

Next, look at ways where the familiar object relates to your product, service or concept and write your own custom analogy.

Here is one example: *Look at a four lane highway as it relates to diversification because by taking four cars instead of one you would be diversified in all four lanes.* Then make the story end on a note where the product or service ties in with the object in the story, such as *diversifying your money over four different styles of mutual funds is like diversifying your journey over four different lanes on a highway. You never know what the fastest lane is at any specific time, but you always have a car in a lane.*

Below, you will find other **Story-Based Selling** examples. Read through them and use them as a guide to help you craft your own great stories.

Tax Deferral:

Tax deferral is like this cup. We can put water, tea, coffee or anything you want in this cup. You can put CD's, stocks, mutual funds or anything you want inside your I.R.A.

As long as we keep your investments inside the I.R.A., the government will not tax you as the money grows. When you pour the money out or take the money out of this vehicle, the government will tax you. That's tax deferral!

An Equity Mutual Fund Portfolio:

An equity mutual fund portfolio is like a grocery bag. When you go to the grocery story, you buy products that you know that are made by companies that you are familiar with such as Coca-Cola®, Kellogg's® and General Electric. If you bought a piece of these companies you would be buying a stock.

When you go to check out of the store, the clerk puts your products into a grocery bag. An equity mutual fund portfolio is a grocery bag of stocks! The grocery cart that you wheel out to the car has several grocery bags in it; this grocery cart is like an equity mutual fund portfolio holding several equity mutual funds.

Why Selling the Sizzle Works

Typically, most prospects and clients will not buy unless they understand why, why they should own the products and/or services that you are recommending. And, if they don't fully understand what the product/service is or what it can do for them they oftentimes will give an excuse, in the form of an objection as to why they don't want it.

The reason why selling the sizzle works so well is because you are bridging the gap between them not understanding the complexities of the product/service you are recommending and the simplicity of something that they have known all of their life. And, you are doing this in the form of a story. Remember, the sizzle is what sells not the steak!

Story #18
Understanding the Reconnection Strategy

One of the most puzzling things that can happen to a financial advisor/agent is during the first appointment process when the advisor/agent seems to be building rapport until suddenly the conversation takes a turn and there seems to be an awkward disconnect.

James T., a veteran financial advisor client of mine with ten years of experience explained that he was recently in a meeting with a prospect who was in a high tax bracket and he had a large sum of money to invest, but didn't want to pay taxes on the money as it grew.

James felt that he knew just the right investment vehicle to recommend and said, *"It sounds like to me you need a variable annuity."* Unfortunately, what James did not know is that the prospect had a distain for annuities, didn't fully understand them and felt that the internal fees were way too expensive. As a result, the prospect responded, *"No, I don't"* and after that it was quite apparent that he didn't want to hear anything else that James had to say.

Understanding the Reconnection Strategy

Oftentimes, advisors/agents can say something that may cause a prospect to disengage. When this happens most advisors/agents try and stress their point or find another way to reconnect. Unfortunately, neither of which are effective. I suggest to my clients to use **The Reconnection Strategy**.

The following is an example of the **Reconnection Strategy**:

1. **Disconnect:** When an advisor asks a question or makes a statement that creates resistance in the prospect it creates a disconnection in any rapport. The challenge is that it's virtually impossible to know what any prospect may feel about a product or service.

Advisor: *"One of the things that I do for my clients is to make sure they have the right life insurance coverage so that we minimize financial risk to the family should anything happen. Can you see why that it important?"*

Prospect: *"We don't need more life insurance, we've got enough coverage to pay for the burial expenses."*

2. **Explain:** When the advisor realizes that something has gone awry it is important to explain why he/she asked the question or made the statement that they did in the first place so that the prospect can understand what the advisor's rationale was.

   Advisor: *"The reason I ask that question is because burial expenses are sadly just the beginning of the expenses not the end."*

3. **Story:** Telling a story helps to take the pressure off of the prospect seeming wrong or having to defend their position.

   Advisor: *"It reminds me of a client that I had that said he just wanted enough to cover the cost of the burial. Unfortunately, that's all he got and later that year he had a heart attack and passed away. After about a year his wife had to downsize because she couldn't pay the mortgage on her own. They moved and the kids went to a new school."*

4. **Reconnect:** Once the story is shared, it is vital to ask if the prospect can relate to the story.

   Advisor: *"Can you see how that affected the family?"*

   Prospect: *"Yes, I see how that impacted them."*

   Advisor: *"How would it financially impact your wife and kids if something similar occurred?"*

   Prospect: *"They would probably have to do the same thing. I guess we should consider taking a look at some more life insurance."*

Why the Reconnection Strategy Works

The reason why **The Reconnection Strategy** works is because it's not about the advisor/agent defending their position, but rather about explaining the challenges others have faced in scenarios that may be commonplace.

By helping the prospect realize that at some point down the road they too may have that same challenge, the reconnection is made as the prospect now understands the advisor/agent has the expertise and knowledge of situations that take place that should be safe guarded ahead of time.

Story #19
The Power of the Pause

We have all heard the saying, *Silence is Golden,* but as advisors/agents do we routinely utilize silence as part of our presentations? Now, you may be thinking to yourself, *"I stop talking every time I ask a question and patiently wait and then listen to their answer."*

While this may be true, it's not exactly what I am referring to. What I mean is to pause or slow down with your dialogue and truly think about what you what to convey, what you want the listener to hear rather than just rambling on with hopes that what you are saying is understood. It is what I refer to as **The Power of the Pause.**

Let's take a look at what a few seconds of strategic silence can do for you.

- **Pausing for Direction:** During one of my Group Coaching Role Play sessions I noticed that some of the advisors/agents seemed to be nervously searching for something to say, trying to fill every moment with a question, statement, fact or story.

  However, what they didn't realize was that they were just filling up the conversation with idle chit-chat. By doing so they were not getting the prospect (we were role playing) to come to a place of understanding regarding the products and services that were being recommended.

  So, I created an exercise, **The Five Seconds of Silence Exercise**, in which the advisor/agent had to pause for five seconds each time prior to speaking. Each round of the game lasted for five minutes. If the advisor/agent broke the five seconds of silence rule, they were immediately eliminated from the game.

  The rounds continued until there was only one winner. The purpose of the exercise was to give the advisor/agent the necessary time to strategically think about the direction they wanted the conversation to go in and what type of dialogue would work well.

After a few rounds, each advisor/agent realized that pausing, even for five seconds, could be just enough time to make a course correction.

- **Pausing for Pace:** A conversation is similar to a dance, as there is always one person who leads and one who follows. If you feel that you are losing the listener because you are speaking too quickly, then it's time to pause.

Slow down and try phrasing a question like this, *"So,"* (wait two seconds-one thousand one, one thousand two) and then continue on with the question, *"Why do you think that is?"* Typically what happens next is that the listener will match your pace and slow down as they answer.

- **Pausing for Impact**: One of the optimal times to pause is when you are about to close the sale. The two or three seconds of silence after starting a question (such as in the earlier example) creates curiosity about what you are going to say next. *"Well?"* (again wait two seconds) and slowly continue with, *"What do you think is the best course of action?"* Then sit tight and wait for them to respond.

Why The Power Of the Pause Works

There is no hard-and-fast rule on perfecting the pause, but if you find yourself disconnected from your client/prospect during a presentation you will be well advised to let a few seconds of appropriate silence enter into the conversation.

Story #20
The Flipside of Foolish

In a recent coaching session, I suggested that Sammy, a financial advisor client with over thirty years of experience, do a little homework before our next session. She had been concerned about prospects not seeing the value in getting an opinion from her on their portfolios and she wanted to know how to convince them that they should.

We had just mapped out a process that I refer to as **Reversing the Dialogue,** which works back from what conclusion you ultimately would like your prospect to come to and the questions path that would most be effective in getting them to realize that conclusion.

In Sammy's situation that getting an opinion from her was in their best interest. *"I will work on it and let you know how it goes."* she excitedly said. *"Actually, why don't you type it out and email it to me then in our next session we can role play with it."* I replied.

The Reality of Role Play

One of two things typically happen when I mention role play to a client, either they look forward to practicing and can't wait to start or they have anxiety and can't wait to explain why they don't want to do it.

"I hate role play" she admitted. *"I'd rather just go out and practice this on prospects and tell you how it went."* I curiously inquired, *"Why?" "Well, it's because I don't want to sound foolish in front of you."* she cautiously replied. *"Ah-ha, you need to understand the flipside of foolish then."* I responded with a laugh.

Understanding the Flipside of Foolish

There was a significant pause on her end before I continued on to explain. Feeling foolish is like looking at only one side of the proverbial coin. There is the negative side, which she had already shared about, feeling embarrassed or inadequate, however on the flipside there are multiple positive reasons why role playing was a smart best practice.

"When it comes to role play, the flipside of feeling foolish is the fact that you WILL learn from practicing with me. You WILL get better at asking questions, moving people down the pipeline and accomplishing your goals. Aren't all of those outcomes worth a few minutes of feeling foolish?" I asked confidently. *"When you state it that way, I'd much rather feel foolish and learn how to do it right BEFORE meeting with clients/prospects,"* she said sheepishly.

Achieving Real Results With Role Play

In our next session I reassured her that there were no incorrect questions and that role play was merely a method that she would learn from.

After two or three role play conversations she became more comfortable and relaxed with the technique of applying (and adjusting) the questions she had mapped out.

"Nice job! You took me down a path of questions to help me understand why I should get an opinion from you. I absolutely felt connected and engaged while you were doing it! I could feel her smile over the phone as she replied, *"I didn't feel foolish doing the role play with you at all. I'd like to do it more often!"*

Why The Flipside of Foolish Works

Often in order to grow our business, we have to be open to leaving our comfort zone to strengthen our weaknesses. Being willing to stretch beyond what you already know and feel comfortable with allows for you to find what your flipside of foolish might be.

Story #21
The First Appointment F.O.R.M

Do you know what prospects love to talk about most during the first appointment process? If you guessed that they love to talk about themselves, you are absolutely right! And, why is that? I believe that it is because self-disclosure can be gratifying. And, what better subject for them to talk about then the one subject they know the most, which is themselves.

Lao Tzu (the founder of Taoism) said, *"Knowing others is wisdom, knowing yourself is enlightenment."*

The Goal of a Good First Appointment Process

The goals of a first appointment process are to discover everything we can about the prospect, uncover any financial challenges that they have and help them understand how your services are the solutions to reaching their financial goals. Once you do that, they are open to the next step in the process, which is the second appointment, where you will be discussing your recommendations.

And, since we know that most prospects are open and willing to share their thoughts and goals around their own financial future then shouldn't we take the time to have a well thought out process for asking better questions?

Understanding the First Appointment F.O.R.M

That is why I created the **First Appointment F.O.R.M**. It is a tool for formulating and preparing for the first appointment. Oftentimes, financial advisors use little or no preparation for their first appointment with a prospect. A legal pad and a few common questions may be all that some advisors feel they need.

However, to truly uncover challenges and sell your solutions to show your value and eventually set the second appointment, you need to have a proven system for crafting the types of questions you will be asking.

Why the First Appointment F.O.R.M is Unique

This tool combines the acronym **F.O.R.M.** (which stands for Family, Occupation, Recreation and Money) and the **Questions-Based Selling Model** (refer to the story **Great Questions Create Great Connections** in chapter 2) to create a strong first appointment dialogue.

By centering the conversation on questions pertaining to family, occupation and recreation, we create the foundation for uncovering how all of these could be affected by money or lack of money. In other words, it uncovers how the prospect's family, occupation and recreation may need money in the short, intermediate and long-term and how these types of needs could affect that money.

In addition, with this tool we combine a process for knowing how to ask the right questions—**Questions-Based Selling** so that we can uncover the situations, concerns, implications of not addressing these concerns and the benefits (from the prospect's viewpoint) of having solutions.

Creating and Customizing the First Appointment F.O.R.M

Let's take a look at how you can create your own **First Appointment F.O.R.M.** by mapping this out on an Excel Spreadsheet with four columns and four rows. The columns will be labeled in the following order: Situation, Problem, Implication and Needs, which is the acronym for **S.P.I.N Selling.**

S.P.I.N Selling (also known as the **Questions-Based Selling Model**) can be found previously in this book under the **Great Questions Create Great Connections** story.

The four rows will be labeled in the following order: Family, Occupation, Recreation and Money. Once you have the **First Appointment F.O.R.M.** fill in the questions into each box.

Four Examples of the First Appointment F.O.R.M Questions

The following is a brief example of some of the questions you could ask when discussing the topic of family. The topic of family can be a great icebreaker when getting to know someone. By leading with this topic you are giving the prospect a chance to talk about people that are most certainly near-and-dear to their heart!

Family Situational-Based Questions:

- *"Tell me a little bit about your family."*
- *"Are you married?"*
- *"Do you have kids?"*
- *"What is it that you'd really like for the family?"*

Let the prospect answer all of your questions and probe deeper by continuing the conversation with questions. That way the prospect is explaining the current family situation as well as goals.

Family Problem-Based Question: Once you have heard the prospects family situation you need to ask yourself if there are any possible problems that you have identified that concern the prospect or are there any problems that you see that the prospect may not. Then, try a simple Problem-Based Question such as, *"What keeps you up at night regarding providing for your family?"*

Family Implication-Based Question: If the prospect has identified one or more problems then it's important to help them understand the ramifications of not fixing the problem. That's why you will want to use an Implication-Based Answer such as, *"What do you think will happen if this concern occurred?"*

Family Needs/Pay-Off Question: By now the prospect has understood and explained to you their concerns when it comes to their family as well as the implications of not fixing those problems. That's why a Needs/Pay-Off Question will help them to tell you the value of your solutions. Here is one example: *"How would it help* *you and your family most if we had a strategy in place to never let that challenge happen to them?"* The answer to that question will tell you the value they place on your solutions!

It is important to note that you do not need to use these exact questions, but rather design your own unique questions around the topics of family, occupation, recreation and money.

Why Using The First Appointment F.O.R.M Works

The reason why this tool works is because with a little thought, preparation and additional practice using the **Questions-Based Selling Model,** for each of the **F.O.R.M** topics you will soon find that you are creating a stronger rapport and a better foundation for building relationships in the first appointment process. And, when you prepare your questions ahead of time you can almost certainly plan to make a better connection!

Story #22
The Power of Preparation

One of the things I emphasize to my one-on-one coaching clients is the power of preparation for themselves and for their clients. A more common challenge that I have heard often during my years of coaching is about knowing what to prepare for prior to a closing appointment.

It seems that many advisor's pre-appointment time is spent on preparing hypothetical illustrations for the products they recommend.

Then, during the meeting they typically talk about their recommendations until eventually their client's indicate if they are interested or not. Thus, more of the advisor's time is spent explaining everything rather than necessarily connecting. It seems that most financial advisors go through a learning curve when it comes to the final appointment process.

Many advisors focus on creating presentations full of charts, graphs and providing literature explaining the products they are recommending. Unfortunately, this is typically where the preparation stops. The problem is that there is much more to the appointment than just the recommendations.

Think of it this way, if you just watch the last ten minutes of a great movie, you might have a very different opinion of it and be wondering why the movie was so bad. This would be because you had not experienced the story that set up the final movie scene. Your presentations are the same way-they need a strong beginning, middle and end.

It takes careful preparation that goes way beyond just planning for the recommendation. You need to prepare everything from small talk, having the prospect answer any questions, comments and concerns to doing a current portfolio review.

Once you have finished explaining all of the features and benefits of your recommendations the final steps are to elicit any objections, resolve any objections and then finally ask for the order.

After many sessions coaching clients, I decided to create a resource that maps out exactly what to do to make a much better connection with a prospect/client so that they want to buy your recommendations, instead of feeling as if they are just being sold them.

Hence, the **Advisor Solutions 2nd Appointment Worksheet** was born!

The following is a brief overview of each step on the **2nd Appointment Worksheet**:

- **Introduction-** (or small talk to connect with a prospect)— most advisors instinctively do this, but you don't want to be like most advisors. Instead, take a minute to think about what conversation starter you can utilize to break the ice <u>before</u> the meeting even begins.

- **Summary/Agenda**— Following the introduction and small talk summarize your appointment so that the prospect understands that there is a beginning, middle and end to it.

    Here is an example: *"I could talk about golf all day, but I suppose I should summarize what we are going to talk about. I have an Agenda Sheet and we will first discuss any questions, comments and concerns that you have.*

    Second, we will recap your current portfolio. Third, I have a couple of questions, comments and two concerns that you should be aware of. Fourth, I would like to show you the recommendations that I put together for you.

    Lastly, we can open up the dialogue for any additional questions that you may have after all of the aforementioned. How does that sound?"

- **Prospect's Questions, Comments and Concerns**—this step is crucial because you want to uncover anything that may come up during your meeting with them. You also want to uncover any additional problems that the prospect may have with their current portfolio or any objections they may have overall.

  It is important to note that the advisor must prepare for this step by anticipating what their prospect's biggest concern(s) may be and position them in the discussion so that they willingly open up and convey how they feel.

- **Current Portfolio**—this is the step in which the advisor summarizes what they learned during their first appointment along with any additional information they may have learned while researching the prospect's current investments.

  It forms the basis for solidifying the relationship because the advisor and prospect are both in agreement of what the prospect has and what they want this money to do for them. It also increases your credibility because they know that you are familiar with their current portfolio.

- **Advisor's Questions, Comments and Concerns**—this part of the process assists in having the prospect question their current portfolio and whether it is helping them reach their goals. It also helps you as their advisor uncover any additional emotional ties to a specific investment such as a stock their father left them with wishes to never sell it.

  Finally, it helps you as their advisor to explain possible challenges that the prospect was not aware of such as a lack of diversification, increased amount of portfolio risk and investment style overlap. All of your questions, comments and concerns lead up to one thing, your solutions.

If done properly you can finish this step by asking this question, *"So based on what we talked about, what do you think is the best course of action?"*

If you mapped out your questions correctly, they should be explaining the type of strategy that you are about to recommend to them. In other words, they already understand why they need your recommendation, you didn't sell any to them instead they bought them from you.

- **Recommendations**—the recommendation process is as unique as you are, but there are some fundamental commonalities that all successful advisors do to connect during the recommendation process.

    o Keep it simple and reiterate the challenges then your solutions

    o Use metaphors, analogies and stories

    o Use trial close statements to close specific issues of the recommendations

    o Use alternative closes when comparing two recommendations so the client can decide which is better for them.

- **Objections**—these are a natural part of the sales process. You want to welcome and actually encourage objections so that you can help the prospect illustrate their concerns about your recommendations so you can move them to the next step, which is the **Objection Resolution Model,** a process to overcome objections (refer to the story **Beyond the Gatekeeper** in chapter 2).

- **Close**— the close is the final step in the second appointment. There will not be any additional looping back to other objections. Ask if there are any additional concerns. If the

85

prospect says no, then ask the prospect to move ahead to filling out the paperwork.

The following story describes a financial advisor who utilized the **2nd Appointment Worksheet** well:

Scott was a newer financial advisor whom I started coaching last fall. During one of our first coaching sessions I realized that he had the tenacity and dedication to do very well with his business. However, one thing was going to keep him from reaching his potential, he was NOT taking the time to fully prepare and organize for his appointments. We spent several weeks reviewing various tools including the **2nd Appointment Worksheet.**

Shortly after, I received this update from Scott:

"Last night I had a client meeting. Unfortunately my computer locked up and I could not show the client the financial plan. Three things made this come out ok: first, I had gone through the presentation several times so I knew it well; second, I had **The 2nd Appointment Worksheet** *filled out for this client; and third I had a letter, with the client's most important concerns in the first paragraph.*

Working from the letter, I was able to describe the client's concerns and get an agreement that these were still their greatest concerns. I was then able to present the information using what I had practiced, along with **The 2nd Appointment Worksheet**, *which in a way is an outline of the meeting. In this way not having the computer, which would have been a showstopper in the past, was simply a large inconvenience."*

I was excited for Scott because it proved to him that taking the time to craft well thought out plans for preparing for meetings can help him feel confident and organized, truly the power of preparation.

In Scott's case taking the time to prepare actually gave him a "surprise" Plan B that he didn't even know about, but it sure did end up assisting him in being able to turn an obstacle into a huge opportunity!

Why the Power of Preparation Works

The reason why The Power of Preparation works so well is because it creates confidence in the advisor/agent. In fact, Scott is no exception to the rule. Some advisors/agents that continuously use **The 2nd Appointment Worksheet** have created an impressive 95% close ratio with prospects!

This tool offers the advisor/agent a step-by-step process for taking the prospect down a path to want to buy. Remember, no one wants to be sold to, but everybody loves to buy! So, the next time you question why you are not getting to the next level ask yourself this question, *"Am I winging-it or am I prepared?"* One thing is for sure, winging it doesn't work! Instead, use The Power of Preparation and you too will see your close ratio soar!

Story #23
The Client-Centered Referral Dialogue

How do you convey your message to a client without seeming "needy" in the process? By understanding how clients think!

Clients give referrals for two possible reasons. First, they want to help you grow your business. Second, they want to help friends and loved ones. Of these two reasons, which one do you believe is a strong reason to give you a referral? If you said to help friends and loved ones, then you are right!

Where the traditional referral asking process, the *"Who do you know?"* question fails, is because it is completely advisor-centered. It revolves around the fact that you are asking your client to help you build your business. It puts the client in an awkward position because no matter how they answer, they run the risk of offending someone. Let's take a further look at this.

If the client answers with a referral, there is a probability that your relationship with the referred could possibly damage their relationship with the referred. If the client answers with no referral, there is a probability that this response could damage their relationship with you!

Let's take a look at the **Client-Centered Referral Dialogue** by understanding the questions as well as the reasoning behind the questions:

Question 1: *Has this been helpful?*

The first question is designed to do two things. First, it is a closed-ended question designed to elicit a "yes" or "no" response. The reason we ask in this way is to let the client definitively admit that they have been helped and second, to identity any shortcomings before continuing with the process. In other words, if they do not feel that they have been helped we need why and how they want to be helped.

Question 2: *How has this helped you the most?*

The second question has three important key elements to it. First, it is an open-ended question designed to elicit more dialogue to get the client to open up. In other words, you are also helping the client take a big picture view of what you do.

Second, when you allow the client to explain their perception, you can later restate their answer to position it as the reason why they want to help others. Third, the word "most" is a presupposition that you have helped them in more than one way and that you are merely curious to unearth the most important way(s) that you have helped!

Question 3: *How do you feel?*

The third question is very powerful! It helps link a positive emotion to the value that the client places on your products and services. When we link the two (positive emotions and your value) we are changing the way they view you! Then, you can also restate their answer to position it as the reason why they want to help others.

Question 4: *Whom would you like to help feel_____ because they have _____?*

The fourth question actually shifts the conversation from you asking about them to you asking about someone they care about. This allows the client to focus on helping others feel the way they do because they are receiving your products and services.

Therein, lies the difference, the conversation is now client-centered. When you incorporate their answers about how they feel and the reason why they feel the way they do about your products and services, you are restating your value by telling them what they said when they answered earlier questions.

Question 5: *Some people like to help their parents, siblings or best friends. You mentioned your _____ who you _____ with, would you like to help _____?*

The fifth question is designed to help the client determine if someone that they have specifically talked about in the past is someone that they want to help in the future. If it is they will be open to making an introduction.

However, if you do not have a person in mind it is important to use a generic question such as, *"Some people like to help their parents, siblings or best friends. Outside of your spouse, who do you spend time with the most? Do you think you would want to help them?"* This question will instantly get the client to think about that person. It will most likely strike up a conversation regarding who this person is and if the client wants to help them by introducing you.

How to Make the Introduction

Getting the name of someone the client cares about is one thing, but getting an introduction to them is another. Oftentimes, a client might say, *"I will have to ask them if they are interested."*

When this happens it's important to keep the conversation flowing by making the introduction easy for them, and teach them how to do it by saying, *"Well, there are two ways to see if they want help. First, you could email them (and copy me) letting them know that you met with your financial advisor today and that you think we should be introduced. I can reply to both of you and see if they are interested. Second, all three of us could grab lunch next week and keep it casual. If he wants help, he will let us know. Of the two ways, which one is better for you?"*

Why The Client-Centered Referral Dialogue Works

By now it probably comes as no surprise that the reason the **Client-Centered Referral Dialogue** works is that it appeals to the reason people give referrals, because they want to help those they love and care about.

The entire dialogue is meant to be just that-a **Client-Centered Referral Dialogue** instead of the usual advisor-centered dialogue with a question that leaves most advisors and agents wondering why they asked, *"Who do you know that you can introduce me to?"* Only to get that deer-in-the-headlights look followed by, *"I can't think of anyone"* response. So, the next time you want a referral use these client-centered referral questions to make a better connection with your clients.

Story #24
Strategically Segmenting Your Client-Base

Building a client-base from scratch can be a lifetime endeavor. Although, you hope that all clients stay with you throughout your entire career the fact is that some will move on or unfortunately pass away.

That's why it is so important to maintain the balance between prospecting for new clients and servicing your existing client-base.

Jim Loehr said, *"It's not how many hours you put in with a client or on a project. It's the quantity and quality of your energy - your focus and force - that determine whether that time is valuable."*

Should all of your clients receive the same level of client servicing when you only have so much time to service an established book of clients?

I believe they should not. And, if you believe this as well then you must also believe that strategically segmenting your client-base is a big part of the solution.

It is surprising how many advisors/agents are unable to tell you the exact number of "A, B and C" level clients they have in their book. The reason is because many advisors/agents rarely take the time to segment their book.

It is important to segment your book early on in your career so that you know how many clients are at each servicing level. If you do not know, you will inevitably service all clients exactly the same way.

The reason this could have a negative impact on your business is because you only have so much time in the day, and if all or most of your time is spent on servicing your "C" level clients then you are doing yourself a disservice. In addition, segmenting the book helps you understand your clients' demographics.

Remember, it takes just as much time to service a big client as it does a small client. In fact, many times it takes more time servicing a smaller client. They may be calling you more often since the money they are investing is a larger percentage of everything they have.

Just to clarify what segmenting your book is all about, I want you to think of it in terms of an educational grading system. When we were kids, we all wanted to get "As" on our report cards.

Much like your report cards, you want to have "A-Clients" in your business book, the type of clients who have a lot of assets, those you like, give you referrals and produce a fair revenue stream. By fair I mean at least a 1% annual revenue stream of assets under management.

And, that is why I have created a tool called **The Client Segmentation Worksheet**. This is a simple tool, which splits each client into four criteria to create the overall "A, B or C-Client Grading system.

Let's take a look at each of the four criteria so you can map out this tool on an Excel Spreadsheet.

Column #1: Assets Under Management

This is the amount of money that you are managing for the client. You must determine what dollar amount is the minimum for each of your "A, B and C-Clients". The important thing to remember is that you can always change the dollar amount that makes up the criteria.

Take for instance Susan K. a thirty-five-year veteran financial advisor who needed help segmenting her book of clients. Originally, she felt that all "A-Clients" had one million or more in investable assets with her.

But, after coaching her over time we determined that her minimum account size should be one million because she had a number of clients that had over five million with her and that her "A-Clients" would be those that have five million or more.

Column #2: Revenue

This means the percentage of annual revenue that you are making off of the assets. A rule of thumb is 1% of assets under management. However, some advisors will discount this based on the asset size.

It never surprises me that most advisors never think to segment their client-base past assets under management. In Susan's case she realized that there were several high net worth clients who were buy-and-hold investors or had their assets in low turnover ratio investments.

Column #3: Likeability Factor

On a scale of 1-10 (1 being worst, 10 being best) how well do you like working with your client. We all end up with a range of client personalities and who have working styles that vary.

Susan was shocked when I explained the likeability factor column and after some thought she realized that there were a few larger clients that were more challenging. Also, there were some smaller clients that she liked so well that she thought of them as friends.

Column #4: Referral Factor: On a scale of 1-10 (1 being worst, 10 being best) how often do the clients pass along referrals. The reason why this is important is because sometimes a smaller client can be great referral source for larger prospects.

When we discussed the Referral Factor she admitted that this was a very difficult subject because she rarely asked for referrals. And, the few referrals that she did get were typically un-provoked.

Understanding The Client Segmentation Worksheet

A client must have at least three out of the four criteria to get a proper ranking. An example would be an "A-Client" having $5,000,000 at 1% revenue with a likeability and referral factor of 7 or higher. If three out of four criteria are filled, then the client is considered an "A-Client".

Why Strategically Segmenting Your Client-Base Works

As you can see, segmenting your book of clients is not an easy process; it does take some thought. The reason it works is because it forces you to determine who really is the most deserving of your time and it is the first step in mastering your client servicing system.

Next, you need to map out what you will do for them or your client servicing levels. Finally, you need to communicate these levels to each client as well as implement what you've promised. When you do this you are sure to retain more clients and have peace of mind knowing they are getting unprecedented service!

Story #25
Being Proactive in a Reactive Environment

Has the recent stock market volatility got you feeling like you are on an emotional roller coaster ride? One day headlines read, *"After historic 1,000 Point Plunge, Dow dives 588 points at Close"* and the next day they read, *"Dow Roars back, Rallies 620 Points!"*

If you find yourself caught between the media hype and hysteria wondering what you should think or expect next don't wait for the market to dictate your actions instead do what other successful advisors/agents are doing and start being proactive in a reactive environment.

Be Proactive With Your Knowledge

We've all heard the saying, *"Knowledge is Power"* and no truer words can be spoken when it comes to understanding a volatile stock market. Your clients look to you to know what is happening and why. In times like these, it is important to not only research the facts (and myths), but to keep current on them at all times. Take time to educate yourself and then your clients!

Be Proactive With Preparing the Story

Knowing what is happening and knowing how to translate that to your clients are two very different things. That is why it is so important to have a process for explaining what the current market story is.

Over the years, I've created many practice management tools for financial advisors and insurance agents. One of the best tools that you can use, especially now, is what I call **The 60 Second Market Story.** It is a process for mapping the past, present and possible future outcomes of the stock market.

If you can explain to your clients what has happened since the beginning of the year, what is currently happening and what your analysts are predicting may happen in the short-term and do it utilizing a story format that your clients can comprehend (without all the industry jargon), you are doing more for them than a majority of your colleagues and peers!

Be Proactive With the Client Calling Process

Once you have prepared what it is you want to share with your clients, it is important to know who exactly to share it with. Take time to create a list of your clients to call with the initial calls to clients whom you feel may be most concerned about the market but you should plan to contact each of your clients. Then, block off a specific time each day to make those calls. Be sure to tell them not to panic if the volatility continues, as it is an expected part of the stock market cycle.

Why Being Proactive in a Reactive Environment Works

Most clients know that market volatility is not your fault, but you do need to remember that client communication is your responsibility. This will help mitigate your client's natural fears by assuring them that you are staying in touch with them, sharing your expertise with what is going on with the market. The reason that this process works is because clients will appreciate that you understand their concerns and an advisor/agent who cares creates loyal clients!

Story #26
What It Takes to Shine

Picture this...you are at a networking event, on vacation or even in an elevator, when you strike up a quick conversation with a stranger and the next thing you know they ask you the inevitable question, *"So, what do you do?"* You immediately try to think of the perfect thing to say. This is your moment to shine! But, do you? Or do you give a generic response such as, *"I'm a financial advisor with XYZ firm."*

During this type of scenario, most advisors/agents panic because they simply haven't taken the time to create a unique "elevator speech". In fact, many do not understand what actually makes a great elevator speech in the first place. I recently read a great definition, *"An "elevator speech" is a short description of what you do, or the point you want to make, presented in the time it takes an elevator to go from the top floor to the bottom floor or vice versa."*

How Do I Create a Great Elevator Speech?

To create a terrific elevator speech you must first understand the formula. I've heard many elevator speeches as well as researched many ways to create them, but I believe the best elevator speeches do the following:

1. Informs the listener of who you are and what your credentials are.
2. States your unique proposition statement.
3. Creates curiosity in the listener to ask questions.
4. Gives you the opportunity to ask additional questions and create a connection.

The Key to Creating Your Elevator Speech

This four-step formula is important to not only understand but to utilize while generating your elevator speech. However, the most vital part of the formula is stating your unique proposition statement.

Your name and credentials are like the appetizer to the main course, they set the stage for the most important information that you want to give—what makes you unique. If done properly, it creates the curiosity needed to further the conversation with them asking questions. If done improperly, it receives an acknowledgement statement such as, *"Oh, I see."* Your question back to them is like dessert, it allows the listener to get engaged in the conversation and make a better connection by telling their story.

Financial Advisor/Agent Unique Proposition Statements

Knowing how to create your own Unique Proposition Statement is a must when creating an Elevator Speech because it needs to be tailored to you. That's why it is important for you to understand the following, which is a series of unique proposition statements to help you better, understand the process so you can formulate your own elevator speech. Use the following examples to get an idea of how to create your own.

Selling the Specifics

Sometimes using specifics about what you do can for your target market can create an incredible amount of credibility as well as curiosity.

"I have a team that specializes in building and preserving wealth for doctors by utilizing the recent Supreme Court ruling."

(Notice the curiosity that you felt? If you were a doctor, you would be asking the question *"What ruling?"*)

Painting the Perfect Picture

In this approach, financial advisors/agents are painting the perfect picture to pull the listener into the conversation by helping them understand what they do through the use of stories, analogies and metaphors. It's a powerful technique when done properly can take a complex business and boil it down to its simplest form:

"You know how a great symphony needs a conductor to organize the musicians or it's just a bunch of noise? Well, I'm kind of like a financial conductor who organizes, recommends and manages all of your financial investments."

The Rhetorical Question

Using rhetorical questions in an elevator speech gets the listener to immediately think about what you are saying. It pulls them in to hear more.

"Do you think multi-millionaires or billionaires manage their own investments? Well, I do the exact same thing for people with $500,000 or more in assets and I can do that with unique technology that I use."

The Problem Solver Analogy

In this technique the elevator speech is designed to solve a common problem, but in a way that uses an analogy or metaphor to help get your point across.

"I'm like mortar. I make sure a family's wealth does not crumble between generations."

Why a Great Elevator Speech Works

Most advisors and agents want to be unique, but rarely do they take the time to practice and perfect their unique proposition statement. The reason why having a great elevator speech works is two-fold; first, it is because it forces you to create your unique proposition statement, it's your stamp to show the world what makes you, you. And, second it also gets you to prepare for the inevitable questions. So, the next time someone asks you *"what do you do"* you can confidently give them your great elevator speech because you now know what it takes to shine!

Story #27
How to G.R.O.W. the Business from Within

I've noticed a recurring pattern with a number of financial advisors/agents with whom I coach. Many advisors/agents seem to go through a cyclical emotional pattern that begins when they realize that their business is not as successful as they want it or need it to be.

This awareness creates anxiety, which if/when it sets in can put them in a "fight or flight" mode; either by working harder, prospecting more and/or doing more business with their current client base (fight mode) or causing them to retreat inward into a state of situational depression leaving them feeling hopeless (flight mode).

Eventually, the advisor/agent gets motivated, works harder (or hopefully smarter) and achieves their desired level of success putting their mind at ease. The problem is if the advisor/agent gets too relaxed they then become unmotivated and as a result do not maintain that same level of success, thus creating the same emotional pattern all over again.

Does this sound familiar? Are you caught up in this cycle?

I have noticed this emotional pattern with my client base in the past. In fact, I have come to expect it with some clients knowing that about once a quarter they revert back to an unmotivated/unsuccessful phase, but for whatever reason over the past several months, more-and-more advisors/agents seem to be experiencing it. As a result, I decided it was time to do a little investigating to find an additional coaching model that might help them break the cycle.

During my research, I had found the **G.R.O.W. Coaching Model**. Wikipedia-an online encyclopedia service- states, *"The GROW model (or process) is a technique for problem solving or goal setting. It was developed in the UK and used extensively in the corporate coaching market in the late 1980s and 1990s."*

This coaching model is based on a four step process for determining both goal setting and providing problem solving. In addition, it allows you to identify options on how to deal with those challenges and what course of action needs to be taken to overcome them.

The following first explains and then illustrates how the **G.R.O.W. Coaching Model** can be utilized by advisors/agents to break the emotional cyclical pattern described.

Goal: The first step is to understand what your goal is. Understanding your goal gives you a concrete objective towards which you can work, and the freedom to start doing so.

Reality: The next step is to look at your current reality. Where are you in relation to your goal? Have you almost achieved your goal? Are you a long way away? Do you need to break the goal into smaller, more achievable goals? It may require a detailed and honest analysis of where you are, but having a deep understanding of where you are provides a very solid foundation of understanding what needs to happen.

Option: Once you understand your goal and your reality, the task is to find out how to start to move the reality towards the goal. At this stage in the process, you examine what options are available to you. This is where the planning takes place. There may be a single course of action, or there may be multiple options from which to choose.

Way Forward: At this stage, we have examined the goal, we know where we are in respect to the goal, and we have examined the various options that we can follow to reach the goal. The final step is to examine the options, and to decide what the best option is to reach your goal. Note that you are not looking at the easiest option, but the best option, which will move you closest towards your goal.

Now here is how a financial advisor/agents could use the **G.R.O.W Coaching Model** as it pertains to providing resolution to their pre-existing fight or flight pattern as discussed earlier.

Goal: To continue with a level of productive activities on a steady basis regardless of my success.

Reality: That I self-sabotage when I am successful by reducing my activities because I am afraid of having too much success.

Option: To surround myself with successful advisors/agents to reinforce a belief system that reaching The Next Level is natural and non-threatening.

Way Forward: Find a mentor who is willing to help me work "smarter" as well as hold me accountable. Find that mentor by the end of the week!

Why the G.R.O.W Model Works

This might seem like a simplistic method, but I assure you it is very effective! Every time I have applied this coaching method with financial advisors/agents, they have determined exactly what course of action needs to be taken. Then, I keep them accountable for taking that action! It gives them the path out of the cyclical pattern and the road to accomplishing their goals consistently.

CHAPTER 3
Advisor Solutions Techniques
Equipping You with the Skillsets for Success

The financial services industry tends to place great significance on having specific sales skillsets to be able to close a sale. And, while I do believe this is important, it's not the only type of skillsets that contribute to success.

Living the life of a successful advisor is about much more than just gross production numbers; it's about developing the skillsets to be able to self-manage while you are managing your clients' finances and relationship with you! And, to do that well, you need a plethora of techniques in your arsenal.

But, what techniques do we need to be our best selves? To know that, we must fully understand what techniques are and to what extent they can be applied to a wide range of topics.

The dictionary definition of techniques is, *"The manner and ability with which an artist, writer, dancer or the like employs the technical skills of a particular art or field of endeavor."* So, if an artist creates art, a writer writes and a dancer dances, what does a financial advisor or insurance agent do besides the obvious? They develop relationships and create connections!

What follows is how my own journey of self-discovery and self-management began.

In the spring of 2009, I had grown my database to over 6,000 financial advisors and insurance agents in just five short years. That database had developed organically by me professionally speaking, volunteering to be a contributing author by writing blogs and articles, and offering free group coaching sessions to investment advisory firms whenever the opportunity would arise.

Just when I least expected it, someone would call or email out of the blue wanting to connect because they saw me speak or read something that I wrote in which I most likely offered a tool or help on how to apply a technique. In other words, they typically had a specific challenge and just needed the solution!

One example of this was a veteran financial advisor with twenty-five years of experience who was in charge of training the rookies in the office. He emailed his request, which said, *"I've got a sales meeting in an hour, do have something I can give my rookies?"*

Immediately, I replied with an article on a topic I thought would help the newer advisors and said, *"I'm happy to explain this technique to them, just give them a copy of the article and get me on the speakerphone in your conference room. I will take care of the rest!"*

He politely declined and said he needed to run it by the branch manager first. He called me the next day and said the meeting went great! And, that he wanted to know if I would speak to the entire office the following week. The next week, he had twenty-eight financial advisors packed into the conference room, all with a copy of a white paper from **The Advisor Solutions S.M.A.R.T Start Group Coaching Program**.

Within the month, thirty-two financial advisors, more than had been in attendance signed up for group coaching! And, about two months later another seventy financial advisors from other branch offices joined as well!

Having thousands of people in the database, I decided that it was time to launch **The Advisor Solutions Monday Morning Motivation**, a weekly motivational email, to everyone to expand on time management, sales, prospecting and client servicing techniques.

What I knew was that I wanted to start with a motivational quote and then expand on it by writing a short blurb on how that quote pertained to anyone in the financial services industry. What I did not know at the time was it was the precursor to developing additional techniques on personal development!

The evolution of **Advisor Solutions** Techniques developed well past the original topics on time management, sales, prospecting and client servicing to topics on, embracing change, learning from failures, getting out of your comfort zone and strategies for creating continuous success.

Some of the original blurbs prompted me to do a deeper dive into researching the topic. As a result, many of the blurbs turned into blogs and articles while others became the basis of a month long group coaching topic in our current flagship group called **The Advisor Solutions Master Class Group Coaching Program.**

For the purpose of this book, I wanted you to understand that the steps, strategies and even the stories should also be viewed as puzzle pieces that fit nicely together to form the "picture" of what a successful advisor could look like.

Unlike the tools section of this book, which focuses on what a successful business could look like, the techniques section is about developing not only business skillsets, but personal skillsets as well.

As you read this section please note that the techniques aren't listed in a particular order as they all work as individual standalone stories, however, when utilized in conjunction with one another, they can and will collectively develop you as a person, which in turn will increase your ability to make effortless connections!

It is my hope that as you read through this book's Technique Section that the stories resonate with you. Their stepwise approach offers granular details to explain them adequately so there is less guesswork. This is the reason why this chapter is so hefty in its length. Any of these techniques can be customized to fit the specifics of your business so that you can create your own unique finished image (puzzle) of what success looks like for you.

Story #28
Protecting Your Inner Peace

Most advisors/agents at some point in their careers get overwhelmed with running their business. As a result, many lose their sense of inner peace. The challenge with this way of feeling is that advisors/agents are trading peace of mind for production and outcomes and they are paying a high price for it.

The Dalai Lama said, *"Do not let the behavior of others destroy your inner peace."* However, can you have a systematic way of not letting negative things that are out of your control affect your mental state of mind? The short answer is "yes".

The key to enjoying your business is found in the power of protecting your inner peace with a particular mental mindset and this is easier than you think.

Step 1: Identify Negative Triggers

One of the most difficult things for advisors/agents to do during an emotional crisis is to stop and evaluate how they got there. It is the first step in moving out of a state of anxiety. The simplest way to do this is the minute you feel your emotions shifting from positive to negative ask yourself the question, *"Why is this shift causing me anxiety?"* which will help you understand your negative triggers.

Matt D., a financial advisor client of mine with over thirty-five years of experience admitted during an individual coaching session that he was in a constant state of stress. We had designed an effective prospecting system, which increased his pipeline to the point where his calendar was full.

As a result, he was working longer hours and on weekends to service his existing client-base as well as prepare for appointments with potential new clients. When I asked him what was causing him anxiety in his business he said, *"I feel like I don't have time to do everything I need to in order to get to the next level."*

Step 2: Understand the Emotional Cost

When advisors/agents are stuck in a challenging emotional state of mind for a long period of time they may not feel that there is a way out. The second step is in understanding the emotional cost that fear and anxiety are producing. Ask yourself *"What is it costing me, emotionally, to continue to feel this way?"*

After tracking his answers over a week's time, Matt realized that the price he was paying was a decrease in his physical and mental health. He wasn't walking his 20,000 steps a day and he wasn't enjoying his work. As a result of this self-awareness, he was now open to a better way of living his life, both personally and professionally.

Step 3: Gain a New Perspective

It is important to put any short-term situation into a long-term perspective because it diminishes the severity of the negative trigger(s). The way to do this is to ask yourself, *"Will this matter to me a year from now?"* A good emotional rule of thumb is don't let anything affect you for more than five minutes if it won't matter twelve months from now.

When I asked Matt this question he laughed and said, *"No! I will have either have figured out a better way to manage all of the activity or I will decrease the level of activity. But, either way it won't matter."* Instantly, he felt better!

Step 4: Action Alleviates Anxiety

I have said it countless times, action alleviates anxiety; however, not just any action. It needs to be strategically planned out to produce optimal results.

I mapped out an action plan for Matt, which included delegating anything that he could to his team. This freed up his time significantly. Also, we set boundaries on the amount of appointments he would have each week so he did not end up overwhelmed.

Next, we scheduled his daily walks so he could have a better work/life balance. Lastly, we incorporated some fun activities as a reward of sorts for keeping the system of managing his anxiety on track. All of this had a profound effect on him and he sustained and was able to maintain the inner peace he was seeking.

Why Protecting Your Inner Peace Works

Protecting your inner peace is not an easy thing to do. However, when you have the four step process outlined above you now know how to do it. The reason why protecting your inner peace works so well is because no amount of success is worth your peace of mind and having a process to attain, sustain and maintain that peace is priceless!

The power of protecting your inner peace lies in understanding the value you place on keeping it; when you do protect it, you enjoy the journey regardless of the weather!

Story #29
Do You Know How to Read Your Gauges?

As a financial advisor we are entrusted with great responsibility—guiding our clients and prospects on their journey to obtain their long-term financial goals via our investment recommendations.

However, since so much of our time is allocated to helping out our clients, oftentimes we forget to take care of ourselves and our needs (both personal and professional).

Understanding Your Gauges

To better illustrate this, think of a car. When you drove to your office today, your car is equipped with plenty of ways to tell you if it was working properly, by the gauges on the dashboard.

Gauges do little to help you though if you do not understand what they mean. For example, when the oil light comes on, it's time to check the oil because you are probably low.

But, if you didn't know what the oil light symbol meant you might keep driving your car unaware that you could be doing permanent damage.

Similar are your own set of personal gauges. If you don't understand the warning signs you may find out too late that something is amiss.

There are many things that could be considered as potential warning signs, let's look at just three of them.

Physical Gauges

When you find yourself exhausted or physically tense, it may be your body's way of telling you that it's time for some much needed rest and relaxation. The body has a natural way of giving you constant warning signals.

While we oftentimes only react to those signals that indicate acute pain, such as a sprained ankle or stiff neck, your physical gauges may be actually sending you more warnings than you realize.

One way to better heed these warnings is to not dismiss any discomfort. Ask yourself if this fatigue, ache or pain seems to out of the blue or if it is recurrent then address it either way with appropriate attention, care or treatment (get more sleep, book a massage, or schedule a doctor's visit).

Emotional Gauges

If you have felt an increase in your anxiety, noticed that you are being overly defensive or even feeling depressed, your emotional gauges are definitely sending you signals.

The cause of why you are feeling this way may be personal and/or business related, but whatever the reason you must find some control over it. Talk your concerns over with a trusted friend or family member or seek a professional opinion.

Relational Gauges

Financial services is a business of relationships, however if you find that you are avoiding clients rather than speaking with them it is time to have a serious heart-to-heart with yourself on why this may be occurring.

It may be that you are taking on too much or feel responsible for things that are out of your control or that you are not working as efficiently and thus effectively as possible.

If this is the case, it may be time to talk to a mentor or business coach who could offer you some insights and suggestions as to how to go about finding your mojo again.

Why Knowing How to Read Your Gauges Works

It goes without saying that the more you know yourself, the more likely you are to take care of yourself. Let's face it no one is going to have a more vested interest in you than you, nor should they.

You are responsible for your own self-care. With that said, the reason why knowing how to read your own physical, emotional or relational gauges works well is because it's the first step in making sure those gauges work. Advisors who are not aware of their own well-being tend to eventually not be well. However, advisors who keep their well-being top of mind are able to take care of themselves better.

Story #30
How Coachable Am I?

I have been a business coach since 2004 and as of this writing have accumulated an estimated 25,000+ hours coaching financial advisor and agents. In addition, I was a financial advisor for thirteen years, with experience in production, so I am well versed in both areas.

I also know that the financial services industry isn't all that different from professional sports in that both coaches (advisors) and players (clients) want to win.

A part of winning at anything in life, whether at a sport you are playing or with a business you are building is the ability to ask yourself the question, *"How determined am I to achieve success?"* If you are honest with yourself and truly want to succeed, then you must also ask yourself, *"How coachable am I?"*

The reason that the latter is such a vital question is because even the most talented and gifted athletes cannot reach their peak without the right type of coaching. Financial advisors and agents are no different.

Over the years, I have realized that there are several commonalities that help define if an advisor or agent is coachable. Typically, these commonalities reveal themselves in how you answer the following questions. Let's take a look at each of the questions and why they are important:

Question #1: Am I ready and willing to succeed?

Success rarely happens by accident! In fact, it starts by having the fortitude to want to succeed. The level of burning desire you have to move forward from your current situation towards your goals can make or break your outcomes.

I can coach my clients with tools, techniques, strategies and solutions to assist them in reaching the next level with their business, but if they honestly do not wish to work to get there, then those methods are useless.

Question #2: Do I know what I want my business to look like?

Goals are more likely to be accomplished when you have a crystal clear picture of what you want the result(s) to be. It is important to note that having a strong reason for setting goals helps you to continue your pursuit of them.

Question #3: Am I open to changing old habits to produce new results?

If you are not willing to make changes in your business then you are not ready to produce new results and find success. Einstein said, *"The definition of insanity is doing the same thing over and over again and expecting a different result."*

Question #4: Am I open to letting go of the fear of success?

Fear of success is rarely discussed but often experienced. If you cannot let go of your present situation then you cannot grasp the future. You must hold yourself to accepting that you deserve success and not being afraid of anything that comes with it.

Question #5: Do I believe in myself?

Sometimes simply believing in yourself carries you closer to your goals then you expect. Your attitude about yourself and your business are by far the most important step in creating the business you have always dreamed of!

Although the questions are simplistic, the answers may reveal a lot about where you are at with/in your willingness to succeed.

The Three Categories of "Coachability"

After reviewing the questions and their explanations you may still be wondering what specific commonalities I was referring to that help define if you are coachable or not.

How you answered these questions puts you into one of three categories of "coachability."

Let's take a look at all three to find out which one you fall into.

The Stressor: The Stressor is a person who likely stresses about everything and is resistant to change; thus, they tend to not do what needs to be done in order to succeed. Instead, they do the bare minimum that they need to do and seem to live in a constant state of stress.

As a result they are typically not coachable because they won't or struggle to apply anything. Ironically, some advisors say that they are coachable but later reveal their true nature when it comes to taking action. If you answered "no" to each of the questions then you are a "Stressor".

The Dabbler: The Dabbler is a person who wants to succeed and is willing to learn what to do but will only apply what needs to be done to the extent that it starts to work. Then, they quit!

Their common battle cry is, *"It worked so well I quit doing it!"* They may also say, *"I know what I need to do, I just need to do it."*

As a result they are partially coachable. They seem to pick-and-choose what tools and techniques they will incorporate. If you answered, "yes" to at least two or three of the questions then you are most likely a "Dabbler".

The Achiever: The Achiever is a person who is serious about success and is willing to learn as well as apply any tools and techniques needed to succeed.

In addition, they eventually turn their newfound knowledge into habits. Their common battle cry is, *"Why re-invent the wheel?"* If you answered "yes" to four or five of the questions you are definitely an "Achiever".

Why Knowing Your "Coachability" Factor Works

Having the right business coach can be a game changer but you must be coachable in the first place. The reason knowing how coachable you are works is because it helps you to determine your level of commitment to your own success. As a coach I know how important that is.

Oftentimes, I tell clients whom I have identified as a "Stressor" or "Dabbler" I can't care more about their business than they do. My hope is that both types move to the next level of "coachability". And, in some cases they do, but only if we work on mastering their mindset first. All coaching begins between your ears.

Story #31
Beyond the Silver Bullet Mentality

Does the thought of how to reach the next level with your business leave you feeling baffled? Do you find yourself looking for the solution that will get you there?

Scott, a fifteen-year veteran financial advisor recently shared that after several conversations with me, he had had an epiphany when it came to making real progress with his business. For years he had searched for the "silver bullet", that one missing ingredient that would change everything and catapult him and his business to success.

However, his recent revelation led him to understand that searching for that one single thing that could bring him growth and success was a recipe for disaster, as that one single thing could fizzle out leaving him with nothing else to go on.

Scott was learning that it comes down to creating a process for multiple aspects of your business, improving upon what you are doing with many not just one area of your practice.

Many financial advisors have a "silver bullet" mentality, hoping that if they find just the right product, say just the right thing or use just the right marketing protocol their business will take off.

This is not to say that marketing and advertising programs do not work. In fact, Scott had invested in a one-hour Sunday morning radio show in L.A. He had been able to attract millions in new assets each time his program aired.

To build a better business you must have the right systems in place, you must evaluate those systems consistently and constantly improve upon areas of weakness. After several discussions with Scott, he began to take a hard look at what was and wasn't working with his radio marketing program and how he could improve upon it.

When he started his weekly radio shows there was a tremendous amount of people calling in. However, many of the calls were not getting picked up because they did not have enough people handling incoming calls. After increasing the number of staff personnel, Scott noticed there were more appointments set. Later, he realized that many of those prospects were unqualified and did not fit his target market. So he designed a qualification script and within weeks he was in front of higher net-worth individuals.

The next challenge was that his staff seemed to be setting appointments for him all over the city and he found himself having to reschedule appointments so that they matched up with other appointments that were close by. He finally determined that the most effective way for coordinating himself was to be in each of the four branch offices once a week and to set appointments accordingly with prospects nearby. The point is that this type of constant and never-ending evaluation was what he needed to work optimally.

Following you will find a summary of some of the steps that Scott and I discussed as he reviewed his experiences. These steps will allow you to evaluate aspects of your own advisory business and assist you as you work on the systems associated with them. This applies to time management, prospecting, sales and marketing components.

Step 1: Identify What IS and IS NOT Working

To make real progress you need to comprehend what your business strengths and weaknesses are. You need to know what the flaws are in your system(s) so you can make changes while at the same time continuing to concentrate on what is already working. In Scott's example he was constantly re-evaluating and identifying what was—and was not working (lack of staff, non-qualified appointments and scheduling challenges).

Step 2: Identify What You Want the Desired Outcome to be

Once you have taken some time to really look at your business, and what is and is not working for you, you need to figure out what it will take to make the changes you want to have the outcomes you desire. It didn't take Scott long to realize that he wanted the phones answered, the prospects to be properly screened and a manageable schedule to be generated.

Step 3: Identify What Needs to Happen to Reach the Desired Outcome

Knowing where you are and where you want to be are crucial steps in reaching your goals, but unless you know what you need to do to bridge the gap, you simply have a wish list. Writing down the steps for this process will help you visualize and focus on what needs to be accomplished. Assigning time horizons for those tasks creates a sense of urgency.

Step 4: Chart Your Progress

Most goals are obtained through well-thought-out plans, careful execution and charting of progress. However, a caveat to remember is that along the way you must be careful not to get too comfortable if things are going well. Just because things are working better than they were before, does not mean that there isn't room for tweaking.

Why Beyond the Silver Bullet Mentality Works

There is no single silver bullet when it comes to running a successful business. Scott could have spent a lot of money and failed miserably with his practice had he not asked himself some tough questions and taken the time and energy necessary to improve upon his systems. This is the only way to make real and steady progress with your own business.

The reason why having a Beyond the Silver Bullet Mentality works is because of the fact that you need more than one solution (or one "silver bullet") for your business. Instead, having numerous solutions and the right systems is vital with a constant eye towards evolving them as your business grows.

Story #32
The Emotionally Intelligent Advisor

Emotional intelligence is essential to building and maintaining a successful financial advisory business because the financial services industry is a people business. If you cannot connect with people, you will not be able to set the appointments, open new accounts, gather assets and build a thriving practice.

There are two distinct types of intelligence- intellectual and emotional- each of which activates distinct areas of the brain. The intellectual intelligence or "book smart" is measured in terms of IQ, while emotional intelligence or "people smart" is measured in terms of EQ.

So what does this have to do with being a successful financial advisor?

Many people feel that having a successful business is about assets under management when "relationships under management" is a better interpretation.

Without the relationship(s) you would never gather the assets and without maintaining a good relationship with clients, you would not keep the assets that you have gathered.

The following are 5 Core Competencies for building relationships and increasing your emotional intelligence.

1. Emotional Self-Awareness

This means knowing what emotions we are feeling at any given moment, and being aware of how our emotions, feelings and personality impact ourselves, clients and prospects.

The emotionally self-aware financial advisor has a high ability to tune into changes in feelings from moment to moment being able to understand when feelings change and why.

This type of advisor has a greater advantage over his or her colleagues because they are able to have a greater level of certainty of how they are feeling and why. This is the foundation of all of the other competencies for building relationships. Managing your level of self-awareness in an emotionally uncertain work environment is the key to controlling your own mental state, your business and your life.

2. Emotional Management

This means knowing how to manage emotional states to regulate emotions that have a negative impact on you, the task at hand and/or your business.

Emotional management is about being able to restrain from emotions that could possibly jeopardize your relationships with yourself and others as well as being able to "bounce back" from any and all emotional setbacks.

Advisors with high levels of emotional management can regulate anxiety, fear and irritability. Typically, these types of advisors do not take rejection personally, but rather see it as a necessary part of sifting through non-qualified prospects to find qualified groups of people whom will one day form a great client base.

Advisors with low levels of emotional management tend to let a host of negative emotions dictate their day and as a result usually wash out of business. When you work in the financial services industry you are working with one of the most emotional subjects that people have…money!

Whatever values your clients place on money, you can be sure of one thing…money elicits emotions both good and bad. To become successful in this business you must be able to regulate your own emotions to not get caught up in theirs.

3. Self-Motivation

Self-Motivation is being able to regulate ones' actions towards the pursuit of ones' goals regardless of perceived setbacks, adversity, discouragements and frustrations. Self-motivation focuses on positive short, intermediate and long-term accomplishments. It is about delaying any activities that promote short-term gratification at the risk of not accomplishing long-term goals.

The highly self-motivated advisor knows what activities they need to do each day to obtain daily, weekly, monthly, quarterly and yearly goals and follows through on those activities.

4. Having High Levels of Empathy

Empathy is a cornerstone of building relationships because true empathy takes the other person's perspective into account and leaves any possible conflict of interest behind.

Our business is a business of trust. To truly be trusted by prospects and clients they must first be convinced that you truly understand what they are feeling. People want to work with those whom they believe understand them.

The highly empathetic advisor is more aware of the clients' feelings and will convey that message, thus building trust. They have honed their listening skills as well as their ability to detect subtle social signals that indicate how the prospect or client is feeling, and they are not afraid to ask the client how they feel. This skill is imperative to being a successful!

5. Understanding Relationships under Management

Being able to manage relationships by managing emotions in others and having the ability to read social situations, communicate effectively and interact with a high level of confidence are all a part of relationships under management.

They can quickly diffuse client conflicts by listening to the clients' concerns, assessing the clients' emotional state, expressing empathy, utilizing reflective listening, and assertively responding to the clients' request. In effect, the advisor controls the emotional climate by controlling their own emotions and managing the emotions of others.

Why Using Emotional Intelligence Works

You use emotional intelligence in your business by understanding and increasing your emotional competencies. In other words, it is not enough to be aware of emotional competencies; you must consciously strive to increase your emotional self-awareness, manage your emotions, and become self-motivated and highly empathetic to increase your relationships under management. The reason why using emotional intelligence works well is that you have a process to make better connections.

Story #33
The Snowball Effect of Solutions

Advisors are faced with a multitude of challenges during the course of their careers. Successful advisors know that there is not just one single solution that is the cure-all. Instead, there are a multitude of solutions, at least one for each challenge. As a result, successful advisors typically have a paradigm shift in their belief systems as well.

Let's take a look at an example of what one advisor did to incorporate a three-step process for creating success.

Step 1: Awareness

It may seem strange to hear, but oftentimes advisors don't realize they have a challenge. Instead, they believe a challenge is just the norm. And, that everyone is doing it. Or, they created a negative belief system and never realized they had done so.

"I didn't think I could do that?" my client Tim K., a twenty-five-year veteran financial advisor responded when I explained to him that the reason he was not filling up his pipeline was because he wasn't asking for the appointment earlier in the relationship. *"I thought I needed to mail a prospect something of value at least twice before I could call back and ask for an appointment"* he said convincingly.

I elaborated on my advice by saying that if he has qualified a prospect, uncovered a prospect's need(s) and shared his solutions then this was the appropriate time to ask for and set the first appointment.

Step 2: Action

Once you understand that you truly have a challenge as well as the solution you must take immediate action to apply the solution. That way you can determine if you are getting a different, hopefully better, result.

Amazingly, in less than an hour after discussing this, I received an email from him requesting a quick call. Curious, I called immediately and I was happy to hear that he had just qualified, uncovered needs, sold his solutions and set a first appointment…all on the initial cold call!

Step 3: Accountability

The final step is to be accountable to someone other than yourself regarding your results. Oftentimes when the results are lackluster there is a tendency to not want to be accountable. However, you may have been missing something in applying the solutions and it helps to be accountable to someone, typically the person who helped you with the solution to make sure you are applying the solution the right way. In other words, you may need a simple course correction.

The following day, during a group coaching session my client told his success story to his peers and was more than happy to report that he had done it again! With this motivation, he was looking forward to the days ahead of finding additional success.

What occurred with this client is what I refer to as the *"snowball effect of solutions"*. It is the light bulb moment when you realize what the solution is and that you are able to make changes and apply a solution to get different (and hopefully positive) outcomes.

Typically, it also corresponds with the moment that you make a course correction in your belief system; in my client's case, this was about changing his belief system that he must mail a prospect something of value at least twice before being able or worthy of asking for an appointment.

I personally believe in my *snowball effect of solutions* theory so much that I wrote a 473 page book around the concept—**101 Advisor Solutions:** *A Financial Advisor's Guide to Strategies that Educate, Motivate and Inspire!* —to help financial services professionals find their solutions and have their own snowball effect of successes.

So, what happened with my client?

He was so excited about his success that he volunteered to mentor anyone in the group and walk them through the process of how he did it. You see, he had spent over ten years reinforcing his old (and unsuccessful) belief system and he now knew that there were others who could benefit from what he had experienced.

Why the Snowball Effect of Solutions Works

Just as any kid on a snowy winter day knows, to make a great snowball you need to keep packing snow onto it. If you keep packing solution-after-solution-after-solution you will create a great business.

The reason why the *snowball effect of solutions* works so well is because you are constantly refining your business by becoming aware of common challenges as well as their solutions, taking action and being accountable for the results. The by-product of this is eliminating negative belief systems and replacing them with positive belief systems.

Story #34
Keep Swinging For the Fences

When it comes to prospecting, you really have two choices, to do it consistently or to do it sporadically. There isn't much gray area. For many advisors/agents, prospecting is a task that a majority of people tends to procrastinate doing even with the knowledge that they need to. They also use various excuses for why it is so challenging. I hear them from 90% of my clients.

Babe Ruth said, *"Never let the fear of striking out get in your way."*

He was known for hitting home runs and for many years was called The Strikeout King. He struck out 1330 times in his career! But, that didn't deter him from taking the next pitch. In other words, he knew the value of giving it his all by continuing to swing for the fences.

If you are not sure how to keep swinging yourself by incorporating prospecting activities into your day, the following strategies will help get you on track.

Strategy 1: Prospect Early In the Day

Start your day off by making prospecting calls. You can't succeed if you don't get up to bat.

Josh M., a veteran financial advisor wanted to take his business to the next level. Typically, he would plan out his daily schedule making prospecting the *last* item on his to-do list. After placing prospecting as his *first* task of the day he rapidly started placing people into his pipeline.

Strategy 2: Focus on Each Call

Focus on each call, all that matters is what is in front of you at any one given time (just like Babe Ruth did with the pitches).

Like most advisors, Josh was told from day one that prospecting is a numbers game, the more people you call, the more success you will have. While that is partially true what he didn't know was that by slowing down and focusing on a current call he could increase his success ratios even more.

As Josh's professional coach, we role played increasing his listening skill sets and how better to be present on each call using a technique called **Empathetic Listening** (refer to the story, **The Empathetic Advisor** in chapter 2)**.**

This process enables the prospect to know that they are being heard. By Josh practicing this, it gave him more confidence in establishing better connection with his prospects.

Strategy 3: Be Professional

Keep in good form by knowing what you are going to say by mapping out a framework ahead of time and know how you will handle objections.

To increase the quality of Josh's calls we focused on a technique known as **Framing the Conversation** (refer to the story **Beyond the Gatekeeper** in chapter 2) as well as four different way to handle objections.

It didn't take long before he realized that prospecting like a professional means to be prepared for making prospecting calls and not to wing them. The quality of each conversation is more important than the quantity of calls made in a day!

Strategy 4: Know Your Value

Speak with confidence and never be afraid to strike out.

After a few weeks of starting each day prospecting, focusing on each call and being prepared by knowing what to say and how to say it, I noticed a transformation in Josh's personality. He was actually enjoying making prospecting calls. His growing confidence was evident in his voice and that element was adding to his success.

Why Consistent Prospecting Works

Babe Ruth knew that stepping up to the plate, focusing on the pitch and putting heart into the game was the only way he was going to reach (or exceed) his potential. He didn't let labels like being called The Strikeout King deter him his next time at bat.

The reason why consistent prospecting works is because it helps advisors/agents hone in on current opportunities rather than past obstacles. The more you persist and regularly manage your prospecting efforts the more success you will find. That can be a game changer!

Story #35
Understanding the Standards Circle

Most advisors/agents want to have continued success. However, very few have a designated system for obtaining it. The problems with not having systems set up are numerous with a significant one being that they leave reaching the next level in your business up to chance.

A common phrase I hear from prospective coaching clients is, *"I want to grow my business but I don't know how to do that."* Does this sound like you? If so, don't be concerned because creating success is merely a process and the process begins when you make a decision to raise your standards!

Thomas J. Watson said, *"If you want to achieve excellence, you can get there today. As of this second, quit doing less-than-excellent work."*

One of the first steps towards achieving a greater level of success is to raise your standards. If you are not happy with where you are then you have to choose to hold yourself to a higher bar so you have something to guide you in the right direction and support that you have to increase the number of activities that your new standards require. In other words, your previous behaviors "supported" your previous standards so by setting new standards you will need new behaviors.

Think of these steps as more of circle than a linear pattern. When you decide to raise your standards, take new actions, turn those actions into habits you will inevitable get better results. After reviewing your results you may want to raise your standards again, which would require a new stepwise approach and habits, thus the Standards Circle continues.

The following is a brief outline of how one client of mine applied the Standards Circle when it came to prospecting. See if you can relate to his experience.

Step 1: Raise The Bar

One of the most common things that advisors/agents neglect to consider when facing an ongoing challenge in their business is to look inward and ask, *"What am I choosing to accept?"* In other words what are the standards (regarding a particular facet) that you have decided are the norm?

Rob D., a client of mine who after months of working from home during the recent COVID-19 crisis stopped prospecting because he didn't think it was possible to prospect in this climate. We discussed the fact that some of his peers were prospecting and how they had adapted to the situation. It didn't take Rob long to make the realization that by upping his bar, he too, could do the same as his fellow colleagues.

Step 2: Change Your Action Steps

Another challenge for advisors/agents after realizing they need to raise their standards is alter behaviors, whether it be doing more of a task that resulted in positive outcomes or changing the type of action altogether.

Rob knew that just knowing what his peers were doing was not enough. Instead he needed to learn a new way of prospecting via phone and zoom appointments, practice and apply it. So, we set realistic goals on who to call, when to prospect, what to say and how he was going to reward himself when he accomplished his prospecting activity goals.

Step 3: Create New Habits

I have seen advisors/agents dabble in applying various solutions, experience some success and then quit doing the activities that got them better results. Unfortunately, this type of process only circles back to ending up with the same challenge. That's why it is so important to continue taking action until these actions become a habit.

After a few weeks, Rob was setting appointments, meeting with prospects via zoom meetings and he even managed to gather additional assets. He was pleasantly surprised and tempted to slow down, but I reinforced the need to continue to reinforce the new habit.

So, what happened to Rob?

Over the better part of a month, he came to comprehend that most of his competition currently had the same standard for prospecting that he once had, they were not prospecting because they didn't think it was possible right now. Fortunately for him, by utilizing the Standards Circle, he now has a tool at his disposal if and when he finds himself at a crossroads (or plateau) again.

Why Understanding the Standards Circle Works

The reason why understanding the Standards Circle works well is because it's a continuous process for improvement. When you apply the process of raising the bar, changing your action steps and creating new habits you can't help, but create better results! And, by using a process for evaluating your standards it helps to keep them high.

Story #36
Embracing Change

Being in the financial services industry you know that there is one thing that you can guarantee, that things are always changing as change is inevitable. It is how we embrace or shun change that defines the difference between having a successful advisory practice or one filled with constant struggles.

The overall solution is to have a consistent process for adapting to and moving through change.

Step 1: Decide that You're Done

Sometimes the hardest part of starting a new process is determining that the old one just doesn't work anymore. It takes being honest with yourself to become aware that there is a challenge and that you are tired of the push and pull.

This is the most important part of changing any aspect of your business—time management, prospecting, sales, marketing, or client servicing. So, the real question you need to pose is—*Are the results I'm currently experiencing with my business ones I'm happy with and if the answer is "no", then am I ready (and willing) to ax the old and embrace the new?*

Step 2: Determine Your New Route

Once you are committed to changing whatever was not working, it is time to determine how you want to change it. The best way to do this is look to others, your branch manager, a trusted colleague, industry authors or even a business coach. You just need to find the most appropriate solutions for you and your business.

Step 3: Take Immediate Action

The biggest mistake you can possibly make once you decide on a solution is not to take immediate action. If you let a few days, a week or a month pass by while you let the process sink in you are wasting time. Let your fear of change melt away with the anticipation of success. Let the mantra, *"Action alleviates anxiety"* become your battle cry.

Step 4: Create Productive Habits

Some say that it takes 30 to 90 days to create a new habit. In many regards this is true, so it is important to have a process for continuing new actions on a daily basis so that you create lasting change and develop those new productive habits. One way to do this is to make a game out of applying action(s); give yourself a prize for winning or a punishment for losing.

Step 5: Evaluate the Progress

The best way to determine if you are moving in the right direction is to continually evaluate your progress. If you have been "playing the game of action" you should easily be able to determine how many times you have accomplished your goals over the past month or so and if the new activities are providing you with better outcomes. If you are happy with your progress, continue doing what works, if not it is time to continue embracing change by making some adjustments.

Step 6: Make Course Correction

There is no shame in admitting that some things work and others do not. In fact, it is a productive part of being open to optimizing your business. Oftentimes, just a slight adjustment to what you are doing can make all the difference. Take time to determine what part of the new process is and isn't working before moving onto the final step.

Step 7: Continue to Embrace Change

Ironically, once you have mastered the previous steps continuing to embrace change actually becomes the easiest step of all because you have already established your process. You go back to step one when something in your practice doesn't feel right. You follow the steps again until your new process is working better than the old. You can apply this series of steps to any facet of your business and see real results in several areas of your business!

Why Embracing Change Works

Change can be a difficult thing for some advisors. The art of embracing change works because it gives you a framework of how to adapt to change instead of neglecting it. When you use these steps you are in fact being proactive instead of having to be reactive when change occurs.

As a result, advisors who actively embrace change tend to feel more in control of their businesses regardless of the situation/s. So, the next time you find that you are not happy with a process or a specific outcome in your business practice the art of embracing change and see how quickly your business transforms.

Story #37
Lug It or Leave It!

We have all heard the term *"emotional baggage."* It is best defined as a metaphorical image in which one carries bags filled with past disappointments, failures and negative experiences that affect how you act/react to events now. So what is your *"emotional baggage"* and does it impact your business?

Typically, when I coach an advisor who has had less than desired results in their business life again and again we find through our discussions that they have created what I refer to as *"emotional business baggage"*, a learned belief system that doing a specific professional activity causes an emotionally painful response.

The following are just a few examples:

With rookie advisors, they often tend to have been rejected often while cold calling; thus, their belief system becomes that *"cold calling = pain of rejection."*

Some advisors put on seminars without gaining any leads; thus, their belief system becomes *"seminars are not effective and I end up with disappointing results."*

Another example might be advisors who have asked for referrals and their clients seem uncomfortable providing them; thus, their belief system becomes *"asking for referrals is uncomfortable and awkward for clients and myself."*

As a result of the three belief systems, these advisors stopped cold calling, doing seminars and asking for referrals. Instead, they carried around their *"emotional business baggage"* of those painful experiences and tried desperately to avoid those painful feelings.

Wouldn't it be nice to lose your emotional baggage? Use the following three step process to do just that:

Step 1: Realize the True Issue

The first and most important step is to understand the true issue, which is that you create your own reality. Let's use the first example of cold calling. If you focus only on the rejection, "the no's", there is no doubt you will feel rejected.

However, if you can use the mentality that *"every no brings me closer to a yes,"* then you won't care (as much) about actually hearing a "no".

A simple switch to looking at the positive in any negative experience as outlined above adjusts your attitude greatly. Try it!

Step 2: Take Ownership of Your Outcomes

The second step in this process is to take ownership of your outcomes by determining what you can control such as increasing your skill sets on how to cold call more effectively.

As you strengthen your own abilities you begin to understand that you are no longer a victim of circumstance, but the creator of your own success! New challenges become new opportunities.

Step 3: Reinforce New Behavior(s)

The third step is to reinforce any new behavior(s) like choosing to focus on the positive within the negative along with what is in your control.

By asking yourself questions such as, *"What is good about this situation? What is in my control? What skills sets do I need to sharpen? What is my desired outcome?"* you continually re-focus, which will keep you on track rather than filling your baggage with more.

The Reason Why Lug It or Leave It Works Well

Let's be honest, having "emotional baggage" is no fun; it doesn't produce any long-term positive results. Instead, it merely weighs you down with unwanted feelings of avoidance and/or despair.

So, why do you keep lugging your "emotional baggage" around? The reason why the process above works well is because it's a process to help you increase your awareness of what the true issues are, which gives you ownership of your emotions and helps you to reinforce new behavior systems. By having this in place you are now more in control of your emotions.

Story #38
Five Strategies for Connecting During the Process

Have you ever gone into an initial first appointment with high hopes of connecting with the prospect only to later realize that you did not make a connection at all? Maybe you have had several appointments like this over the course of your career. If so, you may have been missing one, a few or all of the 5 Strategies for Connecting during the **First Appointment Process** (refer to the story **The First Appointment FORM** in chapter 2).

Let's take a look at what those are:

Get the Prospect's Story

One of the most important things you can do to establish a connection is to genuinely be interested in learning about the prospect. People love to talk about themselves and the best way to encourage this is to strategically map out questions that will help them tell you their life story. If you can do this they will end up explaining the reason for why they are looking for a new financial advisor and what is important to them about finding just the right one.

Show Them How Much You Care

I've mentioned this phrase before, *"People don't care how much you know until they know how much you care"* and I believe that is true. Oftentimes, advisors try to win over a prospect by dazzling them with their stock market and/or product knowledge. Unfortunately, this tends to create more of a disconnection with a potential client.

Don't start the relationship off by telling them what you know, but instead tell them how much you care about their situation. Chances are you have had other prospects and clients experience similar things. If so, then you should share their story with them. Do this and you will set a prospect at ease as they will feel comfortable that you are familiar with their situation.

Understand the Prospect's Pain Points

As you listen to the prospect's story and let them know how much you care, you will probably realize that they have real concerns about their finances–these are what I call the Prospect's Pain Points. Typically, these are the reasons why they came to see you in the first place. If you truly understand their concerns as well and what is most important to them and they know you understand both, it is much easier to build a connection with them.

Strategically Sum Up the Appointment

At some point, you need to strategically shift the conversation into summarizing what you have learned about them from your conversation with them. Try a phrase such as, *"We've talked about a lot of things today and what I'd like to do is summarize what I have heard."* Then, proceed to state their situation, issues/problems and the long-term implications of not fixing those issues/problems. If you do this well, they will be much more inclined to hear what else you have to say because they know you have listened and more importantly heard them!

Sell Your Solutions to Set a Second Appointment

Once a prospect gives you the signs or tells you they are ready it's time to sell your solutions to set a second appointment. Ironically, the strategy that I am about to explain isn't so much about selling as it is about helping them want to buy.

Use questions such as, *"How would it help you most if I put together a full financial plan so that you can understand how much money you will need when you retire, how much income you may have to live off of once you are retired and whether or not you are currently on course to accomplish those goals?"*

Nine times out of ten they will instantly start telling you they would value that by saying, *"That sounds like something I have needed for a long time!"* All you need to do is agree with them and then ask for the second appointment, *"Exactly, then that is what we will do! Are you available this time next week to review the plan?"*

Take a moment to think about what you have just learned. Are you using these strategies in your first appointment process? If not, you now know how.

Why the Five Strategies for Connecting During the First Appointment Works

Making strong connections with prospects must happen in the first appointment process. If you don't connect then you are most likely not going to get a second appointment to show the prospect your recommendations; and as a result they will not be a client.

The reason why using all of the five strategies for connecting during the first appointment works well is because it gives you a framework to create a strong connection. When you get the prospect's story, show them how much you care, understand their pain points, strategically sum up what you have learned about them and sell your solutions to set the next appointment you have a recipe for always moving prospects from the first appointment to the second appointment. As a result, you will find having first appointments becomes easier and easier!

Story #39
What's in Your Whitespace?

In my book **101 Advisor Solutions:** *A Financial Advisor's Guide to Strategies that Educate, Motivate and Inspire,* I suggest to advisors that they read each of the challenges listed and ask themselves this question-*"Is this a challenge that I have gone through, are currently going through or one that I could see myself possibly going through?"*

I then tell them to grab a red pen and circle the solutions that follow then go back and re-read those solutions making notes in the margins as to how they could incorporate those into their own best practices.

What is the importance of making those brief notes? Many times the best way to learn about, retain and apply new concepts is to initially read or hear about them. Jotting down your quick thoughts afterwards provides you with some guidance as we all know we think we will remember our takeaways, but typically don't.

An example of this is a financial advisor client who once said, *"I read all the books I can on how to improve my business. Then, I put them on the shelf and nothing happens."* When I asked him if he understood why, he said, *"It is because I don't actually apply any of the information."*

So, what's in your whitespace? In other words, what are your takeaways from your favorite books, practice management seminars, industry workshops, or from your own or your peer's experiences in financial services? Are you making the most of those takeaways or are you putting them back on the proverbial shelf where they collect dust?

Creating Your Whitespace Strategy

Oftentimes, financial advisors go through the day-to-day operations of working "IN" their business that they don't stop and really take time to work "ON" their business. As a result, they continue to run into the same challenges, follow the same course of action and end up with the same results.

So, how can you take time to work "ON" your business so that you can identify common challenges, find solutions and implement the necessary action to make lasting change? Let's take a step-by-step look at how you can do just that.

Step 1: Find Your Business Pain Points

How many times have you stopped to ask yourself the tough questions such as, "What is not working with my business and why? What do I need to do to reach the next level? And, who do I need to talk to who can help me do that?"

This is the first step in creating your Whitespace Strategy because you need to understand what the challenge/s are in your business that are causing pain to look for the solutions.

Take Jeff G. for instance a ten-year veteran financial advisor client of mine who realized that he wasn't closing enough business even though he was constantly prospecting and adding new people to his pipeline. So, I asked him the questions and what we realized was that he was prospecting enough people, but he wasn't moving them to the next step of the pipeline process because he wasn't asking for the next appointment or the order. In other words, we found his business pain point, which was to keep the prospects momentum moving forward!

Step 2: Find and Map Out the Solutions

Once you know what the challenges are it's important to find the solutions. Since most advisors and agents go through the exact same challenges it is important to not try and reinvent the wheel.

Instead, research the solutions via (as stated before) your favorite books, practice management seminars, industry workshops, or from your own or your peer's experiences. Or, you could ask your business coach!

This challenge was not new to me so explaining the solution was fairly simple. All Jeff had to do was to have a signature close for each step of the pipeline, practice the closing technique and remember to use it to keep moving prospects through the pipeline.

We role played the process and he made notes on the white paper that I had emailed him on the subject so that he could remember his "takeaways".

Step 3: Implement & Assess

Once you find the solutions and understand the steps you must put them into practice by implementing each step. After that you need to assess the results to determine if you have the same challenge.

After a few weeks of applying the steps he noticed that continuing the prospecting momentum had turned into a common occurrence. It was what he did at the end of each conversation by asking for the prospect to take the next step! As a result, he didn't have this challenge anymore and in fact had created a new healthy business habit.

Step 4: Continue the Process

There are only two possible outcomes when you apply the previous step-either it worked or it didn't. Let's look at each:

If you were not able to overcome the challenge then access how well you applied the first part of Step 3: Implementing the Process. It may be that you didn't do each step correctly or even enough.

However, the other possibility is that you may not have found the right solution. If that is the case then go back to Step 2: Find and Map out the Solutions. In either case something was missing, but rest assured you are not the only one who has ever had this specific challenge so there must be a solution for it.

If on the other hand you were able to overcome the challenge then it's time to continue the process by going back to Step 1: Find Your Business Pain Points. What this will do is to continue the Whitespace

Strategy again with a new challenge. As a result, it won't take you long until you realize that all obstacles are merely opportunities to work "ON" your business!

Why Considering Your Whitespace Works

Once you start asking yourself these types of questions and are genuinely interested in finding the answers, you start to open up yourself up to a paradigm shift of possibilities. So fill up the whitespaces in your books and seminar binders and take a moment to write down some of the methods or techniques that you have watched others become successful with or those you desire to utilize to assist you in building a better advisory business.

Story #40
The Focused Advisor

Most advisors/agents struggle with success because they get distracted with unproductive activities. As a result they leave productive activities up to chance. The biggest challenge with lacking concentration is the fact that most people have never been taught ways to get (and stay) focused. In fact, it's more common and oftentimes praised to multi-task.

Bruce Lee said, *"The successful warrior is the average man, with laser-like focus."*

So, the real question you need to ask yourself is, how do you learn to be focused? I use the following process with my coaching clients, which teaches them how to be a more focused advisor/agent.

The first step is to have written goals. Then you need to block out specific times during the day to take action towards those goals. I recommend a maximum of forty-five minutes for any one task. Next, you need to reward yourself for following through so that you associate positive emotions with a job well done. If you can consistently follow these steps you soon will see that successful outcomes are significantly tied to your level of focus.

Let's take a deeper look at each step:

Step 1: Have Written Goals

The first step in any endeavor is to know what you are trying to accomplish. The only way to do that it is to take the time to think about what you want and write it down. This simple step shows a level of commitment.

John T. a thirty-year veteran financial advisor client of mine wanted to have a process for contacting his clients when the COVID-19 pandemic changed and affected so many facets of life.

Together we determined written goals for him on how frequently he would connect with his clients, a process for what he would say and a tracking system so that he would know who he had talked to, about what specifically and when. Once he had all of this in place it was time to move to the next step.

Step 2: Time Block Your Activities

The second step is to commit to when you are going to take action. That means you literally time block a specific time during the day to work towards your goal. As stated earlier, I recommend a maximum of forty-five minutes for any one task. You may need a number of days to complete the task or this process may be ongoing.

John knew how many clients he needed to speak with each day to connect with his entire client base once a quarter, but what he didn't know was when he was going to speak to them. Most advisors/agents get sidetracked with client servicing issues during the day and unfortunately don't get to the tasks that they would like to complete.

That's why he time blocked his "Client Check-In Calls" at 10:00 a.m. each day. He kept that time uninterrupted; not checking emails or voice mails until he was done with client check-in's each morning.

Step 3: Reward Yourself for Taking Action

The third step is simple, but not always an easy one; reward yourself for taking action. Think of ways to treat yourself such as with a cup of coffee, adding money into a reward fund so you can buy yourself something at the end of the month or leaving work fifteen minutes early on days when you achieve your goal.

Sometimes the most difficult part is in allowing yourself to accept the reward. Like many advisors/agents, John was hesitant in giving himself a daily reward at first, but with a little coaxing he started doing so. In fact, we designed a daily, weekly and monthly reward system to create various levels, which motivated him even more.

Why Being Focused Works

The reason this stepwise approach to staying focused works is because it gives the advisor/agent a process to know what to do, when to do it with the added bonus of a reward for a job well done. Like many of my coaching clients, John has found a process that works to connect with his clients during this unprecedented time and both he and they benefit greatly from it.

Story #41
The First Step

At the beginning of each year, it comes as no surprise that many financial advisors have mapped out the goals they would like to accomplish over the next twelve months. The "easy" part is in knowing what those goals are, the harder aspect is actually planning out the tasks and activities it takes to reach those goals.

It's been said that *"The journey of thousand miles begins with one step"* and many advisors have the best intentions as a new year commences, but many fail to even take that first step in making those goals happen for themselves.

Let's take a look at what it takes to set up and actually realize your goals by year end.

Step 1: Set and Clarify Your Goals

Goal setting is relatively an easy to-do, but clarifying your goals so that they are quantifiable and measurable is much more difficult.

One way to do this is to use the **G.R.O.W Model**, which stands for Goal, Reality, Obstacles (or Options) and Way Forward. When you use this model, you will find you are much clearer about what it will take to reach your desired outcomes.

Step 2: Compartmentalize Your Daily Actions

Once you have solidified your goals and written out your **G.R.O.W Model** (refer to the story **How To G.R.O.W Your Business From Within** in chapter 2), it's time to compartmentalize your daily actions.

This will assist you in determining what your first steps should be. Having just one or two steps to focus on can mean the difference between taking action and just thinking about taking action.

Remember, a goal without a plan is a wish.

Step 3: Create Time Horizons

Now it's time to create a time horizon for your activities. The best way to do this is to literally set a to-do item as an appointment in your contact management system. So, if your first action step is to start prospecting make sure that you set a reminder to do that consistently at the same time each day.

When the reminder pops up, set aside what you are doing and be sure to do the task. It is very typical to get distracted and push our tasks aside and tell ourselves we will get to them later. It is also very typical that when we do that, the activity rarely gets completed. So get into the habit of attending to a task once you have it scheduled.

Step 4: Get Leverage to Take Action

Finally, put some "skin in the game" by finding an accountability partner or a person that holds you accountable every day to ensure that action actually takes place. By being accountable to each other, you both are more likely to keep moving forward in the right direction. One way to leverage your success is to assign a reward or punishment to accomplishing or not accomplishing your daily actions.

Why Taking that First Step Works

It's the journey not the destination. Hopefully, by now you've realized that taking steps, especially the first one, is merely a process. And, that by taking each subsequent step, those are a continuation of that process. However, it is important to note that if you are only focused on the destination you will miss out on the journey, which is where the learning and growing always occurs.

Story #42
Ascending Into Greatness

Typically, we start out with the best of intentions and work countless hours. Through hard work, a little luck and by making connections we manage to build a business that generates a level of success that allows us to feel comfortable enough to perch atop an apex.

The only problem is that our business can never stay up there for any extended period because change is the only constant in life, right? My point is there are only two ways that your business can move—forward or backward, sometimes in a rapid trajectory and sometimes at a snail's pace, but either one way or the other.

So, how can you infuse life and passion back into your practice/company/business to ensure it ascends into greatness? Let's take a step-by-step look at how you can do just that.

Step 1: Choose to Succeed

Success is a choice. If make the decision and opt to want to succeed, but then you do not implement the activities/tasks that you need to do you will merely remain at a plateau and more than likely descend and take steps backward away from your desired outcomes.

However, if you choose to succeed and you understand that you need to constantly adjust your attitude towards how to continually find that success, then working towards your goals (short and long-term ones) will be much easier.

Napoleon Hill said in his book **Think and Grow Rich**, *"Whatever the mind can conceive and believe it can achieve."*

Step 2: Re-Assess Your Business Model

Most individuals rarely take the time to ask themselves if their current business model is working, although everyone should. A business model, by Wikipedia's definition, describes the rationale of how an organization creates, delivers, and captures value.

If your business is not growing it probably does not have a strong business framework to guide it; thus, it is time to re-assess and take a look at how you could modify it to make it a better foundation for your business.

You might need to increase your technical expertise, add a specialized member to your team or find a new target market. Whatever the answer is, it is vital to determine your target market, know what their needs are and know how to deliver them solutions. You want to create not only a loyal client base, but raving fans.

Step 3: Re-Make Your Brand

When you take these steps, they should encourage you in adopting a positive mental attitude towards finding your own success and that in turn will showcase your confidence to your current and future clients.

However, your old brand may not reflect the new you! If that is the case, it is important to share your message by first re-making your brand. The key is to confirm that your target market knows who you are and why they need YOUR expertise!

If you have been in the industry for some time, you may not even realize that you already have a brand. In today's competitive environment, a well know image, a great reputation and a unique selling proposition makes your business stand out from the crowd and tells prospects/clients what is special about you. These three components are all paramount in attracting and retaining your ideal clients.

For example, take Samantha J., a veteran financial advisor client of mine who after 23 years in the business decided to get off her business plateau and re-define her brand. Over the years she had worked with many types of clients, but one day she asked herself, *"What type of clients do I really love to work with?"* After realizing that she loved to work with high net-worth women she then asked herself, *"What is it that they need most and why?"*

From those two questions, her "new" brand was born! She determined who her target market was going to be and exactly what they needed.

Next, she mapped out how she was going to help them. Then, she re-worked her messaging and the image she wanted to represent her business. Finally, she began to seek those high net-worth women out and put her plan into practice! Within a few short years her business had skyrocketed and that fueled her passion for what she did every day.

Step 4: Re-Vamp Your Marketing

Once you have re-made or re-defined your brand, it is important to have marketing consistency. Does your logo, website and literature clearly convey the image and benefits of why your target markct should want to do business with you? If not, it absolutely should and can.

All you have to do is find the right people to help you with putting together continuity or a thread that is consistent through all of your materials. For Samantha, she spent time seeking out a qualified marketing consultant who helped her fit all of the pieces together. It is important that you do not think you have to do everything on your own.

In addition, you may want to restructure how you market your business. When I was a rookie advisor, I picked up the phone and cold-called complete strangers. Today, I have a focused and layered marketing strategy.

Samantha, who I mentioned earlier, did just that when she decided that to market herself to high net-worth women she had to strategically align herself with centers of influence such as female attorneys and C.P.A.s with several years of experience in their fields. These individuals had established client-bases, credibility and the trust of their clients. She needed them to help her get introductions to her target prospects.

While I will not give out Samantha's trade secrets, I will tell you that within a short amount of time most of the people in her "Center of Influence" campaign knew who she was. What is even more impressive is that to this day when financial advisors call inquiring about my coaching services wanting to know who I work with I do not hesitate to mention her name, with her permission of course. Although some advisors may not know her by name, all advisors in the city she resides in know her brand!

Step 5: Re-Energize Your Activities

If you follow all of these steps it will re-energize your everyday activities. Your time will be more structured and you will leave the office knowing that the next day's tasks are already planned.

As a bonus, anxieties towards growing your business dissolve because you are consistently assessing what systems and campaigns are working (or are not). You know to always be on the lookout for additional ways of adding value to your practice/company/business and for ways to improve your messaging.

Step 6: Re-Engage Your Team

Most individuals when they infuse the passion back into their business find that their level of excitement is contagious. Whether they have one assistant or are on a team with a number of other colleagues, their enthusiasm spreads like wildfire and they seem to foster the same attitude in others! The level of camaraderie and ancillary learning goes up exponentially! Team members look forward to sharing success stories to help motivate one another to be productive.

Other people will also begin to take notice. They will see that you and your team have a great attitude towards success, a strong business model, a unique brand, well thought-out marketing strategies, increased activities and persuasive energy towards and for the business.

Step 7: Re-Juvenate with Rest and Relaxation

It is important that you embrace taking time to rejuvenate by scheduling vacations or having scheduled time off and by rewarding yourself (and your team) when hitting your goals. I coach entire teams to take some dedicated time to go to dinner together, take an afternoon to go to a ball game or spend the weekend away by coordinating a team member retreat.

Some people find it easy to take time off when they are with others in their office doing so, but remember you should never feel guilty for getting away from it all by yourself or with loved ones. The best thing you can do for your business is take time away occasionally to re-group personally, which will help you re-group professionally as well.

Why Ascending Into Greatness Works

It can be overwhelming to run a business and keep all the details of how to do it most efficiently on track, but with planning, inspiration, solid execution and regular evaluation you can keep the passion and motivation and support the reason you got into the industry to begin with. The reason why the steps to ascending into greatness work is because it's a stepwise approach for reinventing yourself and your business to infuse life and passion back into your practice/company/business.

Story #43
The Flipside of Failure

Have you ever wondered if anything positive could come out of getting a negative result? Let's use the example of the last time you did not close a sale; your hopes were probably deflated as the prospect walked out the door to go home and "think about it". Did you take time to reflect back on your conversation with the prospect and think about what you learned from the situation?

Successful advisors know that the flipside of failure is being able to learn from their mistakes. The following are just of few examples of what you might do to get better results next time.

Step 1: Prepare for the Presentation

Many advisors spend the majority of their appointment preparation time working on a financial plan to determine their recommendations. However, what they don't take time to work on is preparing and practicing the actual presentation or dialogue. As a result, they rush into recommendations, which oftentimes leave the prospect feeling confused or overwhelmed.

Step 2: Make a Personal Connection

People tend to work with people they like. Personality-Based Selling is the art of understanding personality types to make and build better connections. If you don't know much about it, you should do some homework. Remember, you must make the connection BEFORE you can make the sale!

Step 3: Help Them Understand Why They Should Buy

People hate to be sold, but they love to buy. When you map out a series of questions to take them down a "questions path" to understand why they should buy you are helping them come to their own conclusions before you've even explained your recommendations. This is one of the single most important things you can do to help close a sale.

Step 4: Prepare for Objections

You should ALWAYS expect objections! If you don't, you most certainly will get them and not know what to do with them. Take time to write out rebuttals to at least five common objections and practice them well before your appointments.

Step 5: Ask for the Order

A little known secret to sales is that an interested prospect will give you buying signals by asking you questions as if to imply that they are considering owning your recommendations such as, *"How long will it take to move the money over?"* When this happens, you must answer and ask for the order. One of the easiest closes is to say, *"Are you comfortable moving ahead?"* Ask this and you might get another objection, to which you are prepared with a rebuttal or you get the sale!

Why Turning Your Failures Into Success Works

There is much more to each of the five summaries to ensure you find success. It is a proven fact though that you can turn any failure into a success if you take the time to learn from your past errors and find solutions (or best practices) to keep you from repeating them, which will allow you to find the flipside of failure!

Story #44
The Art of Rejection Perception

Chances are you have learned behaviors toward rejection that you have never given much thought about. So ask yourself: *"What are your reactions when a prospect/client says, 'No'"?*

Over 30 years ago, I had the incredible opportunity to pay my way through college by working for a telemarketing firm. A good friend of mine was a manager there, and he convinced me it was easy money. What he failed to tell me was that to make this easy money, I would have to change my belief system about rejection.

During my initial training period, I was given a pair of headphones, escorted into a booth in the center of the calling bullpen and told to listen in on phone calls. As I listened to the eager college students trying to close three times on each initial cold call, I noticed a pattern emerging. Those who were making the sale didn't let rejection affect them while those who were not making the sale were affected. What I didn't understand at the time was how the successful students were preventing rejection from affecting them?

However, now after thirteen years of being a financial advisor and eighteen years of coaching financial advisors, insurance agents, wholesalers, branch managers and agency managers I know what you need to know about hearing the word "no".

That brings us to the five strategies for understanding the Art of Rejection Perception:

Strategy 1: Your Belief About Rejection Will Affect Your Outcome.

Fear of rejection is a learned behavior that many advisors design a belief system around. Your belief about rejection will affect your outcome because it will dictate the type of actions that you are willing to take to avoid or accept rejection. If you have a strong negative belief system regarding rejection, it is time to challenge that belief system to conquer your fear.

Strategy 2: Objections are Merely a Natural Part of the Selling Process.

You must understand this and view rejection as a natural reaction to a prospect's perception of the value of your products and service. Until they fully understand that they have a problem/s and you have the solution/s they won't see your value. All you need to do is inquire about their problems, "sell" them your solutions then set an appointment so you can help them.

Strategy 3: Prospects are Not Rejecting You Personally.

Let's face it, unless the prospect if from your natural market they don't know you. So, they are not rejecting you personally. They are merely rejecting their *perceived* value of the products or services you are offering them. In other words, it is not about you! Keep in mind that often prospect's perception of what value your products or services can add to their lives is completely false. That is because they have not or will not take the time to understand what your products and services have to offer. They may not even realize this or they may not view their lack of curiosity as a problem.

Strategy 4: Your Conviction is Correlated to Your Resilience.

There is a direct correlation between your level of confidence regarding your products, services and yourself AND your level of resilience to rejection. How can you be affected by rejection when you know that your products and services can help prospects with their financial challenges? It is almost impossible to feel the sting of rejection if you know that the prospect just does not understand how much you can help them.

Strategy 5: You Determine Who the Rejecter is and Who is the Rejected.

The law of averages dictates that there are too many qualified prospects to talk to, thus, you must reject those who are not interested in your products and services. When you become the person who is rejecting instead of the one being rejected, hearing "No" has much less of an effect on you.

Why Knowing How Your Rejection Perception Works

Hopefully, by now you have come to realize that the common denominator with each of these strategies is the fact that rejection is merely a matter of your or the prospect's perception. The reason why knowing the art of rejection perception works well is because each of the five strategies listed above help you to reinforce the fact that rejection is only as painful as you choose to let it be.

When you combine all five strategies together you tend to view rejection as becoming less-and-less painful until it becomes almost irrelevant; as a result you eventually will be desensitized to rejection altogether. And, when that happens you've created a paradigm shift, which makes you rejection proof!

Story #45
The Top 5 Myths of Prospecting Procrastination

Let's face it, it's easy to procrastinate from time to time. The problem is when procrastination goes from an occasional occurrence to a daily avoidance that the real challenges set in. With a task such as prospecting for an example, if your business is on a production plateau chances are you bought into a narrative that despite the plateau that you will come off of that without intervention, that your pipeline will trend upwards again soon.

Does this sound familiar? Let's look at this subject from a different perspective. Everything that you may have been telling yourself about procrastination may simply be a myth.

John F. Kennedy said, *"The great enemy of the truth is very often not the lie, deliberate, contrived and dishonest, but the myth, persistent, persuasive and unrealistic."*

I coach advisors/agents every week around these Top 5 Myths of Prospecting Procrastination and hopefully you too can see how those who find success work through them.

Myth 1: I Don't Prospect Because I Don't Have the Time

Not having enough time to prospect is a very common myth because we tell ourselves that the more clients we have the busier we most likely have become so there is no time to prospect. However, the challenge isn't a time management issue as much as it is a prioritization and delegation issue. Advisors/agents that delegate more of their administrative task list to others so that they can prioritize and implement action steps that they should be primarily focusing on find themselves with targeted results and increased positive outcomes.

Myth 2: I Don't Prospect Because I Don't Know What to Say

Unfortunately, most veteran advisors who have not consistently prospected in years may believe there is merit to this myth. In fact, their prospecting skillsets as a result are no doubt rusty. The challenge with this myth is that not knowing what to say should never be an excuse. There is plenty of opportunity to speak with colleagues, mentors, a professional development coach or via workshops to hone the framework of your conversations.

Myth 3: I Don't Prospect Because I Have Call Reluctance

Call reluctance has been the excuse for countless advisors/agents who find themselves stuck with their prospecting process (or lack of). The challenge isn't actually a motivational one as much as it is a mindset one. If your life depended on it you would pick up the phone and prospect. That is an extreme example, but it proves a point that many individuals could in a pinch make those calls. By adjusting your mindset, mapping out conversation architecture and refining your **Objection Resolution Model** (refer to the story **Beyond the Gatekeeper** in chapter 2) you can push beyond and find success during prospecting.

Myth 4: I Don't Prospect Because I Have a Fear of Rejection

The fear of rejection is a learned behavior, you weren't born with it. The challenge with the fear of rejection is not in essence actually being rejected or even hearing objections, but rather it's about your perception of what the prospect is really rejecting. It isn't you personally, but the prospect's perceived value of what your service offerings or recommendations could bring to them. The solution is to find a clear and succinct way to find what challenges they might be having and share some unique insights about how your advice could benefit them.

Myth 5: I Don't Prospect Because People are Uncomfortable With Being a Prospect

When an advisor/agent has a learned belief system that nobody wants to be prospected they are generalizing the attitude of future prospects based on their own past lackluster results. The challenge is not so much that there aren't any prospects that want and need financial/insurance advice as it is the advisor/agent's willingness to find those who are interested and in need. The solution is in defining what you bring to the table that may not be like others in the industry and then prospect with that in mind. You will find those who want and need your expertise.

Why Understanding the 5 Myths of Procrastination Works

Dispelling some of these myths especially around prospecting and procrastination is important because not doing so leads people down a path of continuing the same behavior(s). We should always be seeking to better our best practices and sometimes that means leaving excuses at the door and truly diving into a new methodology that motivates and inspires.

Story #46
Creating a Positive Prospecting Attitude

Many advisors/agents never take the time to think about what is really holding them back from prospecting. While some may say that it's the fear of rejection, I believe it's a deeper issue and more an attitude towards prospecting that determines how well and often you prospect.

Lou Holtz said, *"Ability is what you're capable of doing. Motivation determines what you do. Attitude determines how well you do it."*

Have you ever taken the time to think about what it takes to create a positive prospecting attitude? If not try the following five steps.

Step 1: Find a Mentor

Find a mentor, someone whom you can learn a prospecting process from who is continuously filling their pipeline and enjoy the journey adapting their process for your needs.

Bob K., a financial advisor client of mine with five years of experience had found it difficult to pick up the phone and prospect. I recommended that he find a peer who was excited about prospecting potential clients and find out what steps they were following. Bob contacted his friend who was another advisor in his firm that he had met during training class who he knew loved to prospect!

Step 2: Secure an Accountability Partner

Creating success doesn't have to be a lonely process. In fact, there are plenty of peers and colleagues whom you personally know who would enjoy being an accountability partner.

During our coaching sessions, Bob shared with me the details around Joe's (both his mentor and accountability partner) process and what kept him motivated. I recommended that they keep in contact with daily emails and weekly accountability calls. They both liked the idea.

Step 3: Take Daily Action

Keeping a positive prospecting attitude does require action and accountable on a daily basis. That's why it is so important to have morning rituals!

Both advisors had similar morning rituals to start their day off, setting a positive tone. They would exercise, listen to a motivating podcast and make the first call of the day to a client to just touch base (no stress). Doing these activities made easing into a prospecting mindset a breeze.

Step 4: Gain Confidence With Each Win

Part of maintaining a positive prospecting attitude is to build your confidence. The best way to do that is to take a minute to identify any "wins" during the day such as breaking a record number of dials, contacts, appointments set and held. If you are only aware of the end result, how much business you do each month, you miss out on all of the opportunities to be grateful for all that you accomplish along the way!

Sharing your wins and yes, even losses with your accountability partner keeps you aware and reaching for those wins. That way you reinforce positive behaviors and learn from every loss so not to repeat them.

Step 5: Keep Improving

It's important to focus daily on improving on one part of your prospecting process. By doing this you are concentrating on mastering each step of the way. Eventually, you see that by doing so is a win itself and you notice that constant improvement brings you successful outcomes.

Why Creating a Positive Prospecting Attitude Works

If you follow these steps, you inevitably find that prospecting can be a fun activity that's fueled by your positive attitude. Nothing else can make or break your business more than your own attitude. So, work on it all-day every day and you too will see how it positively impacts your business!

Story #47
Building Rapport

I coach my clients in multiple ways and formats—in Team Coaching sessions when all of the team members are on the call, in Group Coaching sessions when one or two of the team members are a part of a group of other advisors and/or in an Individual Coaching setting when I am coaching advisors 1-1.

Recently, during a Group Coaching session Mike J., a rookie financial advisor was role playing utilizing his cold call techniques. As he went on I noticed that his process sounded more like an interrogation than a dialogue. When the "prospect" would respond with a question Mike would instantly fire off a question in return without making any attempt to answer what he had just heard from the prospect. As a result, the conversation seemed flat, one sided and lacked a connection.

Why Rapport is Important

Rapport is essential in creating an environment of trust. How do you respect and appreciate another person's views while still maintaining your own integrity? How can you sharpen your rapport building skills to build rapport with anyone? To further understand strategies for building rapport we need to take a look at commonalities, which occur when people have a rapport and when they do not.

Three Rapport Building Strategies

During the face-to-face communication process three things are taking place simultaneously. First, words are being spoken. Although you may believe that your words are the most important part in building rapport typically your words are not. In fact, research shows that words are the least effective part of the communication process. Second, voice and tonality are being heard.

Actors focus on honing their voice and tonality skills by practicing a dozen different ways to say the word "no". We unconsciously have this ability, but rarely do we consciously focus on how our voice and tonality are spoken while in casual conversation. Third, body language is being spoken. This is by far the most effective form of building rapport because the listener is constantly unconsciously reading your body language to pick up any non-verbal clues in your communication.

So what does this have to do with building rapport?

Creating a Connection

Effective communication flows when people are in rapport, their words, voice, tonality and body language tend to mirror each other. Although words can build or destroy a conversation, the words you say do not have as much impact as the rest of the message you are sending. What has the most impact is tonality and body language. To build rapport you must have some level of mirroring and matching of voice, tonality and body language.

Matching eye contact is probably the most common and often taught form of building rapport in this country. From childhood we are taught to look someone in the eye when speaking to them. However, we are rarely taught to match gestures, postures, voice tonality, pitch and speed. Oftentimes this type of matching is considered taboo because it is viewed as mimicking.

The Art of Matching is not mimicry, you can use a subtle technique, which is called *"cross over mirroring"* to effectively match the other person. Some examples of *"cross over mirroring"* are if the other person creates wild arm movements, you can mirror with small hand movements. If the other person shifts their body to one side, you can shift your head to one side.

Another successful way to gain rapport is voice matching. Voice matching is done by matching another person's speed, tone, pitch, rhythm and volume. Think of this as a vocal dance and you are leading! As a financial advisor and business development consultant/coach who has spent thirty years (as of this writing) on the phone, I know how effective this strategy is! When people are like each other, they tend to like each other more, and people tend to work with those they like.

There are only two possible limitations to building rapport; your ability to perceive other people's words, voices, tonalities and body language and your ability to do the mirroring and matching.

Improving Your Rapport Building Skills

The following week I had an Individual Coaching session with Mike and he admitted that his cold calling success rate had lacked its former luster. He had been pushing prospects away during his phone conversations because he had not been *"voice matching"*. They had unconsciously noticed this and mistook his eager tone as being insensitive resulting in pushing him away.

After an hour of role playing the same script with three different tones of empathy—less empathetic and to the point, semi-empathetic, acknowledging what he heard and very empathetic, giving examples of how he could relate to their concerns, he realized that he could make a better connection by listening and regulating "how" he was saying "what" he was saying to match them.

Why Building Rapport Works

People tend to work with people that they like and people tend to like people that are like them. That is the reason why the art of building rapport works well. It's because it gives you a framework for connecting with prospects and clients alike. When you know how to consciously use words, voice, tonality and body language to mirror and match the other person they unconsciously tend to feel more comfortable with you because they can relate to you better. In other words, you remind them of themselves.

Story #48
Beyond the Band-Aid

At some point in every financial advisor's career there comes a time when each of us may feel lost, confused and/or unsure about what it truly takes to succeed in this industry. If you have ever felt this way you may have reached out to others for help.

However, the next time you do this, ask yourself this question first, *"Am I willing to go beyond putting a Band-Aid on my situation and dig down to the heart of what's really holding me back or causing me uncertainty?"*

An example of the aforementioned would be Jack a financial advisor with fifteen years of experience who called me one day and said, *"I need help getting new clients. I've been in the business a long time, but I don't feel like I'm getting any farther ahead than I was years ago."*

How Business Band-Aids are Masking as Excuses

After listening to this, we mapped out a cold calling script, determining how to handle objections and started role playing so that he could start prospecting! Two weeks later, as we began our next coaching session Jack admitted that he had not prospected at all. *"I don't think I'm ready"* he sheepishly stated, *"Can we role play again this week? I want to be a little smoother at handling objections before I begin."* Going against my better judgment, we role played once again.

Unfortunately, two weeks later in our next coaching session he admitted that he was still not prospecting. *"I know what I need to do, I just need to do."* he said hoping I would let him off the hook. *"Do you know why you didn't just do it?"* I quickly replied expecting the inevitable laundry list of excuses.*" It's because I've been busy with my clients. The market has been pretty volatile and I've just had a lot going on."*

Realizing the Reality of a "Business Band-Aid Fix"

At this point, it was time for a reality check and I knew that being direct with him would be the best approach. *"Nope, that's not it! It's because we haven't gotten to the heart of what's holding you back."* He paused before he asked *"What?"* *"It is your fear of rejection, once you can conquer this fear, you will get to the next level."* I confidently announced.

Originally, Jack had called me with the best of intentions to help him grow his business. He knew he was rusty at prospecting.

What he didn't know was that just learning or re-learning prospecting techniques was not the solution as doing so was what I refer to as a "Band-Aid Fix"—a temporary solution to ease short-term pain, but not a permanent solution to eliminate a core challenge.

The reason it was a "Band-Aid Fix" is because his real problem was that he was afraid of rejection. All the techniques in the world would not help him if he didn't actually pick up the phone and make a call. So, the solution was to get to the heart of what was holding him back and conquer it.

How to Get Beyond the Business Band-Aid

Now that you understand Business Band-Aids it time to understand what I did with my client to help him face his fear and just rip them off. Here are some steps you can follow to do the same.

Step 1: Admit That There is a Challenge

The first step in overcoming any challenge is to admit that you have one. Then, and only then can you begin to overcome it. Conversely, advisors who make excuses are trying to protect themselves from admitting that they have a challenge in the first place. In reality, this does little to help overcome the challenge because you are merely perpetuating the same actions and consequently getting the same results.

In Jack's case, he could have easily spent additional years coming up with reasons why he should/could not prospect such as market volatility, spending his time client servicing and so forth. Instead, he listened to my theory and made the realization with my guidance that he needed to conquer his fear of rejection.

Step 2: Determine What the Root Cause is

Belief systems—our own personal set of "rules"—are a natural part of our development; evidence, tradition, authority, association or revelation can shape them.

In Jack's case, he told me that his belief that "rejection is painful" was based on the evidence that his first five years in the business were faced with countless hour of prospecting and full of hearing rejection, which he took personally. As the years went on and his business grew, he decreased his prospecting efforts because he was making a comfortable living talking to clients.

This is a common challenge for many veterans that are experiencing a production plateau. They have created a negative belief system towards rejection. It is a learned belief system that prospecting equals pain and for Jack, that pain was so great that for years he had unconsciously chosen not to prospect.

Step 3: Test and Overcome the Limiting Belief System

Once you have identified a limiting belief system, it is time to put it to the test by scrutinizing its validity. The way to do that is by asking the right type of questions known as Socratic Questions—a form of questioning in which Socrates used to create a negative argument to rational investigation. Some examples are as follows:

- What is the evidence that this is true?
- Is this *always* true, each and every time?
- Am I seeing the big picture?
- What is the worst thing that can happen to me?

After explaining this to Jack, I began asking him Socratic Questions. *"Jack, you said that you take rejection personally. What is the evidence that when you got rejected it was because people did not personally like you?"* I inquired. *"Well, I don't know. I just assumed that it must be me"* he cautiously replied. *"Why? Why would someone who has never spoken to you before instantly not like you?"* I probed.

He paused trying to consider the reasoning behind his beliefs, *"I don't know. I guess they don't even know me"* he stammered. *"That's right! They don't know you. And, since they don't, how could someone rejecting you be personal?"* I said. I could tell that it was starting to sink in. *"Well, if rejection is not about me personally then what are they rejecting?"* he curiously asked.

"They are rejecting the perceived value (or lack thereof) that your products and services can provide them. If they think there is value in what you are offering they will meet with you, if they don't see the value they won't. It's not about you personally at all." I replied. *"Then all I need to do is learn how to better explain the value that I can bring to them!"* he excitedly proclaimed. *"Yes! And, that is as exactly how your business will become healthy again."* I confidently agreed.

Step 4: Reinforcing Your New Belief System

To strengthen any new belief system, you must constantly reinforce it. For Jack, it was as simple as continuously reading a post-it note saying, *"They aren't rejecting me, they just haven't seen the value of my services yet. But, I'm confident they will because many have!"* This helped tremendously because he soon built a pipeline of new prospects that turned into new clients!

It is important to note, that although Jack's root cause for not prospecting was his limiting belief system about rejection, your root cause for what is holding you back may be entirely different. That's why it is so important to go beyond the Band-Aid.

Why Going Beyond the Band-Aid Works

It may come as no surprise to you that getting to heart of what's really holding you back or causing you uncertainty is not an easy thing to do. That's why going beyond the Band-Aid works so well because it is a step-by-step strategy for doing just that, getting to and through the root cause of your challenge. Without having this approach you most likely will continue to stay stuck. And, that is an unhealthy way to build your business.

Story #49
The Subtle Art of Helping Prospects Understand

Most advisors/agents have a tendency to tell prospects and clients what they need to do. Unfortunately, this approach creates resistance. Dwight D. Eisenhower said, *"Motivation is the art of getting people to do what you want them to do because they want to do it."*

The common phrase, *"Nobody wants to be sold to, but everybody wants to buy"* is a prime example of what most advisors/agents just don't understand, people buy when they understand why they should buy. In other words, when they realize what the problem is and that you have the solution.

Have you ever taken the time to think about how to help prospects and clients truly understand the reasons why you are recommending specific products and services?

If not, utilize the following steps to help guide you through that process.

Step 1: Understand the Benefits of Your Recommendations

The first step is to write out three benefits for your recommendation(s). If you don't understand the benefits of your recommendations the prospect won't either. Using a tool that I created for my coaching clients, The Question Path Exercise, can do this.

Sean M., a five-year veteran financial advisor client of mine was about to have biggest single day of his career by gathering $7M in total assets. Unfortunately, he had never heard of the concept of Insight Selling, which is about providing a prospect with the insight regarding the benefits of a recommendation so they fully understand why they should buy. I explained the concept and had him fill out **The Question Path Exercise** starting with the top three benefits of his recommendations.

Step 2: Prepare the Right Questions to Ask

The second step is to map out three or four questions for each of those benefits to help them understand that they have a problem and your benefits are the solutions.

Once Sean had his three benefits filled out, I recommended that we design three or four questions around each benefit. The process started out by formulating a question that would prompt a prospect to realize that they had a problem. An example of this is the question, *"Do you know how much diversification you have in your current portfolio?"* We followed it up with two other questions to help the prospect understand that they did not have enough diversification, which is a problem and that they needed more, which is the solution.

Step 3: Summarize Two Options

The third step is to articulate a dialogue that summarizes that they have two options, to keep doing what they are doing or buy a product that has those benefits.

After role playing, Sean fully understood the process, his questions and the options he would share. We continued honing his conversation, which ended up sounding like this: *"So, it sounds like having diversification is important to you?"* in which case the prospect would agree.

Next we summarized the only two options that the prospect has by comparing what he is currently doing to the three benefits he could get by choosing the recommendations. An example of this is by saying, *"You really only have two options: You could keep doing what you are doing or you could get diversification, reduced risk and possibly better returns."*

Step 4: Ask for the Order

The fourth step is to ask for the order *"Of the previous two options which one is better for you?"* At this point, I recommended that Sean use what I call the Ultimate Close, which was just ask for the order. An example of this is, *"Which option do you feel is better for you?"*

Why Helping People Buy Works

Following this stepwise approach can help you map out a presentation that prospects will understand. The reason why helping people buy works well is because it allows them to comprehend both the challenge and the solution and when they realize that they came to the conclusion on their own, they are far more likely to purchase.

So, what happened to Sean?

After practicing the presentations several times, he closed not one, but both of his prospects and gathered $7M in new assets in that one day. That was more than in his entire previous year!

Story #50
Properly Preparing for a Closing Appointment

Most financial advisors wouldn't dream of not preparing appropriately for a second appointment. However, finding out what a prospect needs to do to reach their financial goals is not going to be enough. You need to also properly plan out conversation points to have with them.

Step 1: Preparing Your Questions

It's no secret that first appointments are typically an introductory meeting in which you ask a number of question to get to know the prospect and uncover their specific needs and financial goals to put together your recommendations. Unfortunately, after that first meeting most advisors don't take the time to ask some necessary additional questions.

If you ask those questions before presenting your recommendations, you can actually take the prospect down what I call the **Questions Path** to help them uncover what it is they need; and, as a result they end up telling you what they should "buy".

If you do this successfully they will see the need for your recommendations even before you show them what those recommendations are.

Step 2: Preparing to Listen

It's been said that, "People don't care how much you know until they know how much you care." Try a technique that I call **The 4 Levels of Listening** (refer to the story **Realizing the Importance of the Filler Formula** in chapter 2). When a prospect speaks, oftentimes most advisors mimic what they hear or rephrase what they hear.

While I don't recommend mimicking, I do recommend rephrasing. If you want to make an even better connection reflect back on what a prospect is indicating that he/she is feeling. An example may be, *"That sounds frustrating, is it?"*

After you've started incorporating this try reflecting the feeling and then rephrase, *"That sounds frustrating because it sounds to me that you really aren't sure what to do to reach your financial goals?"*

Step 3: Preparing the Close

Once you use a combination of asking questions and empathetic listening, the prospect will hopefully come to the realization that they need YOUR help. At that point, explain your recommendations, but also reiterate how this helps them fill their need.

Use a question like this, *"Based on what we talked about, how do you think these strategies will help you most to reach your financial goals?"* If you used these techniques they should be able to answer this question. When they do, simple ask, *"What do you think is the best course of action for you?"*

Why Properly Preparing Works

To implement these strategies into your practice use the formula—think Question, Answer, and Filler. Ask a question, let the prospect answer, use empathetic listening then repeat the process. When you prepare your questions ahead of time and practice your listening skills you will make it easy for them to want to work with you!

Story #51
The Science of Service

In our industry, it can sometimes be easy to lose sight of the primary purpose of our business, which is to service the financial needs of our clients. Personal, professional and even corporate goals may lead some of the best financial advisors to occasionally place their focus in a direction that is not in the client's best interest, but in theirs. When this happens, it goes against the Science of Service.

In the short-term this shift of focus may help the advisor accomplish a goal, but typically in the long run it can only be counterproductive because it goes against what should be all about an advisor's integrity. Once this "line" is crossed it is that much easier to cross it again because an advisor's definition of what that "line" is becomes blurred by excuses.

Mahatma Gandhi said, *"The best way to find yourself is to lose yourself in the service of others."* I believe this is very true. However, that begs the question of, "What constitutes service?"

Understanding the Science of Service

Most advisors and agents think that the definition of service is to answer incoming client calls, hear what they need, drop everything and attend to their requests. However, that is a very reactive client servicing system. And, while this type of servicing is necessary at times it is not the only thing that clients need.

Step 1: Having a High Level of Integrity

Over twenty years ago, I asked John M. the most seasoned financial advisor in the office a simple question, *"Can you run a financial advisory practice with integrity and still make a great living?"* He smiled and said, *"You will make more money than you could ever imagine as long as you continue to do the right thing."*

Unfortunately, we have all met prospects that owned products that were inappropriate for them. Instead, the advisor who sold them these types of products probably did so because the advisor was thinking of their own best interests.

Ironically, the "Science of Servicing" begins even before a prospect becomes a client because recommending an inappropriate product(s) is doing the prospect and yourself a disservice.

A level of impeccable integrity must continue when they do become a client!

Step 2: Having a High Level of Product & Market Knowledge

Clients entrust their hard-earned money to you because they believe you not only have their best interest at heart, but that you fulling understand the right investment strategies for them. That's why it is so important to take the time to keep abreast of your product and market knowledge.

An example of this is Paul C. a financial advisor client of mine who spends at least 30 minutes each morning reading something related to the stock market, the economy and/or various products that he recommends to his clients. He says that by doing so he feels well-versed to answer any questions that his clients or prospects have.

Step 3: Having a Pro-Active Client Servicing System

Most financial advisors want to service their clients in the best way possible, but many financial advisors fail to understand "how" to service clients effectively because they do not understand what great service means.

David P. a client was "putting out fires" all daylong, which made him feel exhausted more often than not. That is until we designed a pro-active client servicing system by segmenting his book, clearly defining his client servicing levels, systematizing his client servicing activities and delegating many of the day-to-day interruptions to his staff. It didn't take long before David felt back in control of his day!

Why The Science of Service Works

By now I hope you can relate to the advisors in each one of the examples and realize that what they are doing is not an "art". In other words, it is not subjective. To John M. integrity is the cornerstone of service, to Paul C. knowledge is imperative to keeping his clients informed and having the right investments and to David P. having a pro-active client servicing system gives his clients and himself peace of mind.

To these advisors their activities are not open to interpretation. Instead, they have adopted a Science of Service mindset.

Story #52
Pushing Past the Upper Limit

Have you ever wondered why you are not consistently having record setting years? Oftentimes while coaching financial advisors and insurance agents I have notice specific behavioral patterns that kick in soon after individuals have experienced success.

Gay Hendricks, the author of the book **The Big Leap:** *Conquering Your Hidden Fear and Take Life to the Next Level* has coined a term for this that he refers to as The Upper Limit Problem—which he defines as the amount of success that you are willing to allow yourself to have.

Here is how it works:

We all have an "inner thermostat" that is set on just how much success we are willing to allow ourselves to have before we do something to self-sabotage and get back to our comfort zone. Unfortunately, most people don't know their thermostat's setting much less know a process for inching that setting higher.

How to Reset Your Inner Thermostat and Resolve Your Upper Limit Problem

Hendricks says that to get to the "Next Level" you cannot solve the problem that is holding you back, but rather resolve the problem by gaining a new level of awareness about it. Let's take a look at the four main zones that he refers to that explains where people get stuck.

The Zone of Incompetence

One of the most common zones that I've seen advisors and agents revert to when they start to experience successes is The Zone of Incompetence, which refers to spending time doing activities we are clearly not good at. Take for instance the last time you were having a record month, as the days went on did you find yourself doing activities that your assistant could be doing? If so, it was because you were self-sabotaging your time and activities that could have been contributing to your continued level of success!

The Zone of Competence

Let's say that you are great at doing what should be your assistant's activities, you've done them for years and you find yourself saying things like, *"Well, she's got plenty to do so it's just easier if I do this one thing for my client instead."* The challenge with this is that it's never just one thing. If you are finding yourself doing these tasks, you are in The Zone of Competence. You both could be doing these activities, but the truth is that if you are already having a successful month you essentially are now giving yourself permission to stop doing YOUR job and tackling items that your assistant really should be completing.

The Zone of Excellence

Successful advisor and agents find themselves in The Zone of Excellence, which is accomplishing activities that they do well and getting compensated! Unfortunately, this can create a comfort zone, which long-term will hold one back from reaching their peak potential. In addition, you may find yourself falling into a rut doing what you do well, but not liking what you are doing. In other words, if you are great at public speaking, but are sick of doing seminars you may not be happy and thus need to find things you are good at and like doing. You will burnout otherwise.

The Zone of Genius

At some point, you need to ask yourself the tough question, *"If you couldn't fail at your business, what is it that you really would love to be doing differently?"* The answer to that question will lead you to The Zone of Genius, what you LOVE to do. As a result, work wouldn't feel like work! In this zone time doesn't fly but instead it flows, you are not exhausted, you feel fulfilled. Granted you will still have to "work" to make a great living, but you would also be happy and passionate about your professional life.

Why Pushing Past the Upper Limit Works

Take a moment to determine what zone you are currently in. If you want to live your life's purpose then you must take a big leap of faith and commit to becoming the person you are meant to be by finding what work you love to do.

Then express to your target market your unique abilities and genuine willingness to help them so that one day they too could be in a position to afford to do what they love to do. If you can take this leap, you will have done what Hendricks meant by conquering your hidden (or unknown) fear taking yourself to the next level of work and life.

Story #53
Managing Uncertainty

In the financial services industry few things are certain; more times than not uncertainty is the norm. The one thing that you can count on is that if you don't manage how you react to uncertainty, uncertainty will end up managing you. Being emotionally tethered to events that are out of your control can never be a productive way to run your business.

So, what are some ways you can intervene during uncertain times or unforeseen circumstances to become better balanced with your action/reaction(s)?

Step 1: Determine the Reality of a Situation

Most of the time, when an advisor is faced with wondering what might happen, with the market, the economy, a difficult client et al, advisors tend to distort or exaggerate their view or possible outcome. It is very easy to focus on negativity because when your anxiety is high, equally are your concerns.

Soon those anxieties and concerns multiply into additional thoughts that can spiral out of control. When this occurs it is vital to stop and ask yourself this question, *"What is the reality of the situation?"* It is important to try and stay emotionally neutral when answering this question and you may be surprised to find that the actual reality isn't so bad.

Step 2: Determine Your Desired Outcome and What You Can Control

The second step in this process is to be crystal clear on what you want the end result to be. If you don't determine your desired outcome, you more than likely won't find it. Once you have done this you must also examine what is in your control and what is not. For example: your desire to have a client get better returns.

Now, what is in your control? Can you control the market, their risk tolerance or their ultimate decision to invest in your recommendations? No, however you can decide to give them the best possible advice based on all of the information and expertise that you can provide.

Step 3: Take Action and Track Your Progress

The third step is to take action! Map out your plan and execute that plan right away. There is something to be said about the saying, "*action alleviates anxiety*". The way to sustain this momentum is to keep focusing on your activities by tracking your progress.

Managing Uncertainty Example

Maybe you have a number of clients concerned about the market, you know that the market is out of your control, but you also know that you want them to feel at ease. So, you read your company's weekly market commentary as well as economic reports.

Then, you translate what you have read into laymen's terms and begin calling as many clients as possible to explain to them what is going on. Finally, you track how many client contacts you are making each day. Soon you will realize that your clients are happier just knowing that you are taking the time to connect with them and they will appreciate that you are attempting to assuage their fears/concerns!

Why Managing Uncertainty Works

Now, think about the aforementioned example and compare it to that last time you found yourself emotionally distraught over uncertainty then ask yourself this, "*What type of advisor would your clients rather work with—the one who let's uncertainty manage him/her or the one who takes control of uncertainty as best as possible?*" I am confident you know the answer!

Story #54
The Solutions Formula

Most advisors/agents know that they will be faced with inevitable challenges in their business. However, rarely do they have a formula for creating and applying solutions. As a result they leave overcoming challenges up to chance. A common phrase about challenges that I hear from my clients is, *"I guess there is nothing I can do about it. It is what it is."*

But, what if there was something you could do about it? In fact, what if there was a formula for creating solutions? Thomas J. Watson said, *"Every problem has in it the seeds of its own solution. If you don't have any problems, you don't get any seeds."*

In other words, within every problem lies the answer on how to fix it. You just need a formula for finding the answer. After coaching advisors/agents for over two decades I have established a formula that works. Let's take a look at a step-by-step approach that I call The Solutions Formula to help you find your own solutions.

Step 1: Identify Your Challenges

Knowing what your real challenge is, is half the battle. Unfortunately, oftentimes it seems that advisors/agents focus their attention on the lack of current results that they are experiencing rather than delving into understanding what the underlying obstacle is.

Take William D., a veteran financial advisor that admitted that he had recently had a number of closing appointments, but didn't actually make a close. Instead of trying to understand why he didn't close, he was just frustrated at the fact that he wasn't closing.

So, I had him look at four possible "root challenges" for not closing which were:

He didn't have the right questions to help the prospect understand the benefits of why they should buy.

He was spending too much time telling the prospect/s what they needed to do instead of asking them those right questions.

He didn't come right out and ask the prospect if they wanted to buy by saying, "Are you comfortable moving ahead?"

He didn't have a process to overcome objections.

After giving it some thought William knew that it wasn't a matter of one challenge, but in his case it was all four of the challenges that he had.

Step 2: Identify Solutions & Tools

Knowing the results you want is essential if you want to succeed in any endeavor. However, when you can identify the specific solutions and have tools to apply those solutions you are more apt to end up with successful outcomes.

After William and I had discussed his challenges, it was time to discuss the solutions I recommended:

S.P.I.N Selling (refer to the story **Great Questions Create Great Connections** in chapter 2), which is a process for designing the right questions to ask.

The Question Path Exercise, which is a step-by-step method for asking the questions, so that it flows in a conversational way.

The Closing Question, which is a summary of everything in the conversation and ask for the order.

The Objection Resolution Model (refer to the story **Beyond the Gatekeeper** in chapter 2), which is a proven system for handling objections.

Step 3: Apply & Access Results

The final step is to utilize the tools on a consistent basis and assess and evaluate the results. If you still have the challenge, you would need to find additional tools or make tweaks to your action steps.

In the following weeks, William applied all of these tools. As a result, his close ratio went up over 90%! In addition, he has continued utilizing these tools and is maintaining the same greater level of success.

Why The Solutions Formula Works

The foundation of establishing success on a continual basis is grounded in having a series of proven systems, which are moving you in the right direction. No single solution is the cure all. However, the reason why The Solutions Formula works is because it's a process for identifying the challenge(s) as well as solution(s) and tool(s). So, the next time you find yourself with a challenge, view it as an opportunity to apply The Solutions Formula.

Story #55
The Elephant in the Room

Are you finding that no matter how hard you work there is still something that is holding you back from success? "It" might be procrastination, the fear of rejection, the fear of failure OR the fear of success, overcoming objections, poor closing techniques or a whole host of other possibilities. Whatever your biggest challenge is…let's be honest and give "it" a name; "It" is the elephant in the room.

Recently, during one of my group coaching sessions a financial advisor had an epiphany and shouted, *"That's it! That is the elephant in the room. We all have our biggest challenge that we do not want to admit to ourselves much less to each other. We can't ignore it any longer. These challenges have gotten so big that we need to face them."*

Let's face it; conquering your biggest challenge can be a scary thought. In fact, you may not even consciously realize what your challenges are. All advisors at one time or another in their careers have their own, elephant in the room, and they probably always will unless they apply steps for conquering it.

Step 1: Acknowledging & Admitting a Challenge

Denial is a common response when financial advisors are asked, *"What is the number one thing that is holding you back?"* The reason I ask this is because I want to understand if they know, or can admit that they even have a challenge.

Typically, I get a canned response such as, *"I don't know?"* This is usually followed by me giving them permission to admit that it is okay to have a challenge, *"But if you did know what might it be?"* *"Well, I guess I need to prospect more"*, might be a common response.

Now, we have just peeled one layer of the emotional onion back to discover that there is a challenge. This is important because you must first acknowledge and admit that you have a challenge. But, what if you do not know what your challenge is?

Step 2: Defining the Challenge

One of the most difficult things to determine is your biggest challenge. That's why I created the **Advisor's Business Wheel** (refer to the story **Building A Balanced Business** in chapter 2), a tool designed to uncover how balanced your business is as well as what your challenges are by having the financial advisor rate themselves on a scale from 1-10, (1 being least effective and 10 being most effective) in what I call the 8 Most Important Facets of Your Business, these include, *time management, prospecting, sales, relationship building, client servicing, marketing, product/market knowledge and managing client portfolios.*

Then, I list a number of solutions and tools that I have created that would help the financial advisor get past their challenge(s) and increase their ratings for each facet.

Although this might sound simplistic, it is a very effective process because we are not avoiding the proverbial elephant in the room but instead acknowledging it and creating solutions to move beyond it.

Step 3: Understanding the Next Layer of the Challenge

It is not enough to just become aware of what the challenge(s) are; you must also understand why you have the challenge to conquer it. Take for instance the example of an advisor who admitted the challenge is that he is not prospecting. After asking why, he may also admit because he is truly afraid of rejection.

Eventually, he may understand *the next layer of the challenge*, which actually is his perception that prospects will be rejecting him personally; thus rejection equals emotional pain! So how can he get past his fear? To conquer this and most challenges we must change our negative belief systems.

Step 4: Changing Negative Belief Systems

The secret to changing a negative belief system is to question its validity. By subjecting your negative self-talk or your negative belief systems to rational scrutiny, you break down the belief systems validity, which in turn creates a new belief system. The following is an example:

Negative Belief: *"Rejection is painful because prospects are personally rejecting me."*

Relief Question: *"Is this always true? Have I ever prospected and opened a new account?"*

Positive Counterstatement: *"Prospects cannot reject me personally because they do not even know me. Instead, they are merely rejecting what they perceive to be the value of my services!"*

Step 5: Sustaining New Belief Systems and Applying Solutions

Sustaining your new belief system should be the ongoing process of using relief questions and positive counterstatements. Finally, seek out and apply new tools and techniques to become more effective at conquering your challenge(s).

An example would be for this advisor to increase his cold calling prospecting skills by **Framing the Conversation** (refer to the story **Beyond the Gatekeeper** in chapter 2) so he knows exactly what to say, using **Objection Resolution Models** (refer to the **Beyond the Gatekeeper** in chapter 2) so he can handle objections, and reviewing **The Agreement Close** (refer to the story **Five Elements Of The Agreement Close** in chapter 2) so he can close the sale.

Why Conquering The Elephant In the Room Works

Remember, conquering your biggest challenge(s) is a marathon not a sprint. The reason why these steps work is because when you apply these five steps for conquering your elephant and you continue reinforcing positive belief systems as well as implement new solutions, your elephant will silently disappear.

Story #56
Establishing Constructive Connections

There comes a time in every advisor's career when they realize how important good communication with their peers, support staff, mentors and colleagues is, but how does one know the best practices for establishing constructive connections without a guide?

Matt, a twenty-six-year old advisor was just three years into the industry and found him having to train and motivate a fellow "rookie" on the team, Jeff, who was ten years older than him. After months of training, Matt began feeling that Jeff was starting to resent his help as often his recommendations were quickly dismissed and Jeff continued to face the same challenges.

If this scenario sounds familiar, perhaps implementing the following formula will help you to create constructive communications and better working relationships.

Step 1: Start With the Positives

Let's face it nobody wants to be constantly criticized. Jeff would no sooner finish a cold call and Matt would eagerly be waiting to critique what he had overheard during Jeff's conversation.

I coached both individuals so I knew both sides of the story and thus I recommended to Matt that he make some notes then wait until the end of the day to meet with Jeff in private, then start off their discussion with a list of positive remarks to reinforce Jeff's great calling techniques. One example I suggested was, *"You did a great job today following the format of the cold calling script..."*

Step 2: Transition With an Observation

It has been said that all manner of praise is irrelevant if followed by the word "but". The reason why is because the listener will feel that any compliments given were a lead up to any true sentiments and hence insincere. To keep that from happening, it is important to transition with an observation. An example of this would be, *"What I noticed is that you could be even more effective if..."*

This example lets the listener know that you thought they were good at "X" and that by changing or adding a few things they could get even better results!

Step 3: Recommend & Reinforce with Reasons

If you want to make an impact, you must give the listener a strong reason as to why they should apply your recommendations as explaining your own experience with the subject gives you credibility. Here is an example, *"You should add some of your own personal stories into your conversations. I did this and found that people were more receptive to speaking with me because they could relate and they knew I was having a true dialogue with them rather than reading from a script."*

Putting It All Together

Now, here is how it sounds if you put these three steps together.

"You did a great job today following the format of the cold calling script and what I noticed is that you could be even more effective if you add some of your own personal stories into your conversations. I did this and found that people were more receptive to speaking with me because they could relate and they knew I was having a true dialogue with them rather than reading a script."

Why Establishing Constructive Connections Works

This type of communication doesn't happen overnight. It takes time and preparation but eventually you will find that it gets easier and it is well worth it as creating constructive connections always makes good business sense.

Story #57
Practicing the Principle of Strategic Replacement

One of the most common questions I get asked by advisors who are just starting out with me in coaching is, *"How can I change my business to find more success?"* It's a pretty "broad" question, but with a little probing I can typically whittle things down to specific areas of their business that need the most change.

Some advisors think the answer lies in not contributing to bad habits anymore, for example, *"I'm going to stop procrastinating when it comes to prospecting"* So, they try what I call the "stop technique" for a couple of days, but 90% of the time they end up falling back into familiar patterns.

Instead, I coach them to practice, what I call, The Principle of Strategic Replacement, which states that to change a bad habit we have to replace it with a better one.

Then you need to track your daily progress and be disciplined (and dedicated) enough to do this for at least 30 days to create and establish new patterns. The following steps will assist you in doing just that.

Step 1: Don't Underestimate the Grip of Familiar Patterns

Change doesn't happen overnight and the first step to breaking bad habits is to make sure that you understand and respect the power that they have to hold us to familiar patterns.

A good analogy would be to think of replacing bad habits as equal to the task of removing a tree stump. It may seem like a relatively easy task on the surface, but once you get below ground you may find that there are a lot of roots that were holding the stump in place.

It takes time to dig out those roots, plant seed and carefully and patiently watch new healthy roots take its place.

Step 2: Identify Bad Habits and Root Causes That Need to Change

Identifying bad habits is not always easy because it takes a little soul searching. Take for instance the goal of wanting to grow your business.

If you are completely honest with yourself, you may realize that the reason your practice is not growing is because you are not prospecting, which would be the bad habit you want to change. Now, if we get to the root cause of that bad habit we might discover that you don't prospect because you are afraid of rejection.

Step 3: Change Your Perspective

Once you know the root cause (in the earlier example it was a fear of rejection) it's important to replace it with a new perspective. A good thing to do is to map out all of the long-term consequences of not prospecting along with best practices to managing objections.

Also, replace your fear of rejection with the knowledge that it isn't personal, which should help you to adjust your perception of the rejection. Qualifying prospects is just part of what you do and rejection is a part of that process.

Step 4: Create Strategic Replacements

The next step is to strategically plan out the new activities that will support and promote the "new" good habit. The more detailed you can be the higher the probability of your success. An example would be to prospect business owners for the first hour of each day, map out what you will say, how you will handle objections, track the dials, contacts and appointments set and send that information to a colleague, manager or business coach for 30 days so that you have the accountability to keep you motivated.

Why Strategic Replacement Works

The reason why strategic replacement works is because it is a systematic process for sustaining long-term awareness, action and accountability – becoming AWARE of the root cause of the bad habit and the consequences of continuing with those bad habits, the ACTION or execution of the plan and the continued inspiration to help follow the good habits for 30 days and finally, daily ACCOUNTABILITY to someone else for the action that you took. When you practice strategic replacement you create lasting change by creating healthy habits.

Story #58
Crafting Your Desired Outcomes

At some point in their career path, advisors/agents might look at the success of their peers and wonder, *"Why aren't great things happening for me?"* Some examples might be a colleague taking over a multi-million dollar 401K plan or landing a large rollover or insurance account. While you may believe that luck has something to do with it. The truth is that your actions create your own outcomes.

Chris Grosser said, *"Opportunities don't happen. You create them."*

There are a few elements to consider if you want your desired outcomes to actually occur. Consistently, on a daily basis, you need to implement action steps, this includes getting to tasks that you least like first so that you ensure that they get done. Also learning from both your successes AND failures from the past and mapping out ways to maintain what worked and replace what didn't.

4 Steps to Crafting Your Desired Outcomes

The following discusses some suggestions that I utilize in my professional development and coaching programs. See if you can relate to what the advisor in my example is going through when applying the process yourself.

Step 1: Consistently Implement Action

Most advisors/agents who want better results miss consistently implementing action steps. Take Steve F., a fifteen-year veteran client of mine. During our initial session he admitted that although he wanted to have a record year, he rarely prospected because of the anxiety he felt just thinking about getting rejected. It had overwhelmed and swamped his level of success.

I explained that being consistent in tackling items that are most challenging to you will end up reducing anxiety. Avoiding things that make us uncomfortable will keep you blocking your own way every time. I recommended that he trust me and for twenty business days he had to prospect and record his level of anxiety on a scale of 1-10 (1 being lowest and 10 being highest) to determine my theory. He reluctantly agreed, but also knew he needed to move out of his comfort zone to forge ahead.

Step 2: Do the First Thing First

At this point, most advisors/agents need to prioritize their tasks and unfortunately, as stated earlier, it's the least desirable task that must be accomplished first thing.

To ensure that Steve prospected each day as his #1 task, he needed to begin each morning with having a list of people to call, knowing exactly what he was going to say and how to handle the inevitable objections. That way he was prepared as best he could be. He then needed to make a game out of making the calls by trying to contact ten people before 10:00 a.m. If he did that, he got to reward himself in some small way to motivate him to continue conquering that first of the day task.

Step 3: Look for the Lesson

One of the best ways to change a perspective about any undesirable task is to view doing the task as a learning opportunity. After Steve finished prospecting each day, he would record one lesson that he learned. The next day and so forth, he would review the list of lessons he had documented so that it would reinforce positive activity. It didn't take him long before he started to look forward to adding to his list!

Step 4: Create Accountability

Consistency is important when creating productive new habits and to create consistency advisors/agents need accountability. The reason it is so important is because without accountability it is too easy to slip back into unproductive behaviors/actions. I had Steve begin emailing me his level of anxiety before and after prospecting for each of those initial twenty days. I also had him send me his Lessons Learned List each day. In addition, he had to track his appointments set, attended, individuals in his pipeline and any new business that he landed.

Why Crafting Desired Outcomes Works

After those twenty days, Steve had changed his perspective on prospecting. He realized that following these steps helped him redirect his focus from one of fear to one of faith that he could actually obtain his goals. The reason this process worked was simple, he had a stepwise approach and wasn't winging things, procrastinating or avoiding anymore.

Story #59
Sowing the Seeds of Significance

How do you want to be remembered? We would like to think amongst other things that for most advisors the true meaning of leaving a successful legacy is about changing the lives of your clients for the better.

If you think about it in these terms, imagine the passion that you could infuse into your practice each day. Knowing you are making a difference in people's lives in a very important way is definitely something we should all aspire to.

As any good gardener knows you must take meticulous care when planting and nurturing seedlings and harvest when the time is most appropriate. Planting the seeds of significance and sowing them when the time is right in a business setting is no different.

Step 1: Plant Your Garden—prospecting with the mindset that you want to truly help others is the first step in spreading your seeds of significance. You need to be confident and honest with your intentions. There are more people that need your help then those who do not. All you have to do is help them understand how your solutions and expertise could change their lives.

Be sure to know your target market's common challenges, know what the solutions are for them and know how to ask the right types of questions so that they come to the conclusion that you will bring value to them. When they understand that you are not trying to sell to them, , instead are offering real world and relevant advice the seeds are planted in what will hopefully take root and become a long-term relationship.

Step 2: Nurture Your Garden—once you have a client base you must nurture them with your knowledge, expertise and integrity. Your business is truly like a garden. If you choose to neglect it, it will not bear any fruit; the roots of your client relationships will wither and your clients will simply find another advisor. However, if you are sincere with your communications and dialogue about wanting to make a positive impact in their lives they will sense your genuine interest and continue to grow with you.

Step 3: Harvest Your Garden —although you may never be privy to the full extent of how your advice and solutions impact your client's lives (or maybe the lives of their children or grandchildren) you will know that you have played an integral role in sowing the seeds of significant financial security for your clients (and maybe even future generations).

Why Sowing the Seeds of Significance Works

Taking the time to plant, nurture and harvest your business takes dedication, commitment and an unfailing motivation to continually repeat the process. For those in our industry who do just that, they will find themselves with a bountiful garden.

Story #60
The Value of Vulnerability

Over the past two years, I have had the pleasure of working with a very successful team of financial advisors. As their success has increased so has the amount of advisors that were added to their team; currently they are nine team members.

Each week we focus on a specific exercise to increase their sales skills that I have designed for their weekly coaching session. The advisors learn the exercise, role play it and I, along with the two principal partners, would critique them. We continue to utilize the same exercise for weeks or even months (if need be) until each team member can do it seamlessly.

During a recent team coaching session one of the principal partners told the group that they were not making a good connection during their role plays because they were not opening up and sharing their feelings about the subject at hand. In other words they were not allowing themselves to be vulnerable.

He went on to say that the value of vulnerability is that the prospect makes the realization that you have been in their shoes; consequently, in many cases, you then are able to make a connection!

The following is a simplified step-by-step process in finding the value to be vulnerable:

Step 1: Ask Great Questions

Once you determine that the subject you are talking about is something that is very important to the prospect, it's time to ask additional questions to uncover how they feel about the subject. Try something as simple as this:

Advisor: *"What concerns you most about losing money now that you are retired?"*

Step 2: Uncover the Prospect's Story & Feelings

At this point, it is important to listen, acknowledge what you heard and ask more questions so you can uncover the prospect's story and feelings. Here is an example:

Prospect: *"Well, I don't really want to lose anything. In fact, I'm not sure what I would do if I did lose some of my retirement investments."*

Advisor: *"I completely understand, but how do you think you'd feel if we had another 2008 and your current portfolio reacted like your portfolio did back then?"*

Step 3: Make a Connection

Next, we need to make a strong connection by genuinely talking about how you feel about the subject.

Prospect: *"I would feel sick! I wouldn't know what to do if I lost 20, 30 or 40% of my money. I lost a lot of money back then and it took years to get it back."*

Advisor: *"I would feel sick too!"*

Step 4: Get Vulnerable

At this point, you need to explain why you feel this way by telling the prospect what you have experienced in the past. Here is a brief example:

Advisor: *"My dad retired in late 2007 and I asked him the same type of question that I asked you about how he would feel if he lost money. He said he wouldn't be able to handle even a 10% loss. At that time he didn't need the income and since I knew the market had a great bull run, I recommended that we get very conservative and reposition a good percentage of his assets into somethings that wasn't tethered to the market. We did that and he missed the bear years."*

Step 5: Ask for the Order

In this example, if the prospect is giving you indications that they can relate by smiling, nodding or agreeing that you did the right thing! Try this close:

Advisor: *"We have had a seven-year bull market, how would it help you most if we at least take a look at some alternative strategies so we reduce your risk to the stock market?"*

Prospect: *"I think that would give me some peace of mind. Let's do that."*

Why Genuine Vulnerability Works

As the saying goes, *"It's simple but it's not easy."* The "simple" part is opening up and telling the prospect what you or someone you know has experienced around the subject matter. The "not easy" part is having that topic be something that you genuinely care about.

In other words, if it's not from the heart, you are not going to make a connection. Conversely, genuine vulnerability works because you are discussing something that is important to you and if it's also important to them then you have the foundation to form that connection.

Story #61
Opening the Door to Opportunity

In the financial services industry, advisors/agents need to find all possible opportunities in order to take their business to its next level. I believe that opportunity can find you while you are busy working harder and smarter. In other words, your productive activities attract opportunities that can ultimately result in future successes. Conversely, hoping that an opportunity will fall from the sky is wishful thinking.

Thomas Edison said, *"Opportunity is missed by most people because it is dressed in overalls and looks like work."*

If you think about that quote it comes from a man that is reported to have unsuccessfully invented the light bulb some 10,000 times! However, most people remember him for his successes not his failures.

Let's take a look at a step-by-step approach that successful advisors and agents use to continuously generate opportunities:

Step 1: Know What You Want

It may seem evident, to get what you want you have to first know what you want. In Edison's case, he wanted to invent the light bulb and he was willing to keep trying until he did.

Here is a real time example of how one financial advisor client of mine used this type of process:

Tom P. was a newer financial advisor with less than five years in the industry who was struggling at determining how to best build his business practice.

Our coaching conversations first began with the end in mind so we discussed what a successful business would look like to him. By doing this exercise he got clarity about his target market, yearly asset goals and type of investment products he wanted to provide.

Step 2: Know What to Do

The next step is to know what to do to get what you want. Having coached hundreds of financial advisors/agents I have a few solutions in my toolbox.

So Tom and I mapped out a prospecting process for who to call, what to say and how to handle objections to get appointments. We also mapped out an effective referral dialogue.

We role played each of the two campaigns and soon after Tom quickly started setting appointments. Next, we continued honing his first appointment and closing script. He applied these processes and his pipeline starting filling up!

Step 3: Know How to Track Progress

The final step is to know how to track your progress. Edison not only did this, but he changed his definition of success every time his experiments didn't work by stating, "I have not failed. I have just found 10,000 ways that won't work."

Tom took every "failure" as an opportunity to learn by tracking his activities and results. We would discuss what was working and what was not until we refined his processes.

Granted, this takes time and is an ongoing task however I believe that all advisors and agents with the right attitude can actually uncover their challenges, learn from them and discover and implement solutions!

So, what happened to Tom?

I recently received an email from him in between our bi-weekly coaching sessions that said, "Just wanted to check in and let you know that my pipeline is full. I opened two new accounts this week by both cold calling and asking for referrals, it is working!"

Why a Step-by-Step Approach to Success Works

Too many times, we as financial advisors lose sight of what it takes to get that "big break". Instead, we see others landing a huge account or gathering millions in assets and find ourselves asking, *"Why didn't I?"*

The reality is that those who are successful do the necessary work to open doors. Opportunities sometimes walk through those doors unexpectedly and oftentimes don't "look" the part; the reality is that to open the door to opportunity you must put in the effort and energy to approach them when they do show themselves.

Story #62
Leveraging the Power of LinkedIn

Have you jumped onto the social media bandwagon in recent years when it comes to marketing your business or are you still stuck in the 90s cold calling? I have been in the financial services industry for three decades, and I was reluctant to add one more thing to my prospecting plate such as social media. That is, until I learned how to leverage the power of LinkedIn!

I've recently read an interesting sign that sums up my LinkedIn experience, which read, *"Networking is not about collecting contacts. Networking is about creating and cultivating relationships with your target market."*- Anonymous

There is no better business social media platform to find your target market than LinkedIn, which boasts over 740 million members. It has an average active monthly usage rate of 66 million members in the United States alone!

But, with all of these people using the same platform, how do you stand out and attract your target market? Let's take a look at a stepwise approach to leveraging the power of LinkedIn to help you build your book of ideal clients.

Step 1: Identify Your Target Market

You can't hit a target that you can't see! One of the best ways to identify your target market is by taking the top forty or fifty clients in your book and looking at their demographics to seek commonalities.

An example of this is Joe P. a thirty-year veteran financial advisor client that did this exercise to determine who his target market is. It didn't take him long before he realized that the majority of his top clients were business owners who are between 50 and 70 years of age.

Step 2: Search for Your Target Market

Once you know whom your target market is you can do a search to find how many people fit your demographic that are within your local area. To ensure success it's important that they see that you have some type of connection with someone that they already know, which provides a level of credibility.

In Joe's case we went to the search bar and typed in "business owners" and the city he was located in. In addition, we refined the search by clicking the "filters" button and clicked on the number 2. As a result, we were able to see the business owners that were LinkedIn with current clients and friends of his, leveraging his client/friend connections with their network.

Step 3: Attract and Connect

Once you have a refined list of your target market from your local area, it's important that your profile appeals to them. You may want to get an outside consultant to help you craft the type of copy to attract your target market. Once you have this completed click the connect button!

Joe hired a wordsmith to put the right polish on his profile, updated his picture and then was ready to connect. Since I have beta-tested, using and not using copy, to hundreds of people when connecting, I explained that it really doesn't matter. So, we tried both ways and each way created similar results!

Step 4: Add Value

The secret to cultivating connection is to add value for them without becoming annoying and to get them engaged in a conversation!

Before we started the LinkedIn campaign I had Joe find a weekly digital marketing piece that his company provided on the state of the stock market. Also, he found additional marketing articles on relevant topics for business owners. Remember, the goal is to create value!

Step 5: Be Consistent

To stand out you need to be known as an authority and be consistent with making connections. That means you need to not only message people but also link to worthwhile articles or better yet write one yourself.

Joe stayed on a daily schedule of spending forty-five minutes a day connecting and cultivating relationships and over the course of a few weeks he was then ready for the final step!

Step 6: Make the Call

To ensure success you must pick up the phone and introduce yourself. Since they already know who you are it's not a true cold call, but a warm call connecting with your target market.

Joe was excited to make the calls and set appointments with his LinkedIn connections effortlessly. He put many of them into his pipeline and it didn't take long before he had new clients!

Why Leveraging LinkedIn Works

The reason why leveraging LinkedIn works is because you are reaching out to strangers who are your target market. Letting them see the mutual connections within your network, regularly adding value and fostering conversations. You build credibility before ever speaking with them. So, the next time you want to find new clients utilize your time and energy by leveraging the power of LinkedIn!

Story #63
Connecting the Room

One of life's simple pleasures for me is something that others might dread, public speaking. For over twenty plus years I've had the honor and privilege to speak in front of a wide range of audiences—investors, financial advisors, insurance agents and wholesalers.

A rookie financial advisor client of mine explained that he had held his first seminar and it had resulted in setting several appointments with qualified prospects. However, he was disappointed overall because he said that the audience barely said a word during his entire presentation. Even when he would ask them a question or attempt to interact with them, the room was silent!

If this has ever happened to you, please know that it happens to most speakers at some point in their careers. To combat this challenge, I've developed a solution that I refer to as Connecting the Room. If you apply this technique, I'm pretty sure you will never just hear crickets during your presentation again!

The following is a step-by-step process for Connecting the Room.

Step 1: Ask Strategic Questions

It's no secret that the audience tends to be more engaged at listening when you ask them questions. That's why it's important to map out your questions prior to your presentation so that you have a strategy ahead of time.

Typically, I tend to start off a new subject with a question. An example of this was years ago when I prepared one set of questions for each section of my presentation. Instead of reading the power point slide entitled "Inflation Eats up Your Purchasing Power" I asked a strategic question to the group of retirees which was, *"How many people here paid more for their last car then they did their first house?"*

Step 2: Get the Audience to Take Action

Another great way to help the audience connect with one another is to collectively ask them to take action by raising their hand. After I asked the earlier question I paused and said, *"Let's see a show of hands of who can relate to that. Please raise your hand if you can."*

Immediately, several hands went up!

Step 3: Make a Connection

Next, pick out one person who seems to be paying attention or actively listening so that you can ask them to tell their story to the crowd. Ask, *"What is your name?"* then turn the dialogue over to them by saying something like, *"Joe, when did you buy your first house, what type of home was it (ex: rambler, townhouse or split-level) and was it here in town or somewhere else?"*

Let this individual share the limelight for a moment then continue asking a few more questions. Examples might be, *"What was the biggest purchase item aside from your home that you bought?"* and *"Do you think the prices for items like that will continue to rise?"* Your final question should be a Closed-Ended Question which elicits a "yes" or a "no" so you can emphasize your point. Finish the interaction by thanking the person, *"Joe, thanks for sharing!"*

Step 4: Connect the Room

By now the room will be listening to his/her story and it's time to connect the room even further by asking a general question. *"Who here can relate to Joe's story? Let's see a show of hands."* Pick out the next person and repeat the process if time permits.

Usually a group tends to listen more intently when a speaker is dynamic and uses dialogue versus static and utilizes a monologue. If you sprinkle in these interactions throughout your presentation, your audience will be waiting for them. Use as many as you can and as time permits to solidify your messaging and strengthen your connection with those in the room.

Step 5: Make Your Point

When you feel that the room is starting to collectively relate to each other, move on by asking one final question on this subject such as, *"Does anyone know why things are more expensive today than they were when you bought your first house?"* Let someone answer and then explain such as, *"The reason things are more expensive is because inflation eats up your purchasing power! And, let me show you why."*

Transitioning from one topic to another, this is often the best time to engage with the audience and have the group collectively relate to each other. Be sure your questions are catered to the demographic you are speaking to and support your point of view.

Why Connecting the Room Works

When you use this technique, watch what happens to the people in the room, they speak more freely and are more apt to want to speak with you afterwards and hopefully they are on their way to becoming one of your clients. The reason why the Connecting the Room technique works well is when people feel comfortable they tend to feel connected.

Story #64
Getting Comfortable with Being Uncomfortable

When an advisor asks me if they are a candidate for coaching, I always find myself saying, *"Never wait to succeed!"* Unbeknownst to them, what they are actually telling me is that they are in a comfort zone and that they are not sure if they are ready to get beyond it.

Unfortunately, those who stay in their comfort zone rarely reach their pinnacle of success. Conversely, those who strive for excellence never settle for mediocrity, they do what others won't.

Remember, feeling uncomfortable when trying new endeavors in pursuit of your business goals is a temporary situation. You soon realize that what may have seemed awkward initially turns into your new normal. The secret to getting to the next level is getting comfortable with being uncomfortable. To do that you must first understand the Comfort Zone Model.

Understanding the Psychological States of the Comfort Zone Model

The Comfort Zone Model states that when people are faced with a difficult situation they will overcome and rise to the occasion by learning or growing; thus, lifting out of their comfort zone.

However, I believe that many advisors are stuck in complacency unless they have a strong enough reason for change. The following are three psychological states of the Comfort Zone Model and how it may pertain to you as an advisor.

Level 1: Comfort Zone

The Comfort Zone is described as a psychological state in which things feel familiar and as a result there is a low level of anxiety, stress and feeling of being in control. Advisors tend to get to settle in their comfort zone when they have created a book of business and gross production level, which is acceptable to the company they work for, themselves and in some cases their peers.

However, change is inevitable. Eventually, the market will go down, clients pass away or transfer to other advisors and in some cases the firm you work for will increase their minimum gross production standards. When any of this happens many advisors are forced out of their comfort zone. Or, they are forced out of the industry.

Level 2: Optimal Performance Zone

Although stress and anxiety can play a large part in why an advisor has to step out of their comfort zone the act of doing these new activities can also create new anxiety and stress. However, if the advisor continues focusing on learning and refining new ways of growing and maintaining their business they will soon find that they are in what is referred to as the Optimal Performance Zone, a psychological state in which the advisor is hitting peak performance.

The secret to staying in this state is to continuously want to work "On" your business while working "In" your business. When an advisor is focused on improving their business they learn various tools, techniques, strategies and solutions, which help them work smarter. As a result, they typically start to quickly see positive results!

Level 3: Danger Zone

As I had previously stated, some anxiety and stress can improve an advisor's performance because it propels them towards learning and growth. However, if too much anxiety occurs it can be paralyzing. This is referred to as the Danger Zone- a psychological state where disbelief lives and all actions cease. Performance therefore declines as anxiety and stress increase.

Take for instance Gail Z., a twenty-five year veteran who was told at Thanksgiving that if she didn't achieve the company's minimum gross production number by the first of the year she would be let go. This immediately put her into the Danger Zone and the only thing that got her out of it was by having a strategic plan to follow which helped her accomplish what seemed to be an unreachable goal.

Why Getting Comfortable with Being Uncomfortable Works

It is important to be aware of what psychological zone you are in at any given time. If you feel complacent and not motivated you are most likely in your comfort zone. Beware of complacency because too much of it can have an adverse effect when you are faced with a situation like Gail was.

The place you want to find yourself is in a constant state of forward movement. Being willing to be comfortable being uncomfortable is paramount and will no doubt offer you a leg up as it forces you to continually think on your feet and come up with out of the box solutions.

Story #65
The Mind Space Exercise

During difficult times, some financial advisors find their emotional state tethered to the stock market, when the market is up they are elated, but when the market is down they are deflated.

Norman Vincent Peale said, *"Change your thoughts and you change your world."*

Does this sound familiar? Are you running your internal state of mind based on external events? If so, it's important to note that this can change and you can learn a healthier way to live.

One of the best ways to manage your emotional state is to use an exercise I call The Mind Space Exercise. Let's take a look at a step-by-step process that I had one of my veteran financial advisor clients go through to get and stay in the right frame of mind.

Step 1: Identify Positive Morning Activities/Triggers

Typically, when you have a good day or a bad day it is likely attributed to various recent events. An example would be a day where your alarm didn't go off, you get a flat tire or your biggest client unexpectedly transfers out, those would feel like a bad day.

But, what if you knew the things that were in your control could help you start the day off right? The first step is to identify the top three positive activities (or what I call positive triggers) that you could do each morning to help you set the tone for having a good day.

Joshua K., a veteran financial advisor with twenty years of experience is no stranger to both Bull and Bear markets. He finds himself in a state of situational depression each time the Bear market hits.

Recently, we decided to change that by having him identify his top three positive triggers in the morning before his day begins. He chose meditation, a workout and arriving at work knowing exactly what he is going to do for the day.

Step 2: Rate Your Morning Mind Space Number

The second step is to be aware of how you are emotionally feeling when you start your workday so that you have a baseline of where you are.

Use a simple 1-10 (with 1 being lowest and 10 being highest) AFTER you complete your three positive activities and before you start your workday. I call this The Mind Space Exercise.

When we began The Mind Space Exercise Joshua was typically rating his Morning Mind Space Number at a 1, 2 or 3, but what he found was that by doing his three positive activities each morning he was building new habits, which helped him feel in control regardless of how the stock market was doing.

As a result, his morning numbers gradually increased to 5, 6 and 7, which lifted him out of his situational depression.

Step 3: Identify Positive Afternoon Activities/Triggers

The third step is to continue to stay in a positive state of mind into the afternoon by having three additional positive activities to focus on. Each person is different, but see if you can relate to what Josh did!

He decided that laughter was important and having business success was a must. As a result he said that his afternoon positive triggers were laughing at least once each hour, prospecting every day and having set one appointment with a prospect or a client.

Step 4: Rate Your Afternoon Mind Space Number

The fourth step is to be aware of how you are emotionally feeling at the end of the workday. If your afternoon number is higher than in the morning you are most certainly going in the right direction!

Each day I would receive his afternoon Mind Space Number and I noticed a pattern. When he first began, his morning and afternoon numbers were very low, which was to be expected. They gradually increased as he formed new positive habits. He did plateau, but his morning number rarely dropped below a 7 and his afternoon numbers only on occasion dropped below an 8. Overall, Josh was a much happier person!

Why the Mind Space Exercise Works

When it comes to inner peace you really have two choices, leave it up to chance or have a process for obtaining and sustaining it. The reason why these steps work well is that it gives your mind a task, a focus. And, when your mind is oriented positively a majority of the time, it's most assuredly likely to remain positive!

Story #66
Creating an Effective Email System

Have you noticed that you get more emails now then you ever did before? After constantly being interrupted by emails you most likely have become conditioned to feeling obligated to view each email the minute it arrives.

David Allen, the author of the book **Getting Things Done** writes, *"There are no interruptions, only mismanaged inputs."*

In many respects, this is very true, in that the emails that you receive all day are merely as important as you perceive them to be and the way that you react to them can either be a positive or a negative depending on what type of time management boundaries you establish.

The following steps will help you create an effective email system:

Step 1: Log Out of Your Email

I know that it might sound a bit counter-productive to log out of your email to manage them better but it's the first step on how to effectively manage interruptions because you are choosing when people have access to you.

An example of this would be from Dave G., a thirty-year veteran branch manager financial advisor client who was a slave to his emails.

I recommended that he take the first step and log off from email. He was instantly resistant until I explained that he could set an automatic reply message that informs people that he checks his email only a few times per day.

Step 2: Time Block Email Review

The next step is to know when to log into your email and review your inbox. My clients use a tool called **The Bottom Line List** (refer to the story **Bottom Line List** in chapter 2), which is a simple tool that blocks off five daily activities each of which are for forty-five minutes. In between those activities is a fifteen-minute buffer that I suggest using in part to check emails.

Since Dave had already been using **The Bottom Line List** he knew that his "buffer time" would be a perfect opportunity to review his emails. However, what he didn't know was that I didn't want him to respond to any emails right away. Instead, I wanted him to do something first.

Step 3: Flag or Tag Emails

Once you begin reviewing emails it's important to not get trapped in the same reactive mindset that you have had, but rather take time to organize emails by flagging or tagging them.

Most email contact management systems have some type of color coding process to flag emails such as green, yellow and red flags. By matching a color to the time such as green equals today, yellow this week and red whenever you have ample time, you are constantly keeping in control by prioritizing your inbox.

Dave started the process, but found it difficult at first to understand why he couldn't just respond right away while he was reviewing the emails.

Step 4: Time Block Email Activities

If you have been using "buffer time" to log onto your email account, review and flag your emails then you will more easily be able to start responding when the time is right. For those flagged/tagged with green/today, the best times are before lunch and again before you leave the office for the day. That way you become consistent with cleaning up your inbox on a systematic basis.

It didn't take long before Dave looked forward to responding to his "green" flagged emails and he felt more in control of his time.

Why Having an Effective Email System Works

The reason why having an effective email system works is because you can get more done in less time, with less stress since you are now in control of your interruptions instead of your interruptions being in control of you!

Story #67
The Science of Systems

As a financial advisor/agent, it can be easy to lose sight of what you are doing during the day due to constant interruptions, market fluctuations as well as your regular day-to-day operations. Oftentimes the day unfolds, you get busy and before you know it, hours have passed.

It is important to take a moment or two each day to track what to-dos aren't getting regularly accomplished or obstacles you are encountering and evaluate how effective your present systems are in handling them and ask yourself do you run your business or does your business run you?

Most financial advisors/agents do not take the time to analyze what I refer to as The Science of Systems, which defines that every task that you do should have a system assigned to it and that all systems need to be constantly refined to produce consistent positive outcomes.

The vast majority of advisors/agents use a "wing it" approach, which is a recipe for disaster. To obtain your goals, you need to optimize your systems and not leave your business success up to mere chance!

Orison Swett Marden says, *"A good system shortens the road to the goal."* But, what if you don't have a system for creating systems? If so, use the following steps to develop any system.

Step 1: Determine Point "A"

Point "A" is a description of what you are currently doing or where you currently are in any particular facet of your business.

When I was a rookie advisor I wanted to branch out and try seminars as one of my primary forms of prospecting. At that time my Point "A" (current activity) was that I was doing about three seminars a year maximum.

As a result, I was only earning a small percentage of my new business utilizing this form of prospecting. I had heard that other advisors in the office had built successful businesses via seminars but I didn't know how to manage an affective seminar system on a larger scale. I did know that I needed help!

Step 2: Determine Point "B"

Point "B" can be described as where you want or would prefer to be. In other words, it's your end goal.

In this case, my Point "B" was to have ten seminars a year! That was a lofty goal so I decided to find out what other successful advisors, not only in my direct office but in the company as a whole where doing. Surprisingly, I found a few advisors that were reducing their overhead costs by offering their services to associations and corporations to be a key note speaker at their events. This gave me new insight of how to obtain my goal!

Step 3: Re-Engineer the Steps

The final step is to map out an updated system. Ironically, what I have found is that with any system it is best to actually begin with Point "B" in mind and map out the steps, but in reverse. Let me show you what I mean.

I knew that it took on average about six weeks from start to finish to market, coordinate and plan to put on a seminar. So, I grabbed a calendar and circled all the first Tuesdays of a month excluding the three summer months and December. That left me with eight seminar dates. Next, I backtracked what specific items I needed to be sure had to happen in weeks 5, 4, 3, 2 and 1 and I put those into my contact management system.

Then, I determined that on some weeks I had to work simultaneously on various steps for multiple seminars since there was overlap with back-to-back months.

In addition, I added in prospecting to associations and corporations to see if they needed a key note speaker so that I could add at least two additional seminars during the year for free. Lastly, I setup up my time to work on my seminar system to be at the same time each week so that nothing slipped through the cracks. I did ten seminars that year!

Why the Science of Systems Works

The reason why the Science of Systems works is because you have a repeatable process for attaining goals. I realize that this line of reasoning may sound simple and in essence it is. We tend to make things harder for ourselves when simple solutions exist.

Story #68
The Power of Belief

Successful advisors know that believing in yourself can have a powerful impact on your attitude, motivation and overall success. However, there are times when uncontrollable issues such as market volatility, economic conditions or an occasional poor recommendation can leave you doubting yourself.

If this has happened to you, take comfort in knowing that your clients hired you because they like you, trust you and believe that you have their best interests at heart. Prove your clients right by believing in yourself, in your integrity, your honesty and your commitment to helping them; when you focus on things that you can control, you harness the power of belief.

Norman Vincent Peale said, *"People become really quite remarkable when they start thinking that they can do things. When they believe in themselves they have the first secret of success."*

So how can you increase your belief in yourself to become the advisor or agents that you've always wanted to be?

Let's take a look at a step-by-step approach for creating powerful business belief systems.

Step 1: Understanding Your Current Business Beliefs

The best way to find clarity about your business belief systems is to fill in the following blanks, "What I believe about _____ is _____ because _____." Insert any possible subject about the business in the first blank, the belief in the second blank and the rationale in the third. Now, you've got some understanding about what your belief system is on the subject. The real question is will your current belief system help you or hurt you in the long-run?

Take Frank P. for example, a veteran financial advisor with twelve years of experience who had a belief system that prospecting was a numbers game because most people don't want to make any changes with their money. As a result of his belief on the matter, he would need to double his efforts to double his success.

Step 2: Explore New Possibilities

The next step is to be open to exploring new possibilities that there may be an alternative to a negative belief system. To do this, you need to question any belief system that limits your success. Remember, you weren't born with a specific belief system. Instead, they are learned over time.

In Frank's case, he needed to cope with his fear of rejection by creating a belief system around "Prospecting is merely a numbers game" so that he could eliminate any responsibility for his actions and not feel rejected. In other words, if prospecting is merely the-law-of-averages (you have to speak to "X" number of people to get one prospect) because most people don't want to make changes with their finances than he shouldn't be taking any rejection personally. Now, he had to test his new belief system.

So I asked Frank if working twice as hard is something he wanted to do or was he open to learning how to work twice as smart. He quickly chose the latter. So, I taught him three techniques for handling common objections. We practiced the techniques using role play until he got the hang of them and he was ready to try them out with prospects.

Step 3: Reinforcing Your New Belief System

Once you are open to new possibilities, you must be willing to take action to reinforce a new belief system.

Since Frank understood and could role play these new handling objections techniques he was more confident to give them a try. He made several calls and over the course of a week he realized that overcoming objections is merely a process.

This simple realization was all he needed to reinforce a new belief system about prospecting which was, "Prospecting can be much easier if you are prepared for objections because people are open to a second opinion once they see the value in it."

Why the Power of Belief Works

If you can relate to keeping a negative business belief system that is holding you back, apply these steps to reshape your results. Holding onto something that is not moving you forward is a sure fire way to sabotage helping others. If you can harness the power of belief you will understand how much control you actually have in shaping your own destiny!

Story #69
Striving for Excellence

Oftentimes, we as financial advisors and agents have a choice to make when it comes to the level of energy, effort and efficiency we bring to our businesses. We can "get by" and do just enough to maintain our current level, or we can choose to reach beyond.

Striving for excellence and going above and beyond is a choice and a state of mind that says that you aspire for more. It's not about perfection, but rather about fulfilling one's business purpose by constant and never-ending self-improvement. By adopting this way of thinking there is a higher likelihood that you will succeed at indeed growing and evolving.

Rick Pitino said, *"Excellence is the unlimited ability to improve the quality of what you have to offer."*

Unfortunately, most advisors and agents don't take the time to holistically view all aspects of their business to determine where some work is necessary until they are in crisis mode. Let's take a look at a step-by-step approach successful advisors and agents use to work "ON" their business continually.

Step 1: Evaluate What's Not Working

One of the hardest parts about running any business is to take the time to evaluate what is not working. The reason is that it can be difficult to admit fault or failure. However, when you are open to reflection around areas of potential and realize a tweak here and there can make a difference, you are then more likely to consistently address areas of weakness, especially when the outcomes are positive.

Take Beth T. for example, a newer financial advisor with less than five years in financial services who asked me during a coaching session if she was doing something wrong because a new client called days after opening an account (and transferring their assets to her) complaining that on second thought it seemed kind of expensive to purchase the mutual funds she had recommended.

Step 2: Understand What Works for Others

The next step is to understand what solutions have worked for others. It sounds simple, but many times we think we are the only ones experiencing a scenario only to have a conversation with a colleague or mentor and find out they too have a similar experience.

In Beth's case, I needed to know if this was a pattern or a single occurrence. She said that it had happened twice now in the last few months so that's why she brought it up.

After inquiring about how she explained her recommendations I determined that it wasn't the price of the investments that clients were concerned about, but it was the lack of value that somehow had not been retained. In other words, they understood during the meeting why they should diversify into mutual funds (which was to reduce risk), but completely forgot about it days later when they were thinking about the fees.

The solution was to make sure that Beth had all of the benefits of her recommendations typed out so the client or prospect could refer back to that ensuring everyone was on the same page.

Step 3: Apply & Assess the Process

Once you know what to improve upon, you must apply the process and regularly assess the results.

Beth started presenting prospects and clients a summary page of all of the benefits of her recommendations. She would then give them a copy to take home and keep one in their file at the office.

During client reviews she would add any additional summary pages when there were new recommendations. Prospects and clients liked the new process and Beth never had a client with a case of "buyer's remorse" again!

Why Striving For Excellence Works

It doesn't matter if you are a financial advisor, insurance agent, butcher, baker or candlestick maker if you want to be considered a professional you must adept at honing your craft and the only way to do that is by being willing to accept and work on your weaknesses and develop your strengths.

Story #70
The Significance of Self-Leadership

Being a part of the financial services industry is both challenging and rewarding. Advisors are faced with the enormous challenge of building and maintaining a business that offers monetary and emotional rewards.

And, although many advisors may have resources, mentors or peers that motivate them, success comes down to an individual being fully committed to their own success. I call this practice, The Art of Self-Leadership.

If you cannot or will not lead your own self to be inspired, continually educated and consistently dedicated to your advisory business you certainly cannot (or should not) have the expectation that you will succeed.

So with that said, let's take a look at some of the important qualities that make a self-leader:

Self-Motivation

One of the most vital qualities of a "self-leader" is to be able to motivate yourself day in and day out because without this ability you will not accomplish the activities that lead to successful outcomes. Those without self-motivation do just enough to get by.

To kick start (or maintain) your motivation, here are some ideas:

Turn Everything into a Game

Most advisors have a competitive streak. Competing against others is fine, but what happens when you cannot find a friend or colleague who is interested to "play" with you? Instead, compete against yourself by turning your daily activities into your own personal game.

You can make the rules of the game as simple as say "call ten contacts before ten o'clock" or as complicated as counting every dial, appointment set and any other tasks that make up your day. Be sure that you create your game so that you actually have fun playing it. Then, get skin in the game by setting up a daily reward or punishment system.

Give Yourself a Prize or Punishment

The game of self-motivation is only as important as the reward or punishment associated with winning or losing the game. If you do not have any consequences, then you will not take the game seriously.

So, at the end of the day, tally up your score and immediately give yourself a prize or a punishment. It sounds too simple to work right? However, rewarding or punishing yourself can keep you on track and will ultimately have a lasting impact on you reaching your overall business goals.

Self-Education

Our business is a business of change in which things are constantly dynamic—the stock market, the economy, market sectors, even the addition of new investment products not to mention any personal changes that you may be experiencing in your life while you are trying to manage your practice.

That is why it is so important to keep yourself up-to-date and continually educated on things that can affect your business. Here are some way to increase your knowledge:

Technical Expertise

Technical expertise is the foundation needed to run your financial advisory practice-investment, insurance and financial planning knowledge. Most advisors get some type of training when they begin in the business; most states require that you have your license(s) before you are able to offer any financial advice.

However, what you might not know is that to become even more proficient in our field you need to constantly be challenging yourself to increase your technical knowledge.

Clients deserve an advisor who knows how to help them. One way to ensure this is to constantly learn as much as you can about the products and services you provide.

Conversely, advisors who become complacent with their technical expertise find that their clients may go elsewhere if the competition can prove they have better solutions for their investment needs.

In addition, centers of influence will typically only refer you to their clients if they believe you have a strong working knowledge of varying products and services; it is the advisor who has increased levels of expertise or specialization that get the important introductions.

Real World Experience

There is no substitute for real world experience. You can study, take a test and get a credential, but to help someone you need to roll up your sleeves and find those who need your help. In other words, technical knowledge only goes so far, but combining it with real world experience brings an entirely new level of benefit to others.

Whether you are a brand new advisor or a thirty-year veteran you can still learn from your mistakes. Take for instance Joe F., a twenty-five year veteran that realized he was making more statements than asking questions.

He came to the conclusion that having a process for asking better questions would have made his career much easier as most of the time when he did not get the sale it was because he was going on-and-on about the features and benefits of his products followed by him asking for the sale.

Had he learned from his failures, he would have realized that asking better questions prospective clients want to buy rather than feeling sold to.

So, why would a thirty-year veteran want to learn how to have a better sales presentation? Because he realized that getting additional training could and would help him get to the next level.

Self-Reliance

To manage yourself and activities takes confidence in your own abilities, decisions and recommendations because people look to you as their financial advisor to help them solve complex financial challenges with your investment knowledge and expertise. So, what happens when you start second guessing yourself? Or, what if you don't know how to solve their problems and/or your own business problems?

Knowing what to do is essential in leading yourself to building a better business. Let's take a closer look at two very important concepts.

Problem Solving vs. Challenge Management

All financial advisors are faced with continuous "issues" to manage—client, compliance, and market issues as well as a host of others. During the midst of all of these "issues" you have to ask yourself the discerning question, is this "issue" a problem to solve or a challenge to manage?

A problem is a bad thing. This is something that cannot keep re-occurring. A challenge can be a good thing because it helps you determine that something needs attention. A challenge does not just go away, however knowing how to manage a challenge is a solution. An example of a problem would be buying the wrong security in a client's account.

An example of a challenge would be constant interruptions throughout the day. It is a challenge to manage because we will never solve others needing our time. Using a tool to prioritize interruptions so that you can get back to the most important and urgent ones is the solution.

Once you fully understand the difference between problem solving and challenge management you can view any situation in one of two ways, do I solve this problem or do I manage this ongoing challenge? This increases your ability to make better decisions.

Why The Significance of Self-Leadership Works

Now that you have a better understand of what The Art of Self-Leadership involves, you may be wondering what to do next. Determine which areas your practice may lack direction in? Do you need to get motivated, educated or be more reliant or all three? Next, decide what specific areas you need to work on. Then, take action and over time you will become your proficient as a self-leader.

Story #71
Strategies for Measuring Success

Many advisors/agents measure their success by the end tally of new accounts, new assets and additional gross revenue. Unfortunately, some advisors/agents give up before reaching their set goal! Thomas Edison said, *"Many of life's failures are people who did not realize how close they were to success when they gave up."*

I truly believe that Mr. Edison was correct. However, focusing on the journey towards achieving success rather than the destination itself allows for focusing on productive activities while celebrating accomplishments along the way. Isn't that what we all truly want, to actually enjoy what we do for a living?

Let's take a deeper dive with a stepwise approach that can help you continuously measure progress instead of using the ultimate endgame in mind as your barometer.

Step 1: Compartmentalize the Goals

Goals are an important part of achieving success however if you don't break down your goals into daily actions they inevitably are very difficult to accomplish. That's exactly why Edison conducted 10,000 experiments to invent the light bulb; he just kept at it.

Here is a real world example of how one financial advisor client of mine used this type of process:

Robert E. was an advisor/agent with four years of experience when his boss told him that his life insurance sales had spiraled downward from any other month in production. When Robert and I met he informed me that he no longer had company minimum production standards to meet, upon his four-year anniversary, which he had just passed.

Unfortunately, his boss and the company were taking notice and they were not happy with him. It was time to redefine his goals and map out his daily activities.

Step 2: Create a Game

The next step was to create a game, something that would be fun to do on a daily basis. Having coached hundreds of financial advisors/agents I knew exactly what game would work best for Robert. So, I explained a "cross-selling" campaign that I call the "Oh, By the Way" game.

The title itself was a simple reminder that whenever he was talking to a client he had to look at the account to see if they had their life insurance with him. If not, he began the conversation with, *"Oh by the way I know that we have been working together for some time now, but I see that we aren't helping you with your life insurance, why is that?"* Next, he had to wait for any objections and use one of our **Objection Resolution Models** (refer to the story **Beyond the Gatekeeper** in chapter 2), to overcome it. If he was able to, then he got to mark the accomplishment as a point and then attempt to continue earning himself points.

Step 3: Beat Your High Score

Motivation is an important step in turning daily activities into a habit. The best way I know to do this is to try and beat your personal record and to have daily accountability. At the end of each day Robert would email me how many points he had earned. Every time he beat his high score he would reward himself with some type of motivating reward.

So, what happened to Robert?

At the end of the month, I called his boss to get his opinion on Robert's progress. *"I don't know what you did to him, but he's having the best month of his career!"* his boss proudly exclaimed. In other words, Robert was now enjoying the journey and the bonus was that his business was picking up as a result.

Why the Game Approach to Success Works

The reason this worked for Robert was because he focused on deliberate activities made a game out of those and kept him accountable (both with rewards and by checking in with me). When you change your mindset you can have a good time doing activities that might have seemed like too much work. Viewing it through the lens of a game changed his trajectory.

Story #72
Turning Busyness into Business

Have you ever wondered why some advisors seem to be busy all the time but haven't actually filled their pipeline or secured business closings? Maybe you are one of them. Having a constant list of tasks to accomplish doesn't always equate to having a successful revenue stream. You need to ensure that your busyness translates into business.

Here is the 411 on how to do just that.

Be Honest With Yourself

If you are finding yourself constantly busy and yet not being productive it probably is because you are avoiding something that you feel is or could be painful. An example would be when an advisor says, *"I don't have time to prospect because I'm too busy."*

In reality, most are choosing to accomplish activities that they deem pleasurable to avoid feeling the pain of rejection. In other words, they take on additional tasks to feel or be busy, which enables them to say to others that they have a lot to do although in reality it really is only giving them an excuse to avoid painful activities (in this case prospecting).

Face Your Fears

Recently, I asked a financial advisor client of mine, who owns an independent firm that he wants to grow by recruiting wire house reps, *"Why aren't you setting appointments with them and telling them about your firm?"* He quickly replied, *"I'd like to but I don't have time because I'm dealing with staffing issues and compliance all day."*

By probing a bit, I found out that his past recruiting efforts consistently resulted in the advisors wanting to wait. Once I learned this, I explained, *"Your challenge isn't time management, the challenge is sales and being able to overcome objections and the feeling of rejection when you don't close."*

Once we talked about his fears, we began to focus on what actions could strengthen his sales skills. He's still busy but now he is delegating many of his previous tasks because he feels more confident to be recruiting.

Successful advisors know that there are only three possible outcomes to any task; you can do it, delegate it or delete it, which is rarely an option unless it is an unimportant and not urgent task.

Understand the Art & Science of Task Management

Successful advisors also know that understanding what tasks to accomplish first is one part art and one part science. The art is in being flexible enough to know when it's time to drop everything and "put out a fire". The science is in having a process to determine which fire is the most important to put out first.

Why Turning Busyness into Business Works

The reason why turning busyness into business works is that it's a simple process to evaluate your productivity. The best barometer to know if all of the busyness that you are experiencing is translating into business is to check your scorecard, your revenue! Is your business growing? If so, you're moving in the right direction, but if you are not seeing an increase, then it's time to go back through this article to determine what changes still need to be made.

Story #73
Just Get Out There and Do It!

Years ago, a financial advisor called concerned about his business saying, *"I read all of the books I can, put them back on the shelf, but nothing happens."* When I asked why he thought this occurred, he quickly admitted it was because he did not have a plan to apply anything he read about; thus he wasn't taking action!

Dale Carnegie said, *"Learning is an active process. We learn by doing...only knowledge that is used sticks in your mind."* Unfortunately, the advisor didn't use the knowledge that he learned. Instead, he merely brushed it off and went on with business as usual.

So that you can you apply what you learn use the following steps to just get out there and do it!

Creating Your Action Step Process

One of the saddest things I hear advisors say is, *"I know what I need to do, I just need to do it."* The reason is because they haven't created a process for taking action and unless they do no real change will take place. That's why it is important to apply the following steps to get lasting results!

Let's take a look at a step-by-step approach for creating your action step process.

Step 1: Understand the New Process

You need to understand any new process thoroughly so you know exactly what you need to do to implement it.

Take Robert T. for example-a veteran financial advisor with twenty years of experience who unfortunately had got complacent in his business and needed to start prospecting again. As I coached him though a step-by-step process for turning strangers into clients we realized that he had a clog in his pipeline-he wasn't closing the sale.

So, we worked on a sub-step that I refer to as **The Psychology of Closing the 2nd Appointment** and I introduced him to a tool known as **The 2nd Appointment Worksheet** (refer to the story **The Power of Preparation** in chapter 2) so he could fully understand how to help prospects what to buy instead of trying to sell to them.

Step 2: Create a Deadline Driven Time Horizon to Begin

The next step is to make sure that you quickly take action by giving yourself a time horizon so that you have a deadline to begin and an approximate due date in mind to finish.

For Robert that due date was immediate since he had a big appointment coming up in which he could be gathering a million in new assets if all went as planned. Thus, I had him fill out the worksheet before our next session and we role played it before his meeting.

Step 3: Put Your Plan Into Action

Once you have understood the process and created a deadline the next step is to put your plan into action!

Since Robert knew when his appointment was and had already role played it with me, he felt confident about the process. However, he wanted to make sure so he contacted one of his peers in our group coaching program and role played the appointment again. The extra preparation paid off because he effortlessly helped the prospect understand what he needed and why he should buy; thus, turning the prospect into a client and gathering a million in new assets!

Step 4: Evaluate Your Process to Learn From It

One of the most difficult things for any advisor to do is to admit that they have challenges. However, once they do and are open to learning as well as implementing solutions all that is left is to learn from successes as well as failures.

Robert learned that the process works. So-much so that he used the tools mentioned above and duplicated his success over and over.

Why Getting Out There and Doing It Just Works

If you can relate to the anxiety that Robert was feeling when he realized that he was having a challenge with closing the prospect, know that you are not alone. Most advisors experience anxiety at some point in their business. The best solution is to take the previous steps to determine what to do, do it and evaluate how you did. Taking the right action will alleviate anxiety and soon you will be on your way to success!

Story #74
Redefining Your Reference Point

Most financial advisors and agents settle into a routine after a few years in the business. However sometimes, unconsciously, routines turn into ruts. Many of my clients find themselves wondering why their business is coasting along, but not growing. I coach them that it may be time to take a moment to evaluate and possibly restructure their activities.

If this is happening to you, do not be discouraged, but rather choose to redefine your reference point. Our past experiences can hold us back from future success because they may limit our confidence to try new things.

Pablo Picasso said, *"I am always doing that which I cannot do, in order that I may learn how to do it."*

The secret to redefining your reference point is to think out of the box, find someone who has done what you would like to do, learn from their example and take action!

Let's take a deeper look at each one of these steps.

Step 1: Think Out of the Box

As with most journeys in life, the first step is always the hardest, but you must ask yourself the tough questions to begin such as, *"Where am I now? Where do I want to be? What do I need to do differently to get there?"* Asking yourself these types of questions and analyzing your answers helps you to think out of the box because it encourages the mind to look for solutions.

Jeff K., a veteran financial advisor with twenty-eight years of experience had been on a production plateau for years. After attending a free **Advisor Solutions** Mastermind Session and hearing some of the tools and resources I recommend to other advisors he contacted me to discuss his business. This act of asking for insight was foreign to him since he had never spoken to a business consultant/coach before.

Step 2: Find a Mentor

The next step is to find a mentor who can help you determine all of the steps needed between where you are currently and where you would like to be. This can be a difficult step for many advisors/agents especially veteran ones who may have to consider advice from others who have not been in the business as long as they have. The key is to find a mentor who has proven results and whose opinion you value.

After a quick introduction, Jeff asked a number of questions to hear my backstory. He wanted to find someone who had been in the business, experienced the challenges he had and was able to find solutions as well as get results. In addition, he wanted someone who could quickly assess his challenges and teach solutions to him so he could get off the production plateau. It didn't take long before he realized that "someone" whom he was looking for, was me!

Step 3: Learn From Their Example

To produce the same types of results that other successful advisors/agents have you must find out what they have done to accomplish those positive outcomes. It is very important to fully understand their step-by-step process so that you can tweak for yourself.

Once Jeff explained his situation to me I knew we needed to map out a great prospecting campaign and since he had a large client base I explored the possibility of prospecting by asking for referrals. Over the years, he had tried numerous times to get referrals, but ended up very disappointed with the results. I detailed out the process for him, we role played the dialogue and I coached him on the reasons why a focused referral system works. After hearing that another client of mine had received 27 referrals in one month, he was ready to begin!

Step 4: Take Action

The most important step is to take action, without it everything else is just wishful thinking.

Jeff began the **Client-Centered Referral Process** right away and within a week he reported to me that he had received 5 referrals! That is more than he had gotten the entire previous year. He was so excited about it that he gave me a referral to his boss who he believed needed to hear this process and whom ended up having me teach it to his entire region.

Why Redefining Your Reference Point Works

The key to creating success is to constantly be redefining your reference point because it keeps you open to exploring new ways of improving. The reason why redefining your reference point works well is that by having a constant and never-ending improvement mentality you are in a fact constantly evolving your business systems to keep getting better and better. And, when you have effective business systems you have an efficient business!

Story #75
What Every Genius Knows

Albert Einstein, whose name is synonymous with "intelligence", is not the only genius to acknowledge that whether the subject is something as vast as the universe or as microscopic as an atom, everything has a deliberate design to it. However, he does sum up the philosophy best with his quote *"There does, in fact, appear to be a plan."*

In other words, for something to work effectively it must be rooted in a foundation of a successful process. Your business is no different. For you to be effective in building, running and maintaining a successful business, you need to have well thought out systems. You can operate your business in one of two ways, leave your success up to chance or map out your methods and procedures.

Successful advisors/agents know that mapping out a new system, method or procedure is a process in and of itself. Let's take a look at specific steps for how you can incorporate new stepping stones into your business future.

Step 1: Understanding Where You Are

As a professional development coach, I said it often, that when it comes to your business you must be completely transparent with yourself. That's why it is important to look at every aspect of your business and ask, *"Where am I with this?"* In other words, what is working, what is not working and why.

John D., a twenty year veteran financial advisor who realized that most of what he was doing in his business was reactive in nature, in areas such as time management, client servicing, prospecting and even with his sales process were all facets of his business that he didn't have a systematic stepwise approach for.

Ironically, not having a process was his process so when a client called with a question or request, he dropped everything and took care of it. When he did decided to prospect by asking for referrals he typically would say, *"Who do you know that I could introduce myself to?"* This was followed with the client replying, *"I can't think of anyone, but if I do I will let you know."*

It's interesting to note that in this example he actually did have a process for asking for referrals. However, it was not at all effective.

Step 2: Understand Where You Want to Be

Sometimes it can be difficult for an advisor/agent to realize that they have been running a reactive business simply because they have never been taught any other way.

In John's case, I explained that successful advisors/agents have a pro-active business model because they have an effective and repeatable methodology for everything! As I went into the details John began to recognize that having this type of business was exactly what he wanted (and needed).

Step 3: Learn & Implement

Then it was time to map out and create a business systems manual. That way John could refer to it at any time when he found himself wondering how to manage something. This is best done by taking each facet of your business finding a colleague or mentor who has an effective approach that you desire to emulate.

So as to not overwhelm John, we started with time management. I showed him tools and techniques for architecting structure for his day, a way to prioritize interruptions and make a game out of sticking to the steps with a daily reward and punishment incentive.

It didn't take him long to start feeling more in control of this time! Once John felt he had a handle on one business facet we went onto another one.

Why Running a Business like a Genius Works

Repurposing another's successful systems means you don't have to craft something from scratch, which can be overwhelming. You do have to implement and follow whatever steps you outline for yourself. Having a plan makes sense and you don't have to be Einstein to know that!

Story #76
Mastering the Art of Excellence

Obtaining excellence with any endeavor is rarely an overnight occurrence. It typically takes years of tenacity to master a craft. Many advisors/agents let outside influences and short-term setbacks detract them from acquiring excellence in many facets of their business. On the journey to becoming your best, you must sometimes take things one step at a time.

The key to mastering the art of excellence is to focus on each of those steps whether that is defined as learning how to cold call, close a sale or ask for referrals. It is important to concentrate on your ability to be more effective on each particular "step" before moving on to another.

Eventually, those "steps" string together and form a way forward and you realize that you have traveled farther than you ever thought possible. Aristotle said, *"Excellence is an art won by training and habituation."*

In other words, we create excellence by continuously learning and honing the activities we do until they become a habit; thus, excellence is merely a by-product of doing such.

Here are some suggested things to consider as you strive for excellence in whatever areas you seek:

Step 1: Commit to a New Level of Greatness

If you want to excel at anything you must commit to a new level of greatness. It doesn't matter whether you are a financial advisor, insurance agent or professional athlete, every successful person knows that the first step is to decide without a shadow of a doubt that they are fully committed to putting in their best effort.

James T., a twenty-year veteran financial advisor was stalemated as his business had reached a production plateau. When I began coaching him he was absolutely committed to learning how to unclog his pipeline. All he needed was to unearth the clogs, implement the right processes and put those into place and take action.

Step 2: Model the Masters

Success doesn't happen overnight, but it will happen a lot more quickly when you model those who have mastered whatever it is that you would like to succeed at.

In Jame's case, I had coached many financial advisors/agents on a methodology to find specific clogs at every stage of the pipeline, so we quickly found what challenges he actually had. Next, we discussed solutions that have worked for other successful advisors/agents. Then he began to apply the activities that were necessary on a daily basis to put those solutions into place. Over time, these activities turned into habits and voila, his pipeline moved along well and converted for him in many cases.

Step 3: Map Out the Milestones

The final step is to track your progress or what I refer to as "Map out the Milestones". That way you can see accomplishments (or obstacles) that were made during each leg of the journey. The following is a brief description of milestones that Rob experienced.

Initially, I had explained to James that my pipeline process had Four Stages: Initial Contact, First Appointment, Second Appointment (or Closing Appointment) and Getting Referrals.

James knew that he had a clog in each stage, but some were bigger than others. So, we began working on **Stage #1-the Initial Contact** because he was not filling up the pipeline, which was vital. Soon, he was setting more first appointments then he had ever done previously.

Then, we worked on **Stage #2-the First Appointment** because he said that many prospects weren't securing a second appointment with him. I taught him how to help prospects see the value of a second appointment and he was able to make those happen!

Next, we worked on **Stage #3-the Closing Appointment** because he was not strong at closing prospects. After a number of weeks he reported that he had closed 9 out of 12 prospects!

Lastly, we worked on **Stage #4-Getting Referrals.** Once we role played what I call the **Client-Centered Referral Process,** he had a framework or structure for his conversation around getting referrals!

Why Mastering the Art of Excellence Works

The reason why Mastering the Art of Excellence works is because who wants to settle for mediocrity? Being just "okay" with your business is not okay; finding techniques that work is imperative to getting your business firing on all cylinders.

Story #77
Stretching Beyond Your Business Limitations

You are the sole architect of your business. You and you alone are the only one that can create, construct and care for the business of your dreams. Your responsibility to fulfill this dream lies with no one, but yourself.

Abraham Lincoln said, *"Always bear in mind that your own resolution to succeed is more important than any other."*

Unsuccessful financial advisors/agents let obstacles not opportunities dictate their outcomes while successful financial advisors/agents have learned that the secret to stretching beyond their business limitations is in making a conscious decision to succeed. This then leads to unearthing strategies that reach beyond their present situation and to creating the future they desire.

Any challenge that you have in your business can be overcome by believing there is a solution and directing your energies toward pursuing it, applying solutions, assessing progress and continuing the process until you find yourself accomplishing objectives.

What follows is a process I use with my clients and how that process was used with one financial advisor who was feeling limited and stagnant.

Step 1: Identify Your Challenges

The quickest way to get past your own business limitations is to acknowledge that you have them. A lack of honesty can absolutely deter progress on many levels. You must admit where you are to first go in the direction of where you want to be going.

Take James K., a veteran financial advisor with twenty-five years of experience who wanted to take his business to the next level, but couldn't bring himself to prospecting because he believed that after being in business for so long that prospecting wasn't something he needed to do.

After an extended coaching session he admitted that his real challenge wasn't the amount of new business in the pipeline but that he had this negative attitude towards prospecting that he was aware needed adjusting.

Step 2: Believe in the Solutions

The next step is to be open to exploring new possibilities of what worked for others and the reasons why. It's important to note that just understanding what the solutions are is not enough. You must delve into each step in the process and comprehend its importance. Then you need to believe that they can work for you as well.

In James's case, I needed to work on helping him understand how other veteran advisors manage prospecting. They leverage existing relationships via centers of influence, networking, prospecting their natural market and through referrals. After I explained each form of prospecting and mapped out a proven step-by-step process, I had him pick out two prospecting methods that he would like to utilize and implement. I then had him listen to two audios of clients who had applied these methods so that he would believe that the solutions worked.

Step 3: Apply, Assess and Deploy

The final steps are to apply the process, assess how it is going, make course corrections if need be and repeat them until you ultimately get your desired results. This might seem like a daunting task, but once you follow through, it gets easier and easier. In fact, each time you apply these steps it helps you to tweak routinely, which is the difference between working harder and working smarter.

Since James understood what to do, I immediately had him take action, record daily progress and debrief me on his prospecting efforts each week. It didn't take long before we identified a few steps that needed some customizing, but once we did he was filling up his pipeline and closing new business. In addition, he was open to exploring additional business limitations.

Why Stretching Beyond Your Limitations Works

If you can relate to having limitations that are holding you back, apply these steps and find yourself on the right side of the results spectrum. It may seem a simplistic method and mindset, but I assure you that it is effective because you are refocusing your attention from the current undesired outcomes to a proven system.

Story #78
Creating an Attitude of Gratitude

Gratitude can be defined in numerous ways. Some view it as an attribute, which has the power to decrease fear and attract abundance while others view gratitude not just as verbal expressions, but also as a constant awareness that one should live by.

Successful advisors/agents know that showing gratitude has a profound effect on themselves, others and their business. The secret to creating an attitude of gratitude is to continually be looking for the opportunity to be thankful and to express that appreciation in communications and actions with clients, colleagues and even with ourselves.

Melody Beattie said, *"Gratitude makes sense of our past, brings peace for today, and creates a vision for tomorrow."*

Let's take a deeper look at some best practices for how you can incorporate gratitude into your business:

Best Practice #1: Gratitude for Clients

I truly believe that the #1 reason why clients leave their advisor/agent is because they feel their representative doesn't seem to be acknowledging and catering to their unique set of needs. When a client has not been contacted regularly they tend to feel unappreciated and neglected. This inevitably ensures that they will eventually move their business to another advisor/agent.

Let's look at what one successful advisor is doing to avoid this happening to him.

Steve C., is a twenty-five year veteran financial advisor who had lost his motivation. After discussing why he is in the business he said that he loved his clients. However, he also admitted that he wasn't contacting them as often as he knew he should be.

Steve immediately went on a large-scale client servicing campaign to contact all of his clients every three months to check-in and see if they had any questions, comments or concerns. In addition he developed a systematic way of scheduling client reviews. Within a few months his client-base began to take notice and he was feeling the effects of their appreciation as well.

Best Practice #2: Gratitude Towards Colleagues

One of the most overlooked opportunities is to be thankful with colleagues. The reason is because most advisors/agents get caught up in their own day-to-day activities that they don't take time to express their appreciation towards those who have helped make business a success.

In Steve's case he started to realize that there was a number of people that he relied on however he rarely had taken the time to express his appreciation. So, he made a list of the "Top 10 Colleagues to Thank". He wrote down the reasons why he was grateful and then he made it a point to call each of them and let them know specifically how much he had appreciated their help.

Best Practice #3: Gratitude to Yourself

Most people are hardest on themselves and thus very infrequently do we take the time to consider why we are grateful for our own actions or wins.

After Steve transformed his relationships with his clients and colleagues, I suggested there was still one more person he needed to appreciate, himself. For years he had put tremendous pressure and set up unrealistic expectations for reaching his goals.

But to be truly happy in this industry he needed to be less demanding on himself and more loving. So, I had him make a list of the top ten qualities that he believed he possessed that were the reason why his clients worked with him. He was to keep that list handy and affirm those qualities often.

Why Creating an Attitude of Gratitude Works

The reason why creating an attitude of gratitude works is because the focus is on adopting a positive perspective for why clients work with you and colleagues assist you. It's this conscious act of looking on the bright side that directs your energy towards successful outcomes.

Story #79
The Science of Success

Struggling advisors/agents oftentimes feel that creating a prosperous business is based on luck or timing. However, it is my belief that luck and timing have very little to do with consistent business growth, it is more about the science of success.

Oscar Wilde said, *"Success is a science; if you have the conditions, you get the result."*

Let's face it, if you prospect on a regular basis using a proven systematic process that has worked for you or others, it will work again. The problem is that most advisors/agents don't view growing their practice with this methodology.

Read below the seven steps of the scientific method that I utilize with my coaching clients around challenges that they have in their business.

Step 1: Question the Challenge

The first step in the scientific method is to query the challenge that you need/want a solution for. In other words, why do you have the challenge in the first place?

Ellen D., a thirty-year veteran financial advisor client of mine couldn't understand why her business had been stagnant for years. That is until she was really honest with herself. She admitted that she had never liked prospecting and thus she rarely did it. Any incentive to push herself out of her comfort zone was non-existent.

Step 2: Conduct Research

The second step in the scientific method is to conduct research by finding someone that you know who has overcome the same or similar challenge and learn how they tackled finding a way to conquer it.

Ellen began her research by speaking to a friend and colleague who was the most successful advisor in her office. She concluded that her friend's success was the result of turning prospecting into a game. Her peer played the game of prospecting for forty-five minutes every day. Her reward was her first cup of coffee, which motivated her to do it as her first task of the day. She blocked off her calendar so that it was like an appointment. Conversely, if she did not prospect first thing, she had to go with no coffee that day.

Step 3: Form a Hypothesis

The third step is to form your own hypothesis (an educated guess) around the outcome you are hopeful to have if you implement change in your methodology or technique. That way you have an idea of what to expect when you integrate the research that you have conducted into your own process.

Ellen's hypothesis was simple, if she stuck to her reward system, only getting coffee if she took action each morning, she most certainly would prospect and get it done.

Step 4: Test the Hypothesis

Step four is to test your hypothesis to see if you are correct. If you are not, go back to formulating a new one until you find one that works well for you (a little more art than science sometimes). If you are correct, you proceed to the next step.

Ellen was excited to test her hypothesis and had a list of prospects that she had accumulated over the years. Most of them knew her already so calling them wasn't as difficult as she expected.

Step 5: Make an Observation

Step five is to observe what happened while testing your hypothesis to gain additional insight.

Ellen's observation was that her hypothesis was on point and she was more motivated to make calls when using a reward system. However, she concluded that the punishment system of not getting coffee unless she prospected was more motivating because her punishment was more painful than prospecting itself.

Step 6: Track Your Results

Step six is to track results so you have a record of your success (or not). With results, some tweaks to your process are often necessary to fine tune.

Ellen continued prospecting each morning for a month tracking the dials, contacts and appointments that she had set. She also tracked her rewards and punishments and she looked forward to reviewing her progress.

Step 7: Communicate Your Findings

Step seven is to communicate any findings from your process so others can benefit as well.

Ellen reported to her friend that her new system was working. She was motivated to prospect each day. She also said that focusing on planned out activities alleviated her anxiety about growing her business because her pipeline and client-base were finally growing.

Why Using the Scientific Method for Success Works

The reason why using the scientific method for success works is because it offers a stepwise approach that can be used for any area of life you would like to find success in.

Story #80
What Is Your Focus?

Recently, I had a coaching session with Tom Y. a financial advisor client of mine who has only been working in the industry for five years. We have been working together just under a year. He had hired me as part of his plan to shift gears (and his focus) to upright his success rate. By doing so, he has gathered over $17M in new assets since the beginning of the year. It had not always been this way. In fact, in his first four years in the business he only averaged around $2M annually.

When I asked him to sum up the major difference in his first four years versus this past year, he replied, *"I consciously decided to focus on how to make my everyday work more fun!"* Tony Robbins sums up that positive train of thought well, *"Where focus goes, energy flows."*

Daily activities can become rote and routine, but only if you let them. Tom had been trying too hard to get ahead and find success and in the process lost what had initially interested him about being an advisor.

As my coaching sessions with Tom continued each week, I asked him to think back and paint a picture of what his business had been like when he wasn't focused on how to make his professional tasks more fun. He described that he was in a constant state of anxiety, and full of worry and doubt; after four years of struggling he had come to a place where he wasn't sure if he was cut out for financial services and had considered giving up.

I then asked him to share how he made the decision to change up his focus. I wanted him to hear out loud in his own words what his catalyst or turning point had been versus simply getting out of the biz. After listening to him, we chatted about how what he had done had fostered his growth and ultimate success rather than doing what many unsuccessful advisors/agents end up doing by finding another career path.

The following is a brief outline of talking points from our discussion.

Daily Structure

Some of the things, a majority of advisors/agents who have struggled have in common are with time management tasks. They haven't outlined a scheduled structure to their day nor do they have a method to manage interruptions.

Tom had admitted that once he started time blocking his day and prioritizing his to-dos he got way more accomplished in less time. Previously, he had been "putting out fires" all day long. He is now way more in control of his time, which has diminished his level of stress and that is always a "win".

Prospecting / Sales Systems

Another commonality for advisors/agents that are chasing success is that they haven't created productive prospecting and sales systems. Instead most days they are "winging it!"

Tom had said that his approach was centered around the philosophy that prospecting and sales was a "numbers game" so the harder he worked the more clients he would subsequently close.

That hadn't been the reality. Once we worked together to break down each aspect of his prospecting pipeline and Tom practiced what to say during each phase, he realized that working "smarter" was a far stronger way forward.

Know Your Value

I have seen advisors/agents grapple with self-worth because they let a lack of business drive their perception of them lacking value.

Tom said that once he understood that he knew that most prospects have holes in their financial plans and gaps in their coverage, but that his clients didn't, he just needed to change his narrative so that his value was clear as day. This upped his confidence factor and his conversations with clients and potential clients were far easier.

Manage the Milestones

Unfortunately, when an advisor/agent is attempting to reconcile why their outcomes have not been what they desired, it is difficult to be reminded of failures and to learn from them.

Tom mentioned doing exactly that, listing out his weaknesses so that he could set up being accountable for those areas instead. In his case, he did that for daily time blocked prospecting activities and it motivated him to achieve his monthly goals because he knew that if he stuck to the process and had a reward/punishment system, it would inspire him to fill his pipeline.

Why Having a Focus Works

Oftentimes, it is challenging to be grateful during adversity or a plateau period where goals seem to be slipping away. You are always able to adjust your attitude and make a choice to focus, as Tom was able to. It isn't always an easy mindset change, but setting an intention and putting in effort to see it come to fruition is always possible.

Tom had fun this past year and though from the outside looking in, some might say it was because he had a banner monetary year. I view it from this perspective, the reason Tom was having such a great year was because his focus became less about the outcome and more about how he viewed and what he did each day, focusing on what motivated him rather than on what wasn't working made all the difference.

Story #81
Action is the Antidote to Anxiety

Financial advisors/agents can find themselves tangled up in their fears, which can limit any level of future success. As a professional development coach, I refer to this as the "teeter-totter effect" where on one side sits anxiety and on the other sits results.

It goes without saying that when results are up, anxiety is down and when results are down, anxiety is up.

So how does someone get off this "ride"? Well, action is the antidote to anxiety. Dale Carnegie said, *"If you want to conquer fear, don't sit home and think about it. Go out and get busy."*

There are many ways to take action. First, you have to make the decision that you are tired of feeling hopeless, helpless and/or fearful. Then you need to map out what action or change of focus you should be implementing.

Create leverage for those actions or focus by writing down a reward or punishment that you would give yourself at the end of the day if you follow through (or not). Then, get going and do it whatever "it" is that you have concluded needs to be done.

You also need to be conscious that this process is ongoing and dynamic. You need to evaluate and tweak accordingly as what you move forward doing now may not be what you need to be doing a few months down the pike.

Be Solid in Your Desire to Change

Change can be a frightening thing. The thought of the unknown can seem more terrifying than complacency. One of my financial advisor clients was in need of change. Here is his story:

Aaron P. has over forty years of experience in the industry and was comfortable only working with his client-base. He didn't feel the need to prospect. However, as his clients aged he was faced with the reality that his client-base was shrinking and consequently, so was his income. One day he called me and declared that he knew he needed to prospect, but after all this time of not, he didn't know how. By letting himself get rusty, he had created for himself a fear of rejection.

Take the Time to Determine Your Direction

In Aaron's case, he needed to first conquer his fear of rejection by determining how valid that fear was. So, I asked him a series of questions until he came to the realization that any rejection that he might experience while prospecting was not of a personal nature. Rather, they were rejecting the value of his services.

He needed a stepwise process so that he could ensure he was adequately explaining their value and his veteran industry knowledge. We mapped out what type of prospecting he would do, when he would do it, who he would call, what he would say and how he would handle objections.

In Order to Create Habits, You Must Create Leverage

Like Aaron, once you have a plan, you must have a strong enough reason why you need to follow it to get motivated, create momentum and have it become part of your protocol. In other words, you need leverage.

Aaron had plenty of reasons why he should prospect; his client base and income were shrinking. However, to pick up the phone and make that first prospecting call he needed to have a reward to strive for or a punishment to avoid.

Make those items meaningful enough and speak to what you would like to work for (or against).

Taking Consistent Action Requires Commitment

Once you have decided to make change happen, determine your direction and create leverage and accountability, you need to be consistent.

Aaron did just that! Within weeks he was filling up his pipeline again. When I asked him what he thought about his prospecting system he said he wished he would have started sooner.

Why a Well Thought Out Action Plan Works

Following this approach can lessen your anxiety or eliminate it altogether. The reason why a well thought out action plan works is because it refocuses your energy to view things as opportunities not challenges.

Story #82
Listening to Your Wake-Up Call

Millions of people begin their day hearing that ever so-familiar sound, their alarm clock. Whether waking up to your favorite radio station or the clock's buzz or ring, the alarm is meant to do one thing, wake you up. Similarly, your business is constantly setting off alarms, however, you might not have noticed.

Take for instance, if one day you realize that you have a pipeline that is dry, a production level that is low, continuing education credits that are due in a week, and you forgot to contact a client recently. The next thing you know there is a transfer notice that your client is moving her account to another firm. All of these are common examples of your business setting off alarms. Unfortunately, you may not have been listening.

Much like your personal alarm clock, with your business alarm clock you really only have three options; ignore it, hit the snooze button or get up. Let's see how these wake-up strategies apply to your business:

Step 1: Ignoring Your Business Wake-Up Call

My definition of a business wake-up call is any activity or lack of activity that is or may cause you emotional pain. One way to determine if your business alarm is going off is to ask yourself this question, *"What is the number one challenge in my business?"* Let's say that you answered this question with *"I am not growing my business."* That is your business wake-up call because you know to prosper as an advisor you need to grow your business.

The challenge with ignoring any business alarm is that the law of cause and effect will catch up with you and your business challenges will not just go away. Instead, you reap what you sow, find yourself getting negative results and your business challenge(s) will just get larger and larger.

The most effective solution for getting past ignoring your business wake-up calls, is to do the "Dickens' Exercise". In the Charles Dickens' classic **A Christmas Carol** the main character Ebenezer Scrooge was visited by three ghosts, the ghost of Christmas Past, Christmas Present and Christmas Future. What motivated Scrooge to make lasting change was the vision of what the future "could" be like.

Similarly, you too can change your present activity (or inactivity) by doing the "Dickens' Exercise", writing out all the possible effects of continuing to ignore your business alarms.

Step 2: Hitting Your Business Snooze Button

Most financial advisors hit their "Business Snooze Button", but few know they are doing it. Take for instance our previous example, the wake-up call of *"I am not growing my business"* where the solution is to start prospecting to fill up the pipeline and grow the business. So you fill up the pipeline, close prospects, have a good month and then stop prospecting thinking you can coast, that is hitting your "Business Snooze Button".

The challenge with this type of start-and-stop method for running your business is that you will constantly find yourself on an emotional roller coaster. Once your business is down, negative emotions such as anxiety and fear kick in long enough for you to take action.

Once you take action and your business productivity goes up, positive emotions such as excitement and joy kick in long enough for you to hit your "Business Snooze Button" reducing your action(s), thus starting the emotional roller-coaster ride all over again.

The most effective solution, for getting past hitting the "Business Snooze Button" is to make your business actions a habit. In other words, if you schedule prospecting as the first activity that you do every morning (regardless of how good or poor business has been) you will consistently have a robust pipeline.

Step 3: Listening to Your Business Wake-Up Call

The first step to listening to your business wake-up call is ask yourself the question, *"What is the number one challenge in my business? Why do I have this challenge?"* Let's take the example of *"I need to grow my business."* After asking yourself "why", you may realize, *"I have a fear of rejection and as a result I would rather ignore the fact that my business is down than do something about it."*

Now you must understand the implication of not addressing the problem so that you can understand that not addressing the problem will be more painful than tackling it. You can do this by asking yourself, *"What are all the things that will happen if I do not address this problem?"* Make a long list and feel the pain.

Next you need to spell out the solution(s) by asking yourself these types of questions, *"What needs to happen in order to get past this challenge?"* And, *"How can I apply these solutions on a consistent basis?"* If you are not sure how to find the solutions to your business challenges than find someone who does know.

Taking action and applying the solutions is the only way forward. One way to consistently take initiatives towards implementing solutions is by having a strong enough reason why to succeed and a strong enough reason on why not to fail.

Why Listening To Your Wake-Up Call Works

Now that you understand what your business might be telling you, it is vital to actually listen to your business alarms and design strategies for dealing with them. The reason why listening to your business wake-up call works is because you are not only aware of what your specific business alarms are but you are taking action to keep them from constantly ringing.

Story #83
No More Excuses

In the financial services industry, we as advisors hear excuses on a daily basis. "I'm busy, I didn't get the information in the mail, can you send it again? I received your information, but haven't had time to read it." And let's not forget..."call me after the holidays."

Using excuses to mask fear is not exclusive to your clients. By now, you may have already created a number of reasons (or excuses) why you are not implementing and reaching your own goals. "I'm too busy to prospect. My clients are demanding all of my attention. Or, I forgot to set up my seminars this year" are all common examples of what many advisors say to avoid engaging in and completing activities that they perceive to be difficult, painful or time consuming.

Most advisors at some point in their careers are faced with the reality that they are not satisfied with their level of success. If this sounds familiar, rest assured you are not alone. However, the truth is that you are probably in part where you are (if you are not where you want to be with your business) because of excuses; the market is too high, the market is too low, cold calling doesn't work, prospects aren't interested in a second opinion...whatever the excuses are you must stop making them.

Use the following steps to make the transition to eliminate excuses:

Step 1: Understand Your Excuses

Most advisors don't really understand what excuses are much less give them any thought. However, excuses are your mind's way of defending your inaction to help you avoid the perceived pain of taking action. In other words, it's a defense mechanism.

It might feel good in the short-term to avoid those activities, those you know you need to do but just don't want to do but eventually it will feel bad in the long-term because your business will take a hit and become stagnant.

Understanding what excuses really are helps you to increase your awareness that your mind is just trying to protect you. It also helps you to know it's time to get to the next step.

Step 2: Admit That There is No Time for Excuses

As you know if you do specific activities, you get specific results. It's cause and effect. And, if you admit to yourself that the result of buying into excuses means eventually equates to a lack of results then you must also admit that you have no time for excuses. In fact, giving yourself excuses is like giving yourself permission to fail because you are not even going to try.

Don't put yourself in that position. Instead, realize that you only have so much time in the day and choosing to procrastinate until the last minute is actually more painful than taking action, no matter what the activities are.

Step 3: Acknowledge That You Need a Better Way

Once you've admitted that there is no time for excuses the next step is to acknowledge that you must start learning better ways to utilize your time doing more effective and efficient activities. By doing this you are in fact changing your focus from the challenge (the excuse) to the solution (a better way to spend your time). What this does is that it helps you to use education to get beyond the excuse.

One way to do this is to become a student of building a better business by educating yourself and understanding everything you can about how to be effective at each of the following facets of your business: Time Management, Prospecting, Selling, Relationship Building, Marketing, Client Servicing, Product/Market Knowledge and Portfolio Management. Then, put your newfound knowledge to the test by taking action. Your new action will create new reference points and soon you will eliminate any doubt of your own abilities.

Step 4: Know What to Do Next Time

Will your mind continue trying to make excuses even after you have a better way of being productive? Absolutely! But, the next time this happens you test your excuse. And here is how:

At the first sign of procrastination or avoidance, ask yourself these questions-"What concerns me most about doing this? And, why?" or you could put a positive spin on your question by asking, "What would I need to do right now to have fun accomplishing my goal?"

Getting in the habit of asking these types of tough questions is never easy, but it will help you understand the feelings that are holding you back from taking action.

If you find that your first answer is vague such as-"I just don't want to do it. Or, I'm just too busy" you need to continue to dig with questions to get through your own "smoke screen objection" and get to the heart of the negative belief systems that you have. Use questions such as-"In addition to that is there anything else that is holding me back? Or, why do I feel this way?"

Why the No More Excuses Steps Work

Let's face it, you either have a process for eliminating excuses or you don't. The reason why the No More Excuses steps work is because it's a process to remind yourself that excuses are merely your mind's way of protecting you. You don't have time for excuses, you have (or can have) a better way to take action and if all else fails ask better questions to understand your own feels then repeat the process. In other words, it works because it helps you move forward instead of staying stuck.

Story #84
Taking Action is THE Key Ingredient

Taking action is the single most important ingredient in obtaining your goals. Without sustainable and consistent action, goals are merely a wish list. One of the core elements is in understanding the value you place on the steps you need to take. If you perceive an action to be pleasurable, you will most certainly begin right away however if you perceive an action to be painful, you most certainly will procrastinate.

Andrew Carnegie said, *"There are two types of people who never achieve very much in their lifetimes. One is the person who won't do what he or she is told to do, and the other is the person who does no more than he or she is told to do."*

To manage your level of activity assign a "carrot" or reward for fulfilling action items and a "stick" or punishment for when you don't. This process will inevitably change your value system and help you in remaining motivated.

Read on for a more detailed stepwise approach for how you can eliminate inaction and procrastination as it pertains to your business.

Step 1: Define the Value of the Task

Most advisors/agents have a multitude of tasks that "should" get done every day. As stated, pleasurable tasks get done and typically are accomplished first while painful tasks either don't get checked off or are delayed in getting accomplished. Unfortunately, this process neglects the fact that sometimes short-term pleasure can create long-term pain.

Ken C. is a ten-year veteran financial advisor who felt overwhelmed and exhausted most days. After a decade of prospecting he found himself spending most of his time servicing clients when they called him. He did receive pleasure out of making his clients happy, which is why this had been a priority. As a result, the more arduous task of prospecting was neglected most days and his business growth had grown stagnant.

After a number of queries, Ken admitted that he hated getting rejected, realized the long-term result of not prospecting meant the pain of never becoming a top producer. So, we discussed the client servicing activities that he could delegate to his licensed assistant who was qualified to handle those activities. This resulted in freeing up time for him to prep and tackle prospecting.

Step 2: Schedule an Action Date

Typically, goals are much more likely to get accomplished when the tasks associated with them are assigned a time horizon, an action time and date. So, we mapped out Ken's day to prospect first thing in the morning for forty-five minutes. All client service activities that didn't directly involve discussing investments with clients were to be delegated to his assistant while everything that was investment related but wasn't time-sensitive were to be done after his time blocked to prospect.

Step 3: Create Leverage

The easy part is in creating the process, but the harder part is sticking to it. To ensure that you continue to take action on a consistent basis you need to create leverage by assigning a reward system for accomplishing the activity or a punishment system for not doing the more difficult activity.

Ken was a coffee lover and to him the morning didn't start until he had finished his first cup of coffee. After he told me this, I knew exactly what type of leverage he needed. He was to use coffee as his reward system, if he started prospecting he could pour himself a cup of coffee if not he couldn't. At the end of the day, he would send me an "accountability email" to share the day's results. It took a few weeks of consistently prospecting and delegating to get into a groove, but it did become easier and easier.

After a month or so of daily "accountability emails" Ken's prospecting paid off and his business started to grow again. In addition, he was feeling far less overwhelmed and excited about his outcomes.

Why Having a System for Scheduling Action Items Works

The reason why having a system for scheduling action items works is because it generates an awareness of what is important about the task, it sets aside dedicated time line for accomplishing it and then promotes keeping you accountable for the results. Oftentimes the simplest of solutions pays off in spades.

Story #85
Where There is A Will, There is a Way

Most advisors/agents at some point in their careers find themselves doubting their own ability to get to the next level in their business. A common phrase about self-doubt that I hear all too often from my coaching clients is, *"I should be further along in my business by now. I don't know how I'm every going to get to where I want to be."*

The problem with this "philosophy" is that the advisor/agent is choosing doubt over discipline, which results in a self-fulfilling prophecy. Elon Musk said, *"When something is important enough, you do it even if the odds are not in your favor."*

The key to conquering self-doubt is to have a proven and disciplined strategy. Start by answering the question, *"Why do I want to succeed?"* which will help you understand what your motivation is. Then, ask the question, *"Who do I know that has been at my level of success and reached the next level?"* Next ask that person, *"What did you do to reach that next level?"* Then follow their lead by incorporating what worked for them into what you do, acknowledging that you may need to modify or tweak to make it a fit for you.

The following is a step-by-step process that I have utilized with one of my veteran financial advisor clients to conquer his self-doubt and initiate the necessary actions to achieve a new level of success.

Step 1: Know Your Why

The first step is to articulate your "why", why you desire to reach higher. Unfortunately, most advisors/agents don't take the time to define their inner drive. It is vital to take some dedicated time to get at the heart of what motivates you.

Peter K. had 25+ years of experience in the financial services industry and he confessed to me that he was unmotivated. He had a thriving practice and by most accounts was considered successful.

However, he oftentimes questioned why he was even in the business after all of these years as he just wasn't passionate about it anymore.

When he began his business, he was seeking to become financially independent. After achieving that goal, he found it more and more difficult to stay motivated. That is until we had a coaching session and he came to the conclusion that he wanted to help family, friends and clients become financially independent as well.

Step 2: Model Your Mentor

The second step is to know what you need to do and find a way to integrate that into your daily systems. As stated earlier, finding a mentor who has overcome the same or similar challenges as you have is imperative.

Although Peter knew how to help his clients build wealth, he had never approached the subject of "why" it was so important to him that they experience financial freedom. Also, he rarely worked with friends and family because he didn't want to jeopardize those relationships if their investments lost money. One of his first mentors was Bob L., who after 48 years was still passionate about helping others.

Step 3: Schedule Your Success

The third step is to stick to a daily routine that supports success by scheduling what you are going to do and when you are going to do it.

After meeting with Bob, Peter quickly realized that he needed to have a heart-to-heart talk with clients, family and friends to explain that his mission was to help them become financially independent. He scheduled the first hour of each business day to be devoted to spreading his message. It didn't take long before his calendar filled up with appointments. He also expanded his service suite to include insurance and estate planning experts to round out his client's total wealth planning. By doing these things, he conquered his self-doubt and reignited his passion and purpose.

Why Having Tenacity Works

When you find your passion and purpose it greatly encourages living up to your potential. The reason why having tenacity works is because it's a driving force. Without it, it is a challenge to find yourself with successful outcomes. So, the next time you find yourself filled with self-doubt follow this process and you will find that your will to find a way is stronger than your unwillingness to change.

Story #86
Building Your Business in a Bear Market

If you are in the financial services industry your business is tethered to the market. When the market is up so is your business, but when the market is down, so is your business. It's inevitable especially if you have a fee-based business. When the market and your assets under management drop it also means your gross commissions drop.

When this happens, do your business building activities necessarily need to follow suit? The answer is "no". However, many advisors stop prospecting because they don't have a good strategy for continuing to do that task during a Bear Market.

If you are viewing a Bear Market as an obstacle rather than an opportunity you certainly won't reach the next level.

Warren Buffet, one of the best investors of our time had the right mentality regarding investing in a Bear Market when he said, *"A market downturn doesn't bother us. It is an opportunity to increase our ownership of great companies with great management at good prices."*

This perspective carries over and supports connecting with prospects when other advisors won't. And, when the market is down it's an opportunity to increase ownership in your own business.

Let's take a look at a five step strategic process for building your business in a Bear Market.

Step #1: Master Your Mindset

Your mindset is the most important part of the process. If you don't get into the right frame of mind you won't apply any of the other steps. The big question is, how do you get into the right frame of mind? By reframing your reference point.

In 2001, I hired my first business coach because after experiencing my first Bear Market I was at a loss at what to do. I really didn't want to do anything. My business coach helped me to pinpoint a different reference point and look at the opportunity within the obstacle by understanding that all Bear Markets eventually end.

He asked me to start thinking about what I would want to happen when it did end. That changed my reference point! I knew exactly what I would have wanted to do, which was to speak to my clients and prospect daily to build my business when nobody else was.

Step #2: Master Your Time

Once you have a positive mindset and are ready to begin building your business in a Bear Market you need to make time to do it! In other words, you need to create a habit of prospecting. The best way to do this is by using two time management tools that I have created, which are the **Bottom Line List** (refer to the story **Bottom Line List** in chapter 2), and the **Time Matrix To-Do List** (refer to the story **Being Passionately Productive** in chapter 2),. The first helps you to have structure in your day because it maps out the top five daily activities that need to be accomplished-each activity scheduled for a forty-five-time block. The second is a tool for prioritizing your tasks and interruptions so that you know when you will work on them.

Typically, the best time to prospect is at the start of your business day because that's when you are more productive on the phone. Since my target market was business owners, I wanted to catch them early so I put prospecting as the first activity on my **Bottom Line List**. When I would get interrupted I would put the interruption on my **Time Matrix To-Do List,** prioritize it into one of four categories which are: today, now, this week and whenever. Then, I would go back to prospecting.

But, just making an effort to prospect isn't enough; you need to go to the next step.

Step #3: Master Your Prospecting Process

Once you have a positive mindset and you have developed your time management system you need a good prospecting process. I recommend three prospecting tools that my clients use to find success:

1. **Framing the Conversation**
2. **The Smoke Screen Technique**
3. **The Objection Resolution Model**

I mapped out my business owner cold call script using a technique called **Framing the Conversation** (refer to the story **Beyond the Gatekeeper** in chapter 2) so that I knew what to say within the first seconds of the call.

Then, I mapped out how to handle objections that I believed just weren't the truth such as "I'm busy" or "Send me some information", by using **The Smoke Screen Technique**. Then, I stumbled across a technique called **The Objection Resolution Model** (refer to the story **Beyond the Gatekeeper** in chapter 2) for handling what I considered to be the real objections. Once I had my prospecting process mapped out I started making the calls and setting appointments.

Step #4: Unclog the Pipeline

All sales pipelines have a clog in them and the way you can find any/all clogs in it is to use a tool I created called **The New Business Strategy List** (refer to the story **New Business Strategy List** in chapter 2).

This tool shows you what stage of the pipeline each person is in. And if there is a pattern of a number of prospects that don't move to the next stage, you've found your clog. Once you find the clog you need to find and apply the solution.

After a few weeks of prospecting, I found the clog in my pipeline; I was not closing the sale because I wasn't preparing for objections.

So, I used the same handling objections tools for setting the appointment to master closing the appointment. And, my close ratio went up!

Step #5: Master Your Tracking System

Now that you've got a system down for building your business in a Bear Market all you need to do is keep track of your progress.

Eventually, I realized that I needed to track my successes so I created some new columns on **The New Business Strategy List** for assets gathered and gross commissions closed. This helped to determine my progress at any given time.

Why Building Your Business in a Bear Market Works

As you know, getting comfortable with being out of your comfort zone is difficult to do. The reason why building business in a Bear Market works so well is because it gives you direction when everyone around you is directionless.

Story #87
Beyond the Blame Game

In today's climate, many sources are quick to place blame on the reasons for changes in our economy and overall market volatility. Likewise, many advisors/agents have a tendency to do similar when having to explain to others the state of their business; statements such as, *"If the market would cooperate, I would be doing better"* or *"Clients don't see the urgency in getting together while the market is doing well"* are examples of excuses for not taking responsibility. The consequence in making those excuses is the possible outcome. Attending to your clients and their portfolios during both up and down markets is vital.

Ralph Waldo Emerson said, *"No one can cheat you out of ultimate success, but yourself."*

Successful advisors/agents know that true growth is really up to oneself, regardless of what is going on both in and out of your control. You must be willing to be honest about what is working AND not working for you presently.

Then, you must be willing to adjust and adapt to changing conditions. Next, you must decide on what actions will actually guide you towards positive results. Implementing those activities and continually assessing your results will keep you accountable to yourself and prevent the "because of everyone else" blame game.

Let's take a look at specific steps for how you can incorporate responsibility into your business.

Step 1: Be Completely Honest

Honesty truly is the best policy and what better person to be honest with than yourself. However, many advisors/agents find it difficult to admit that they themselves are the true cause of their own not-so-great results. Let me share with you about one advisor that I've worked with to identify his shortfalls and some solutions we utilized for replacing them.

Bill T. is a fifteen-year veteran financial advisor who found himself on a production plateau. After years of building up a client-base he stopped prospecting. His rationale was that he had "made it" and that anyone with his number of years of experience should not have to prospect. However, his company did not share the same point of view and thus was not happy with Bill's level of production.

So, during one of our coaching sessions I asked Bill a number of questions to determine his honest view about prospecting. It didn't take long before he realized that he needed to change his perspective about prospecting from one of an obstacle to one of opportunity.

Step 2: Adjust and Adapt to Changing Conditions

One of the hardest things to do once you face the truth is to make the necessary shifts in both attitude and tasks. The best way to do this is to create a well thought out action plan. Take time to develop it and be realistic about your own expectations. In Bill's case, he knew he needed to get back to prospecting, but had no idea where to begin since it had been quite some time since he had prospected. So, we mapped out an action plan together.

We first determined his target market, which was business owners. Then, we worked on how to approach them by scripting out a formula for what to say during the initial contact. Next, we worked on brainstorming every possible objection he might hear and how to overcome them to set appointments. Finally, we practiced the process so that his first call would sound flawless.

Step 3: Implement & Evaluate Your Action Plan

Now it is time to implement in real time and constantly be evaluating (and tweaking) your action plan to fine tune it to make it work optimally.

This is best done by determining what time of the day you will do particular tasks and sticking to that blocked time. You also need to allocate the time to record your daily activities and record the outcome on a monthly, weekly and daily basis.

After several weeks, Bill realized that his pipeline was starting to fill up with qualified prospects that were interested in meeting with him. Organically, he began turning those prospects into clients. His company took notice and asked him if he would be interested in teaching other advisors/agents how he had turned things around.

Why Taking Responsibility Works

The reason why taking responsibility for your own success works is because it's not anyone else's responsibility that you succeed. Choosing to blame the economy, the market, your firm or others will always result in a losing game.

Story #88
Building Healthy Business Habits

Have you ever wondered how successful advisors keep reaching new levels of success? Some might say that it is just luck while others might say it's about skill. I believe that it comes down to one simple but powerful process, which is all about knowing how to build healthy business habits — habits that provide consistent action towards achieving goals.

Brian Tracy, a popular motivational speaker and author of over eighty self-help books says, *"Successful people are simply those with successful habits."*

Over the course of coaching hundreds of financial advisors and insurance agents since 2004, I've found this to be true. The main difference between those who want to succeed and those who do succeed comes down to consistently applying the following steps that create lasting change.

Let's take a look at a five-step process for building healthy professional habits:

Step 1: Realization

I know that it might sound strange to hear, but you can't form a healthy habit unless you realize that you have unhealthy ones. You must understand any challenge before you can apply the solution(s).

Stephen R., a fifteen year veteran financial advisor client of mine who was in a constant state of anxiety when it comes to managing his client-base while also trying to prospect. After our first coaching session he admitted that he had no structure for the day and no way to handle interruptions; he was putting out fires all day and not prospecting.

Step 2: Information

Once you realize your challenge it's only natural to want to find the solution.

Since Stephen understood that for him to master time management he needed to incorporate structure into his day I showed him two tools to do just that, **The Bottom Line List** (refer to the story **Bottom Line List** in chapter 2), which time blocks five hours into forty-five minute time blocks and the **Time Matrix To-Do List** (refer to the story **Being Passionately Productive** in chapter 2), which is a tool that prioritizes interruptions.

Step 3: Implementation

The next step in the process is to implement the solution(s). Otherwise, you know what to do, but you don't put it into practice. That's why turning these tools into a game, attaching a reward or punishment system and having my clients send me an accountability email at the end of each day for at least thirty days helps solidify these new habits.

Stephen started the process and soon realized that when he applied the tools they actually worked. Unfortunately, short-term success is not a guarantee of long-term success unless you apply the next step.

Step 4: Dedication

This step is the most important step in the process because many people don't have the dedication to continue doing the activities they need to do and know they should do to turn them into habits.

After a month Stephen had tremendous success so he decided that he didn't need to send the accountability emails anymore. However, after six months he had the same challenge again because he stopped being dedicated to implementing the tools. So, he went back to applying them and sent accountability emails every day for the next three months.

Step 5: Transformation

The final step is the by-product of the four steps. Real transformation doesn't happen overnight and it is rarely an eventful moment. Instead, transformation is the result of consistently applying the activities needed to get the desired results.

After three months of getting back into sending accountability emails Stephen admitted that he had no anxiety regarding managing his client-base and prospecting.

Why Building Healthy Professional Habits Works

The reason why building healthy professional habits works well is because each step builds on the previous step. Most people do the first two steps they realize the challenge and find the solution.

Some people take the next step to implement the solution(s) and quit as soon as they achieve success. That's like losing twenty pounds and going back to eating unhealthy only to gain it all back. Those who become dedicated to applying the activities needed each day will experience success and true transformation by building healthy business habits.

CHAPTER 4
Advisor Solutions Transformational Moments
The Evolution of Success

The financial services industry is a place of constant and never ending change. The stock market, economy and even your client base are in some state of fluctuation all of the time.

The economy while maybe not as volatile as the stock market is either expanding or contracting and your client base is either growing or shrinking.

Living the life of a successful advisor is about applying the right tools and techniques to create transformational moments that have a lasting impact on your business as well as yourself.

What **Transformational Moments** are helpful towards becoming our best selves? To know that, we must fully understand what **Transformational Moments** are and to what extent they can be applied to a wide range of topics.

The dictionary definition of transformation is, *"The act or process of changing completely: a complete change."* So, if change is inevitable and we are actually in control of it, what creates a transformational moment that results in positive change? For many, it is the feeling of success.

It's the moment we realize the positive results (or successes) of applying what we learn, that's when we have the epiphany that what we are incorporating is actually working.

What follows is how one of my advisory clients discovered a series of **Transformational Moments** for himself:

In the spring of 2022, I had a group coaching session with a number of advisors and agents who had been participating in the **Advisor Solutions Master Class Group Coaching Program** for about six months. We begin each group coaching session with what I refer to as an "accountability check-in" having each advisor/agent explain the results of applying a tool or technique from the course or from individual coaching that they were to apply the previous week.

Bill K., a 30+ year insurance agent client of mine began his "accountability check-in" on an unusual note by saying, *"Instead of telling you what I was supposed to apply this past week can I tell you what I learned during one of my first appointments?"* Collectively, the group said. *"Sure what do did you learn?"*

"After I finished a first appointment with a prospect, I was driving back to the office when it dawned on me, that that appointment had been easy! I asked myself, why? Why did the conversation flow so smoothly and how can I have every meeting go like that?"

I smiled knowing the answers, but asked, *"Do you know why?"* He laughed and replied, *"Yes! That's why I wanted to share this story with the group. It's because I had been using the tools and techniques that we talk about in our coaching sessions that need to be applied in the first appointment. And, I realized that in the meeting I had applied at least four of the techniques and that's why it was so easy!"*

What I realized was that the evolution of **Advisor Solutions Transformational Moments** happens more often than not. Since that "check-in" session with Bill, I have made it a point to ask each of my clients what tool or technique created a **Transformational Moment** for them. What I have found was that no two advisory clients have the same story. However, all of my advisory clients have experienced several **Transformational Moments** and the underlining commonality is that they can happen at any time.

For the purpose of this book, I wanted you to understand that the stories in this section should be viewed as puzzle pieces that have already been assembled together to show you the finished product or what the picture on the box looks like. Or, in this case what success looks like once you apply the tools and techniques to create **Transformational Moments.**

Unlike the tools section of this book, which focuses on what a successful business could look like and the techniques section, which is about developing not only business skillsets, but personal skillsets as well, the **Transformational Moments** section is the byproduct of utilizing both tools and techniques to create real and lasting change.

As you read this section please note that the **Transformational Moments** when utilized in conjunction with one another, can collectively develop you as a person, which in turn will increase your ability to make what I call effortless connections.

It is my hope that as you read through this book's **Transformational Moments** section that the stories resonate with you and that you apply what you learn in this book to your own business so that you can create your own unique puzzle of what success looks like for you.

Story #89
Writing the Next Chapter

As a new day begins, you may be wondering what it holds in store for you and your business. Will this be the beginning of your breakout year—a banner year that takes your business to the next level? Or, will you find your business in the same place next year?

The story of your future success is yet unwritten so it is up to you to begin writing the next chapter. Here is what I mean.

The financial advisory business is essentially made up of a series of chapters, which are compiled during one's career. Each chapter brings a new and hopefully greater level of awareness, accountability and action as we learn and grow from our previous chapter's experiences.

Oftentimes we may not realize we have moved into a next chapter until we have a defining "a-ha" moment, but it certainly does not nor should not take an "a-ha" moment to start or end a chapter; more subtle wins and losses contribute to transitions and change too.

These life chapters come in varying formats and sizes and they typically evolve when we least expect them. One example of this happened to me over thirty years ago when I was just starting in the business and I made the realization of "how" I had set a recent appointment. I had set several appointments prior, but I never understood "how" I was setting them. The conversation went like this:

"I think I'm all taken care of. I have mutual funds already" said Mary, a middle-aged business owner. *"What kind?"* I curiously asked. *"They are the XYZ Funds. I've had them for years"* she stated. *"Oh, so your advisor is from XYZ Securities? Did he mention that he got paid a higher commission for selling you his company funds? And, with the universe of funds to choose from, why would those funds be the best fund family for you?" "I don't know"* she quietly

replied. *"That's exactly why I want to get together with you."* She paused and then said, *"What time?"*

After that conversation, I realized the importance of asking the right questions. I began mapping those out prior to meetings and then applied those questions during them. I held myself accountable for reviewing those conversations so that I could tweak my process and continue to get better at it; thus, I began a new chapter by changing the way I communicated with prospects and clients.

Why Writing Your Own Chapter Works

Remember you are the sole author of your "book" about your business and your life. You can consciously choose to turn the page on your next chapter and wrap its' ending if the moment speaks to that.

Story #90
Do What You Love and Love What You Do

I'm sure it comes as no surprise that the old saying *"Do what you love and love what you do"* has been paraphrased in various forms from all sorts of people. The same type of message has come from Henry David Thoreau as well as LL Cool J., with each of them putting a unique spin on it.

However, what you might find surprising was what Nicki, a financial advisor client of mine shared when we were doing a check-in during a coaching session. I noticed that Nicki had been having a tremendous amount of success by absorbing my coaching curriculum, implementing what she learned immediately and reporting her success stories back each week. I was hoping this trend would continue and was eager to find out if it had.

"I'm closing so many people that I'm feeling guilty!" she said laughing. *"Are you serious? Are you really feeling guilty?"* I replied. *"Yes, I am because it's so easy to figure out their personality type and then connect with them during the closing appointment that I feel guilty."*

Just months earlier she was trying to figure out how to find success and now she was feeling guilty because succeeding had become "easy" for her, *"But seriously, my big concern is that I love what I do and if I keep continuing to close people like I have been that in five years I will have such a large client base that I don't know if I'll have time to continue prospecting and growing the business."* she said with a hint of concern in her voice.

"Nicki, doing what you love and loving what you do is vital to your ongoing success." I assured her.

Find Your Passion

The first step in doing what you love has to be in recognizing what fulfills or drives you.

If we boil a financial advisor/agent's business down to its basic elements we commonly find two—prospecting and working with clients. Now, here is an analogy that better explains this. If you think about it, advisors/agents essentially have two jobs—as both a hunter and a farmer. The hunter's job is to find food while the farmer's job is to grow food. We as advisors/agents have to find new clients and then keep the clients we have.

Do you get a rush trying to find the next big client? Or, do you get a bigger rush out of finding the next solution for an existing client, possibly an investment or an insurance recommendation?

Refine Your Passion

It's no secret that part of loving what you do is also about doing it well. Unlike in golf where you can be a terrible golfer, but still love playing it, your career isn't the same since if you are terrible at it, no matter how much you might love what you do, you still could be fired.

So, refine your passion by learning how to be better at it. If you love to prospect, do what Nicki did and learn how to be a better prospector. If you love to manage money, study and get the designations to be a money manager. An investment in yourself pays the highest returns and offers the greatest potential impact for you and your business.

Acknowledge What You Don't Love

As a business coach, it can sometimes be difficult to determine what an advisor/agent may not love. An example could be an advisor/agent who says they need to prospect, fill their pipeline and start closing new people.

They eagerly attempt to learn the technical aspects of how to prospect, but if over the course of a month or two they seem well aware of all the aspects of prospecting, but have not added anyone to their pipeline. You have to connect the dots and accept that they are a farmer who thinks they should be a hunter, but actually hates hunting.

You first need to come to some level of recognition that there may be some things that you just don't like to do. You may need to still do them, but you can better prioritize to ensure that those things you do like to do that motivate you are capitalized on.

Find Someone Who Has a Passion for What You Don't

Teams come in all sorts of combinations, but the best teams are two people coming together with opposite interests or passions. A hunter that knows he/she is a hunter and prefers to hunt and a farmer that knows he/she is a farmer and prefers only to farm.

I have found that there is no set rule for who should be a hunter and who should be a farmer. Some would say that only rookies should be prospecting because veterans need to manage their book of clients. But, I've seen veterans with over 25 years of experience that can't wait to close the next prospect and rookies with less than 5 years of experience who can't wait to put the next financial plan together and manage it. Don't rule out any possibilities when it comes to your team members.

Why Do What You Love and Love What You Do Works

It may come as no surprise that when you find your passion and go one step further to refine your passion you can find success. Also, when you are honest with yourself on what you don't like to do and find someone who complements you because they love doing the aspects of the business that you hate, it creates the perfect combination for a great team.

The reason why doing what you love and loving what you do works so well is because you are able to be your authentic self—you get to be you. And, there is no better person for you to be.

Story #91
The Will to Succeed

"Who wants to take the referral challenge?" I asked a group of financial advisors at the end of a recent group coaching session. They had just finished up a discussion about effectively creating, maintaining and sustaining a referral campaign.

During the hour they had heard me share a story about Sean K., a rookie financial advisor who was asked the very same question in a previous group a few years back.

Sean had quickly taken me up on the challenge, which was to use the material he had learned during coaching and ask for one referral a day from his clients.

A week later he proudly reported that he not only asked for one referral a day, but that he found himself asking numerous clients for referrals all throughout the day and because of that, he had actually received eight referrals that week.

Understanding the Will to Succeed

So, when I asked my current group the same question, you could have heard a pin drop. Why? I believe it comes down to what I refer to as "The Will to Succeed" which I define as having the drive and determination to better yourself and succeed at whatever it is that you would like to improve on.

Now, you might be wondering if any of the advisors were even interested in asking for referrals. I assure you that previous to me asking the group *"Who wants to take the referral challenge?"* they had each stated how important getting referrals was and that they all wanted to be better at it.

This brings me to the inevitable question of *"What is it that drives some to take action in pursuit of their goals and not others?"*

How the Fear of Failure Stops Success

I believe the underlining factor that stops some in their tracks is fear of failure. It is the perceived fear that taking action will be more painful than not taking action. Typically, this results in procrastination or avoidance until it gets too painful to procrastinate any longer.

A common example of this is having a productive month followed by a disappointing one. While having a great month, the thought of prospecting, setting new appointments and putting new people into the pipeline seems painful, *"Why do it if you don't have to?"* is a common attitude. That is until the next month comes and you realize that you don't have anyone in the pipeline. Then, you find yourself scrambling to prospect again.

How to Increase Confidence and Conquer Fear

This brings me to another important question, what can you do to increase your will to succeed? The answer lies in increasing your confidence level so that you lessen your fear of failure and here is how to do it.

Building confidence is really a two-part equation; first, you need to increase your technical expertise and second, you need to gain experience in actually applying what you have learned.

In the case of Sean K., he believed that the new technical expertise that he had learned in group coaching would get him a better result than what he had done in the past.

However, what Sean did unlike the recent group members was to actually apply the material and gain the experience. As a result, each new referral reinforced his new belief system that asking for referrals was not painful, but fun! Remember, you can't win the game if you don't play.

Why Having The Will to Succeed Works

I believe there are two types of advisors/agents— those that have "The Will to Succeed" and those that don't. Now, it's not so say that someone who does not have it can't change and acquire the will. In fact, if you tap into your core reason "why" you are in this business you can use that to increase your drive and determination to succeed. However, you have to want to change.

The reason why having "The Will to Succeed" works so well is because it overpowers the fear of failing when applying what you learn. Take Sean K., the reason why he was successful at asking for and getting referrals was that his will to succeed was stronger than his fear of failing. In other words, he focused on the possibility that a new process would work better than anything else he had tried in the past. And, he was right.

Story #92
The Paradox of Pain in Your Practice

We have all heard the phrase, *"No pain, no gain,"* but how often do you actually look forward to adding "pain" into your practice? My guess is probably not very often. However, your attempts to consciously (or unconsciously) avoid that "pain" might create headaches for you and your business down the road. This is what I call *"The Paradox of Pain in Your Practice"* and it is much more common challenge facing advisors/agents than you think.

Identifying the Two Kinds of Pain

There are several kinds of pain in life. Some can propel you forward while others make you take a step back. It has been my own experience while being in production for thirteen years and coaching financial advisors/agents for over twenty years that most advisors/agents choose the "pain" that is seemingly less severe when it comes to how they run their practice. However, it is ironically the wrong choice.

The two kinds of "pain" we are talking about with regards to your business have names: *Discipline* and *Regret*.

Understanding the Pain of Discipline

"I know what I need to do, I just need to do It." is a common response when a financial advisor/agent learns a better process, but are paralyzed to take action in applying it. That is because the "pain" of discipline is firmly ingrained. Take cold calling for example. You can learn a proven method for cold calling, master how to handle objections, secure a list and yet not pick up the phone. Why?

Because the thought of getting rejected is probably a memory that you care not to repeat you would rather avoid taking action altogether. But, is that the best choice? You know the answer. The secret to overcoming the "pain" of discipline is to learn from your past and other's mistakes. You will find that once you implement it (whatever "it" is for you), you slowly become desensitized to the "pain" and the pleasure of success takes its place.

Understanding the Pain of Regret

"I wish I was more successful" seems to be the mantra of those who feel the "pain" of regret. Unfortunately, the short-term pleasure of not taking action turns into the long-term regret of the business you have not built. This is by far the more painful of the two because regret never really goes away and can linger for your entire career.

Why the Paradox of Pain In Your Practice Works

The reality is that the "pain" of discipline is fleeting. Soon what seemed like painful activities turn into positive and business building habits! Those cold calls become appointments, appointments become prospects and prospects become new clients. All because you managed your "pain", picked up the phone and prospected. You do have a choice, discipline or regret. Which one would you choose?

Story #93
Are You Only Tuned into Station W.I.I.F.M.?

At the beginning of each of my one-on-one coaching sessions, it is standard procedure to request a recap of all the activities that an advisor has accomplished since our previous session. Jim F. and I had worked preparing for his upcoming "big appointment" the last time we spoke.

Jim had been anxious about the meeting because he knew that closing this prospect would mean the difference between experiencing a bad month versus having a good one.

Since he seemed to be just surviving and not thriving with his practice, a close would most certainly give him both the financial and emotional confidence that he needed.

"Well, how did it go?" I asked hopeful. *"Not very well"* he admitted. *"I had prepared, but I was nervous during my presentation. I just wanted to close him, but I did not. I don't think I will get another chance either since he seemed to be in such a hurry to get out of my office."*

Tuning Into the Wrong Station

This is a common story for many financial advisors and agents who are new in the business. The anxiety, nervousness and fear of making the sale can overwhelm them during their presentation and prospects can most certainly sense it.

I paused and asked Jim the inevitable question, *"Do you know why you didn't get the sale? I guess it's because I didn't prepare enough."* he quickly replied. *"No, that's not it,"* I assured him. *"It's because you are tuned into station W.I.I.F.M. "What?!?"* he snapped back. *"It stands for "What's In It For Me,"* I stated.

In other words, what Jim was doing was listening to the little voice inside his head that continually repeated the message that he needed to get the sale because his success was dependent upon the commissions that would be generated from it.

As a result he was feeling anxious, nervous and fearful. The prospect had picked up on it and regardless of how great the recommendations may have been those cues pushed the prospect away.

Tuning Into the Right Station

The solution for Jim and all advisors who find themselves tuned into the wrong station is to change your frequency—go into each phone call, appointment and/or networking event—with the willingness to find out and convey "What's In It For Them" because at the end of the day you should be saying "What's In It For Them" IS "What's In It For Me".

One example of this would be that during each appointment envision the prospect/client having the acronym W.I.I.F.M. written on their forehead.

This will help remind you that somewhere inside the mind of your prospect/client they are tuned into their own station and you need to be listening to it too. If you can you will soon find that individuals will be very willing to work with you because you have their best interests in mind.

Why Tuning Into W.I.I.F.M. Works

The reason why changing your frequency to the prospect's station of W.I.I.F.M. works well is because being in the financial services and insurance industry is not about what you can get out of it, but what you can put into.

When all you care about is yourself, you fail to care for others. Conversely, when your focus is primarily on caring about others, people will sense that and they will be more apt to work with you. Remember, their success is your success and when you come from a place of wanting to give instead of wanting to get, everybody wins!

Story #94
Reaching Beyond Your Limiting Belief System

Recently during a coaching session, my client Samantha announced that after 27 years in the financial services industry she had had a record month of gathering assets and had officially broke *The Bannister Barrier*.

Elated I congratulated her and then asked the most obvious question, "What is *The Bannister Barrier*?" She went on to explain that in 1954, Roger Bannister was the first man to run a four-minute mile. Soon after, a number of other runners also ran faster than a four-minute mile.

Intrigued, I did some research to find that as of April 2021, 1,663 athletes have broken the "four-minute mile barrier"! Today, it is actually the standard for professional middle distance runners.

What is even more amazing is that in 1964, Jim Ryun became the first high school runner to break the barrier. By 2022, seventeen other high school students have done so as well.

Understanding the Bannister Barrier

Samantha explained that *The Bannister Barrier* is a phrase, which she uses to refer to breaking through mental obstacles that hold one back from reaching their true potential. Once Roger Bannister did the unthinkable, other runners reached beyond their limiting belief systems to reach the same goal (or better) too.

Samantha had a goal of gathering $25M from retail clients during a twelve month period—a goal she believed was the pinnacle of her potential. In our coaching session, she proudly announced that this month alone she gathered $12M in new assets from new clients—a personal record asset month.

However, what was even more amazing was that she did so by opening just four new accounts, thus, putting her over her year-end goal with three months to spare.

Her limiting belief system had been that she thought she could only gather $2M a month. As a result, she had been reinforcing her belief system by averaging that number. Also, she had believed that since her average account size was around $500,000, she would need to open four new accounts.

Realizing the Reality of Breaking Through Limiting Beliefs

However, after opening up two accounts of $5M each and two accounts of $1M each she broke her personal *The Bannister Barrier*. In other words, her previous limiting belief system is now a thing of the past as she realized that the apex of her true potential is really a product of how much she believes in herself.

In addition, she went on to tell me that clients of the $5M accounts she had acquired had originally told her that they had an advisor and that they were all taken care of. Undeterred, she had continued keeping them on her mailing list and followed-up from time-to-time with phone calls until they finally agreed to meet with her.

Both clients eventually felt they were not getting the level of service they had been promised with their advisor and thus Samantha was the person they both thought of when they decided to take their business elsewhere.

Never Adopt Another Person's Limiting Belief

This brings me to another point about limiting belief systems. While most advisors would have let their limiting belief systems hold them back from continuing to prospect investors who were "all taken care of", she did not. She knew that if they were one day unsatisfied, she wanted to be the first person they thought of, she didn't let anyone else's limiting belief systems become her own.

Why Reaching Beyond Your Limiting Beliefs Systems Works

Can you relate to Samantha's success story? If so, then you may be asking yourself this important question... *What happens when I reach the pinnacle of my potential*? Typically, the answer becomes apparent when you realize that you now have a new reference point for what you are capable of doing. Then you can focus on pushing beyond your limiting belief system to obtain a whole new level of success.

Story #95
Heroes to the Rescue

As I began a coaching session with my client Carol, I picked up on a touch of despair in her voice. She had openly shared that she had doubt, concern and fear about ever finding success as a financial advisor.

Our conversation gravitated towards the turmoil that had been stirring inside of her for months and there wasn't anything that I was going to be able to say or do that would necessarily change her mindset, at least initially.

So, I decided to ask her one very important question, a question that I had never asked any of my other clients *"Do you want me to call a few of my women clients who at one time felt the same way you do and have found success, maybe you should hear their stories?"* Carol immediately said, *"YES"!*

Calling in the Cavalry

I told Carol I would make some calls and hopefully get back to her later that morning. I knew that she would be eagerly waiting to talk to anyone who could help.

I picked up the phone and called the first woman I could think of that fit the profile I had mentioned—Gail a thirty-year veteran who just a few years ago had been struggling with her business.

Through a steep learning curve, applying solutions that she learned during our weekly coaching forums turned her business around increasing her production 60% in one year. Almost two years later Gail was up 75% from her previous year numbers. After explaining Carol's concerns to Gail, she couldn't wait to offer up her success story.

Next, I called Viola, a twenty-year veteran who just three years ago had similar feelings of being lost and alone in an office full of other advisors. She had been looking for direction, structure and a way to reach the next level. But, she had nobody to help her until we met and began weekly coaching sessions.

We mapped out a plan to find the right advisor who was open to getting out of the business and structuring a deal to buy his client base. After many months (and meetings) she was able to buy a book of clients, which doubled her assets.

The following year she spent building relationships with the new clients while continuing to service her existing ones.

The plan worked and it didn't take long before implementing client servicing systems, adding structure to her daily tasks and handling interruptions proactively translated into her doubling her production! When I asked Viola if she would share her story with Carol, she replied enthusiastically, *"absolutely, count me in!"*

I made one last call, this time to one of my clients who was a new advisor. Janet had just six months ago transferred to a new firm. She had been a referral for me from one of my best clients and she and her business partner were open and eager to build a solid team structure.

Now, with systems in place and their increased connections, their pipeline was growing. *"I would love to tell her she isn't alone and that she can make it in this industry!"* Janet said. I then arranged a time later that afternoon that was convenient for everyone.

Assessing the Battlefield

I arrived on the conference call line to find Carol nervously waiting. Soon the cavalry arrived and I made brief introductions. *"Thanks for being here everyone,"* I then briefly explained that the primary reason for the call was to help Carol hear that it is very common to have challenges in this business.

Second, that for every challenge experienced, there is almost always a solution. Lastly, to let her know she wasn't alone with her fears and struggles. Every one of the women on this call understands what you are going through and have been able to rise above their challenges to apply the appropriate solutions and find success.

I asked Gail to tell her story first. She quickly jumped in and described what her life had been like when she was full of anxiety, fear and angst; how not having the right processes, structure and sales expertise had held her back.

Before Gail could explain how she turned her business around, I asked her to hold her thoughts until we heard from the others. Oftentimes, people need to hear the same message more than once and that's why I wanted the other women to get a chance to talk about their hardships before sharing about their successes.

Next, Viola explained how she too had been lost and alone. Finally, Janet explained that her frustrations revolved around not knowing where to begin. The magnitude of things that needed to be done to have a well-run business had felt overwhelming to her. Carol listened and with a little coaxing from me opened up to tell her tale. They could relate to her feelings of fear.

Creating Your Battle Plan

The interesting thing about success is that when people with integrity start to succeed they can't wait to help others succeed as well. Each woman patiently waited while the others explained how they turned their businesses around, what they were continuing to do to succeed and what they recommended to Carol to do as well.

The "how", while very important, was not the message that I wanted Carol to absorb. I knew that we would customize solutions to fill her needs. What was important was that she understood that these other woman had felt similarly and yet were able to turn those obstacles into opportunities for their businesses.

I could hear the anxiety in her voice fade away as she became engaged in asking questions. By the end of the call Carol had a renewed sense of purpose, confidence and faith that she too could do the same as these women had.

Why Becoming a Hero Works

Within minutes of hanging up, Carol had emailed all of the women thanking them for providing reassurance and being "hero" figures. Since then, communication between the women has continued and a *Monthly Think Tank* is being developed. I am confident that one day Carol will also become somebody's hero.

So what does any of this have to do with you? Maybe it's time you became somebody's hero. If you are a successful advisor think about a colleague or young advisor that your story could provide a boost to.

Story #96
You Are Not Alone

During a recent group coaching session, *Defining Your Business Purpose*, I noticed that an overwhelming majority of the advisors had similar responses when asked, *"What was your single take away from today's session?"* Most if not all of the advisors who were in the group replied, *"That I am not alone."*

Their responses were not an echo of each other as many advisors had their own specific "single takeaway", but each seemed to comment on whom in the group had provided them with a newfound nugget of wisdom; be it their colleagues or me.

Advisors replied with answers such as, *"I could relate to what, (so-and-so) said about _____...."* or *"I really liked what, (so-and-so) said about having a challenge with _____ because I thought I was the only one who had this challenge."* These types of responses only masked what they were really attempting to say, which was that although as an advisor you may feel isolated in your challenges, you are certainly not alone.

This group was not unique. Many advisors experience a sense of camaraderie and ancillary learning during discussions in a group coaching setting. What was unique was their understanding of the commonality between them and their colleagues.

The following are a few of the truths that I share with my coaching groups.

1. **All Advisors Face the Same Challenges at Some Point in Their Careers.**

    It doesn't matter if you are in Denver, Dallas, Detroit or Davenport…at some point in your career you will face similar challenges than those of other advisors. The reason is because common challenges such as fear of rejection, handling objections and filling the pipeline, just to name a few, are universal.

2. **Many Advisors Feel Isolated in Their Challenges.**

   Again, you are not alone. You may think you are alone because of the independent nature of our business (and often because of the reluctance to discuss our obstacles), but in reality you have colleagues and friends that are going through or have gone through the same challenges that you are. Thus, many of your colleagues feel they are alone and isolated in their challenges when that just is not reality.

   Your isolation, as well as those of your peers could easily be overcome by finding a mentor or mentee. There is someone right now who needs your help. You could create your own Mastermind Group or join one to help yourself and others.

3. **Solutions are Available, but Many of Your Colleagues Are Not Looking for Nor Apply Them.**

   The truth is that many of your colleagues may have hurdles that they are facing, but they may not be willing to find or implement solutions. Those that do find solutions may not be willing to make the necessary changes to implement them, which could/would create a long lasting impact on their business. As one advisor stated in a recent coaching session, *"I read all the books I can on improving my business. Then, I put the books away and continue having the same problems."*

Why Knowing You Are Not Alone Works

The reason why knowing you are not alone works is because you now know some of the truths about your peers, that all advisors at some point feel the same way, many feel like they are isolated in their challenges and many of your colleagues are not looking for the solutions much less applying them. Knowing these truths can help you move forward out of a feeling isolated and into doing something to feel more connected.

The way to get connected is to do something about it. Reach out to those who truly need your help by creating or joining a Mastermind Group. Or, ask for a helping hand by finding a mentor or hiring a coach.

Story #97
What is Your Why, What, When, Where and How?

During a recent group coaching session, Jeff S. a veteran financial advisor explained that what was working well for him when talking with clients and prospects was finding the answer to the question, *What is Your Why?*

The group members were quiet as they tried to figure out what Jeff actually meant, so I asked Jeff to elaborate. He explained, we all have a *"Why"* or a reason(s) that motivate(s) us to do what we do. However, few advisors truly take the time to uncover their own *"Why"* or that of their clients. Instead, advisors merely explain their recommendations to the prospects and/or clients and expect them to agree.

Let's take a closer look at this concept of and how What, When, Where and How also fit in.

Understanding the *"Why"*

People hate to be sold to, but they love to buy. The reason they buy is because a product or service appeals to their motivation. So how do we find out what is motivating them? We ask questions such as, *"What do you want this money to do for you and why? How will you feel when you accomplish that goal?"* and, *"What's important about having that feeling?"*

Now, their answers tell us a lot. Take for instance possible replies to the preceding questions: *"I want this money to be for retirement so I don't have to sell my house. I will feel more comfortable knowing I have a cushion to fall back on if need be and, what is most important about having that is a feeling of security to not have to rely on others."*

These answers or motivations focus on *"why"* the value they place on having money equals having security.

Understanding the "*What*":

Once you understand the "*Why*" you must now help them understand the "*What*". The "*What*" is the product or service you can offer that will help them accomplish their goals. At this stage in the conversation it is important to connect the two. Here is an example:

"It sounds to me like you want to make sure that you get some growth in order to have a cushion to fall back on, but you don't want to take a lot of risk because you may need this money. In order to do both, I recommend we take a look at X or Y."

Understanding the "*How*":

Once you explain the "*What*" (the product/service) that will assist them in reaching their goals, you need to explain *"How"* those connect with their motivations (their "*why*") so they will want to buy. They may also have questions about "*How*" the process or procedure works. That is why it is vital to help them fully understand step-by-step all the details of your specific recommendations.

The "*Where and When*" can be comfortably inserted into the "*How*" as follows:

"If this seems like it makes the most sense in helping you get the growth ("why") *as well as security for your retirement dollars without taking a lot of risk, then* ("what"-insert investment recommendation) *is the vehicle that I recommend because* ("why and what"-insert all of the reasons*).*

In order to do that we would need to ("how") *open a new account card, fill out the paperwork and transfer the money from* ("where") *your other brokerage account. This should take about* ("when") *a week or two to have the money transferred. Are you comfortable moving ahead?"*

Why Figuring Out Your Why, What, Where, When and How Works

The reason this is so powerful is because you are helping them understand the *"Why, What, Where, When and How"* to accomplish their goals. The only thing I have left out is the *"Who"* will help them to do it however if you have mapped out this entire process to fit your own discussions, your clients and prospects will undoubtedly realize that YOU are the advisor for the job.

Story #98
Lasting Lessons

The saying goes that hindsight is 20/20 and I think we can collectively agree that in many cases this is true. So with that in mind, let's picture the last day of your career. You have spent many years in the financial services industry and now it's time to retire. In fact, picture shutting the lights off, locking the office door and walking to your car.

What would your older self, on that final day, offer as nuggets of wisdom to your younger self? What are some lasting lessons you think you would share? Many times if you think along these lines, you come up with are things you already consciously or unconsciously know you should be utilizing NOW.

Let's take a look at some solid advice that I have received from veteran advisors over my last thirty years in this business.

It's Not About the Money, It's About the Mission

At some point in your career you will go from just trying to survive to feeling comfortable with your level of success. When that day happens, you will realize that it's not really about the money, it's about your mission, whatever your purpose is for deciding to be in this business. For many advisors, their mission is to help people prepare for financial security. If you are not in the business for the mission but for the money, you won't last long as your clients will eventually figure that out and take their assets elsewhere.

You Never Help Others by Holding Yourself Back

There are no excuses for failing to be successful. The fear of rejection, complacency, insecurity, lack of technical knowledge and expertise are all challenges that others have faced and overcome. You can never help others by holding yourself back with excuses. The key is to figure out, sometimes with the assistance of a mentor, colleague or coach, what your challenges are, then research the appropriate solutions and implement them.

Action Alleviates Anxiety

The antidote for a worried mind is to fill your day with productive activities. If you don't have enough in your pipeline, get busy prospecting. If you do, you will soon find that your anxiety is replaced with the excitement about opportunities presenting themselves.

You Determine Your Own Success

Success is a choice! Nobody can succeed for you. It is your responsibility to become dedicated to do so. There are many tools, techniques, strategies and solutions that have worked for hundreds of financial advisors that I've coached over the past decade but only you can choose to take steps towards determining and defining your own success.

Why Considering Some Lasting Lessons Works

Take a moment to think about what lasting lessons you would like to begin incorporating into your practices now rather than waiting until you wrap up your professional days. Sometimes by thinking ahead, sometimes way ahead, you can climb out from under the clutter of the present and gain clarity on what your focus truly should be from now into the future.

Story #99
Groomed for Greatness

Have you ever wondered why some advisors build thriving businesses while others struggle to keep theirs afloat? For some advisors, their success is in part a bit of luck like being in the right place at the right time or taking over an existing book of clients handed to them by a relative or retiring colleague.

However, while coaching advisors for almost three decades I have gathered and identified some key qualities that all successful advisors possess. Follow their lead and you too can be groomed for greatness.

A Passion to Help People

I have asked countless top producers why they are in the financial services industry and their answers all revolve around helping people. For many, making sure that individuals have strong financial security for themselves and their families is an inspiration and motivation.

In addition, several top producers have also mentioned that providing for their own family while maintaining business integrity is a secondary motivator. However, I have never found a top producer to place himself or herself first at the expense of others.

A Willingness to Learn

Recently, I said to a financial advisor client of mine who has $200M of assets under management, *"You are good at selling, but you are not great at helping people understand why they should buy. I want to be great!"* she said, *"What do I need to learn?"*

Successful advisors never stop wanting to learn. Constantly evaluating your strengths and weaknesses is a good way to ensure you are consistently engaging in areas of growth.

The Humility to Find Help

Great athletes know that the right coach can take their game to the next level. Successful advisors have the humility to find help for the same reason. *"The value that you as my coach bring to the table is to help me to define my challenges even if I'm not sure what they are and to provide solutions that work for other successful advisors"* said a million dollar producer.

An Abundance Mentality

Successful advisors aren't intimidated or threatened by the so-called "competition". *"There are enough quality clients in this city for anyone to succeed if they want to"* said a top producer to a room full of "competitors" during an FPA statewide association meeting. It's this type of abundance mentality that creates greatness because there is no room for feeling like a victim.

The Ability to Bounce Back

Years ago I literally was bucked off a horse. Battered and bruised and with a black eye a famous quote came to mind, *"When you fall off a horse, you have to get right back on."* The reason is because if you don't get back on the proverbial horse the fear of getting bucked off again will overtake you and you will never "ride" again.

Successful advisors are very resilient and they learn from their mistakes. There are many key qualities that help characterize those who are successful, but find a few, like the ones above and focus your energies on fine-tuning them.

Why Groomed for Greatness Works

I believe that everyone has the ability to be great in this business. I also believe that there are some slight differences between those that are great or on their way to becoming great and those that are not and typically will never be. The main difference is to (consciously or unconsciously) embrace these qualities. If you find yourself on a production plateau, review the list of qualities to identify which areas you need to improve on. Then, find a colleague, mentor or coach to help you.

The reason why being Groomed for Greatness works so well is because it's the combination of these five qualities, that fuel advisors to reach the pinnacle of their success. And, those that truly want to get to the next level and beyond need to first apply these qualities.

Story #100
The Seriousness of Success

During a complimentary group coaching session with sixty financial advisors, I made a special announcement that for a limited time we would offer a very low monthly payment plan option on our upcoming group coaching series to anyone with five years or less in the business. I did this to try and help those in need who did not have the necessary funds for coaching.

The caveat to this deal was that we were only taking the first ten people who emailed me with their interest. Within minutes, we had more than ten people contact me. However, only one ended up actually signing up for our group coaching program.

My first thought was that the others didn't see our follow-up email with the registration link. After calling the entire list twice and speaking with many of the advisors I made the realization that the real reason they were not following through on their initial interest was that they were not serious about their own success and it had nothing to do with money after all.

The following are just of few examples of what I have found with my successful client advisors:

They Are Serious About Commitment

Successful advisors know that making a commitment to "own" their success is not a gray area—either you are committed to succeeding or you are not. This doesn't eliminate setbacks, but instead redefines them as opportunities to learn and move forward.

Steve K. was a rookie financial advisor with only four years of experience when he became a client. In our first individual coaching session, he explained that he was very serious about learning how to get to the next level and that he would do whatever it takes to succeed.

It was that level of commitment that catapulted his assets from only $12 Million under management at the end of year four-(when we started) to $25 Million under management at the end of year five!

They Are Serious About Character

Successful advisors know that doing the right thing for the client is much more important than earning a commission. They say what they mean and they stick to their word.

Kimberly G. was a twenty-year veteran financial advisor-client who did a portfolio review for a prospect and liked the investments. However, she didn't know how close the sale was since she didn't think the prospect should make any changes.

I explained that we need to "close with character"- in that she wants to manage the portfolio, but doesn't want to make changes at this time. Apparently, the prospect had not spoken to their advisor in years, felt neglected, and wanted an advisor with integrity. As a result, it was her character that got the sale!

They Are Serious About Consequences

Successful advisors know that they are responsible for their own success, not their firm, their clients, the market, or the economy. They realize that it is pointless to blame others.

Julie T., a thirty-five-year veteran financial advisor was given an ultimatum by her boss in November-either you get your production level up to the company's minimum requirements by the end of the year or you will most likely be asked to leave.

Instead of placing the blame on others, she got serious about her own success! As a result, she not only accomplished her goal by the end of the year, but continued her activities and a year later she had increased her production so much that she was asked to be one of only twenty-five women to be on their company's "Woman of Distinction" panel to help other women who needed to succeed!

They Are Serious About Collaboration

Successful advisors find others to help them build and maintain a thriving practice. They utilize their firm's resources and expertise. They oftentimes build teams with other like-minded advisors or hire junior advisors to delegate activities to that they themselves don't like to do.

James D. was a twenty-five-year veteran financial advisor-client who had built a successful business, but found himself on a production plateau. He had long given up on prospecting because he didn't enjoy it. I advised him that either he needed to prospect or find someone that will.

He asked me to speak with his thirty-year-old son who was interested in getting into the business. I quickly realized that his son would be a great fit and within a few short weeks of coaching him he was consistently setting appointments for his father!

They Are Serious About Control

Successful advisors know what is and is not in their control. They CAN control their attitude, activities, and actions. They don't worry about things that they cannot control such as their clients' attitudes, the market, and the overall economy.

Jason L. was a ten-year veteran financial advisor-client of mine who had applied the Advisor Solutions tools every day. He had been doing so for years and using those tools became a habit for him. When he explained that his mother-in-law was very sick and that their entire family was concerned I asked how that translated into his business-was there a lack of motivation. He said, *"Not at all. I control what I can control and don't try to control things that are out of my control."*

Why the Seriousness of Success Works

I'm not saying you can't have fun in your business, but I am saying that if you want to get to the next level with your practice it's time to get serious about your own success! The reason why the seriousness of success works is because ultimately if you are not serious about your own success then who is? Nobody else can or will do it for you.

All successful advisors know that their commitment, character, consequences, collaboration, and what they can control is a responsibility that falls directly on them. Those that do not understand this early on, rarely make it in the business. Those that forget this well into their careers tend to stay on a production plateau. However, those that never forget that their success is solely their own responsibility continue to reach new heights.

Story #101
Put Me In, Coach!

Being a financial advisor is a lot like being an athlete. If you have ever played on a team you can probably relate to the feeling of anticipation while waiting to play and all you wanted to say was, *"Put me in, coach!"* Once you got in the game it was up to you to make the most of the moment and shine.

One example of using this analogy is Amy R., a ten-year veteran advisor who wanted to succeed and she needed my help to do it. As her business coach, I helped her determine what her goals were and what actions it would take to work smarter rather than harder.

Next, we practiced by role playing so she could get back to actually prospecting. However, it didn't take long for her to realize that she was not applying what she had learned because her fears where getting in her way and thus, she would rather sit on the sidelines than risk losing the game.

If you've ever felt this way or are feeling this way now, don't worry because most advisors/agents have or have had the same feeling. It's more common than not!

Let's look at all of the ways of thinking and taking action that I utilized with Amy to help her to create her amazing comeback and want to win.

Be "All-In"

What Amy was experiencing is very common for veteran and rookies advisors alike. It's easy to want to win, but it's not always easy to risk the possibility of defeat. Many advisors choose not to even try. In other words, it's like asking the coach to put you into the game, but choosing not to be "all-in", playing the best you could once you were in because you don't want to make a mistake and contribute to a loss!

The first way to create a comeback with Amy was to get her to commit to taking action and dedicate to being "all-in" when it came to her own success. So, I had her make a list of reasons why she wanted to get to the next level and what would happen in one, three, five and even ten years from now if she continued not prospecting. After realizing the pleasure she would have by being a top producer and the pain that she could have by being a low level one, she committed to getting back to prospecting!

Think on Your Feet

All athletes know that sometimes plays don't go as planned. You may practice the play over-and-over again, but on game day anything can happen. So too is practicing for an appointment and realizing the conversation isn't going in the direction that you want it to. That's why you must be able to think fast on your feet.

Amy realized that setting appointments with new prospects was getting easier, but from time-to-time she was getting caught off guard with specific objections.

I assured her that this is natural and all we needed to do was to increase the tools, techniques, strategies and solutions to handle any objection that came her way. It's not about memorizing what to say, but understanding the formula of how to say it. Once we did this, she could easily adapt to any conversation path!

Assess Your Actions & Results

All great coaches know that the best way to take their players to a higher level is to help them assess their actions and results. That's why most teams watch game films, so they can duplicate their successes and learns from their errors.

Within weeks, Amy was excited to tell me that her pipeline was full! She had eight appointments set for the week and had already turned a few prospects into clients since our last session!

Why Wanting to Win Works

Let's face it, you really only have two choices while playing in a game, setting an appointment or closing a prospect, you either want to win or you don't!

The reason wanting to win works so well is because it forces you to be completely honest with yourself. Now, most people would say the obvious answer would be *"Yes, I do want to win,"* but if you are truly honest with yourself you must also ask, *"Am I willing to do what it takes to win?"* When you commit to being "all-in", learn how to "think on your feet" as well as assess your actions and results you will soon find that winning is just a natural bi-product of playing the game so well.

Story #102
Winning the Inner Game of Business

Successful team athletes know that they face two opponents in every game; the other team and an inner opponent, the little voice in their head. Similarly, successful financial advisors know that most sales are won from the inside out, as growing a business is really about having a strong mental skill set to create and then maintain steady successes.

Joe, a financial advisor with fifteen years of experience is a current coaching client of mine. When he initially contacted me to discuss his challenges I quickly realized that this was a man whose inner opponent was clearly defeating him.

So I explained that the solution was to increase his mental skill set for winning his Inner Game of Business. Once he could master that, he would be back at the top of his game.

I was curious to know more about Joe and the evolution of his business to get a better idea of his situation so I asked him to share what happened during the first five year period of his career.

"In the first five years I was consistently having record years." he explained with a smile. *"As a result, I loved the business and had a positive attitude towards my future."*

He then paused as the smile disappeared from his face, *"But, from years six through ten my business plateaued and I later realized that it was because I was comfortable and thus complacent."*

Unfortunately, that resulted in a decrease in his business each year for the past several years until he found himself doubting whether or not he should continue on or move into another career field altogether.

I commented that typically when a professional athlete is in a mental slump they don't throw in the towel, but instead they may seek out a Sports Psychologist who would work with them on what's known as a performance pyramid, which has three levels to sharpen metal skill sets:

Increase Your Basic Mental Skill Sets

Sometimes the hardest thing for anyone to do to make a comeback is to accept that they need to get back to the basics. In other words, a professional football player doesn't want to be told how to hold a football properly.

Similarly, advisors in a slump don't want to be told to change their attitude towards prospecting. However, the first level of the performance pyramid is about rebuilding a strong mental foundation by focusing on essential mental skill sets such as having a positive attitude, finding motivation, setting goals, establishing accountability, making a commitment and increasing communication.

"Joe, what is the most important thing that you need to do everyday to turn your business around?" I asked hoping that he would state the obvious. *"I need to get back to the basics of using the goal setting and motivational tools that you have taught and using them every day in order to get my head back in the game."* he said.

So we clearly defined what successful outcomes would be and what each of these mental skill sets would look like and we went to work on putting a plan into action.

Increase Your Preparatory Skills

It didn't take long for Joe to start feeling better about himself. I decided we needed to go to the next level by sharpening his preparatory skills, which are the mental skill sets that athletes use immediately before they perform.

Examples of that would be a professional golfer taking practice swings or a professional basketball player taking easy shots at the basket. The two most important activities at this tier are Positive Self-Talk and Metal Imagery.

For a financial advisor that may include telling yourself you will get the sale and mentally picturing the prospect signing the paperwork to become a client.

In order for him to customize his preparatory skills I asked him, *"Joe, if you were going to shoot a free throw what would you do first?" "I would probably dribble the ball a couple of times, exhale and then shoot. Why do you ask?"* he cautiously replied. *"Because that's what we are going to do next- increase your preparatory skills so that each and every time you have a meeting with a prospect you are ready to take your best shot!"*

Joe quickly embraced the process but was admittedly amazed at how taking five minutes before a meeting with a prospect made him feel much more confident.

Increase Your Performance Skills

The third level of the performance pyramid focuses on what an athlete (or in Joe's case an advisor) does during the big game. Joe's "big game" happened when he had a second meeting with a million dollar referral.

To help him close I explained that there are three ways to increase performance skills: focus on managing anxiety, emotions and concentration.

For Joe to accomplish this, I knew he needed to not only prepare for the appointment, but to role play every step of it so that he was conditioned to successfully close.

Why Winning the Inner Game of Business Works

Joe went into the meeting with a new level of confidence. He was focused, calm and genuinely excited to help the prospect. He asked the right types of questions, made a great connection and effortlessly closed.

The reason why winning the Inner Game of business works well is because you are working your way up the performance pyramid to increase your mental, preparatory and performance skill sets to face your inner opponent head on, which will increase your confidence and chances of closing the sale.

So, the next time you step onto your business playing field, be sure to tap your inner game by preparing for it and sharpening your mental skill sets. That way you are on the road heading towards victory.

Story #103
Creating a Childlike Curiosity

We have all heard the saying, *"Curiosity killed the cat"*, that it is better to mind your own business. However as advisors/agents do we truly believe that that is the best course of action to make a connection?

I think it's safe to say that most of us think that we ask a lot of questions. Unfortunately, I've found that many of the questions that we ask are merely designed to uncover facts and not to truly understand the prospect or client's situation and how they feel about it.

Young children have a genuine and innate curiosity when they want to get to know someone and they seem to have no problem asking a multitude of questions. Let's take a look at how this type of curiosity can benefit you and your prospects/clients.

Gives You Time to Think

During one of my Group Coaching Critic sessions, in which we role play our group members as if they were on the phone with prospects, I noticed that one advisor used what I call a "curiosity question". It was, *"That's interesting could you tell me more about that?"*

This was in response to a prospect who gave him an objection about how he didn't like to use certain investment products and thus wasn't interested in setting up a meeting. After using his "curiosity question", his prospect relaxed, opened up and ended up telling us a story about his investment experience. This gave the advisor more time to think about what direction he wanted to turn the conversation towards.

Uncovers Important Information

The prospect revealed some interesting information about his concerns regarding a financial advisor he had worked with because years ago one advisor put him into a product that he perceived as expensive and he had lost him money when he was told that it was safe. As a result, he felt that he was misled and that consequently all advisors would mislead him. This helped my advisor client truly understand that his prospect's real objection was trust and not about a specific product at all.

Shows That You Care

After listening to the real objection about trust, the advisor acknowledged what he had heard by summarizing how it must have made the prospect feel by saying, *"That sounds frustrating, was it?"* The prospect quickly shared with him how frustrated he was and the advisor in turn showed he cared by being even more curious and asking, *"Why is that? Why do you think some advisors don't take the time to fully explain their recommendations?"*

Creates a Connection

By now the advisor was creating a connection because he was open to getting to know the prospect and the prospect was connecting because he felt that he was being heard.

After a lengthy conversation the advisor inquired, *"I'm kind of curious, if we met and I did give you a second opinion on the investments you own would you be open to speaking with a couple of my clients to hear what type of experience they have had working with me? It's free and maybe it would help you see that all advisors are not alike?"* It didn't take long for the prospect to reply, *"Yes, I would like that."*

Why Childlike Curiosity Works

It's no secret that people want to be heard. The reason that childlike curiosity works is because when you truly exude through your choice of words and tone that you care, prospects are more open to telling you a lot more about themselves. Everyone has a story, so get genuinely curious and find out what it is.

Story #104
The Reality of Creating a Record Setting Year

Do you believe that achieving a record production year in your business happens by chance or design? If you said design, you are right.

However, while most advisors start off a new year with big dreams few finish reaching them. The reality of creating a record setting year is more than just great intentions and luck; you need thorough and consistently used systems.

As a rookie financial advisor over thirty years ago, I struggled my first year. During my second year things were a bit better because I gathered three times the assets, but I was still in no position to stop eating ramen noodles. It wasn't until my third year that I made a commitment (and a plan) to creating my success.

As a result, I tripled my income from the previous year, then repeated the process the following year and was able to double my income following the exact same system. I'm telling you this not to impress you, but rather to impress upon you that you cannot leave success up to chance.

The following is a brief outline of how you too can plan for your success with a little upfront work:

Create an Unwavering Commitment

It was a simple statement to myself, *"I'm never going below $10,000 gross per month this year"* that led me down a path to changing my belief system that I could actually do it. I used this same strategy years later, but doubled the number and was able to hit a personal record high production month five out of the first six months of the year.

Why? Merely because I choose to believe that it WAS possible. Remember, the more you believe in your own potential the higher the probability that you will hit your goals.

Daily Discipline of Prospecting

Part of that unwavering commitment was to start every day prospecting. And, one of the best quotes I've ever seen on the subject of having daily discipline is what John C. Maxwell said, *"Motivation gets you going, but discipline keeps you growing."*

This may seem like a no-brainer, but it's not easy unless you do one important thing, learn to enjoy doing it. It might sound crazy, if you make a game out of how many dials, contacts and appointments you do while prospecting it can actually become a lot of fun.

A Systematic Way of Selling

Although hope is a good thing, it's not the best strategy for sales success. Instead, you need a systematic way of selling so that you can duplicate every step of the way, from the initial contact to closing the sale. In my third year, I also learned from a top producer Tom D. how to cross-sell to my client base.

When I asked Tom how he consistently grew his business he confidently said, *"I always look for ways to help my clients with additional products and services. So, each month I'm calling clients with a new idea."* This opened my eyes to how to gather additional assets and commissions, but more importantly to increasing my value to my client-base.

A Detailed Tracking System

Years ago, I read a quote by Peter Drucker, the "father" of modern management. This is a theory, based on research, that employees work for numerous reasons, such as achieving satisfaction, happiness, and desired lifestyles. Peter says, *"You can only manage what you can measure."* He is the author of 38 books translated into 30 languages.

To keep the momentum of activity and results going it was important for me to create a great tracking system that was simple enough to fill out during the day, but effective enough to keep a tally and tell me if I was going to achieve my monthly goals.

I created a **Daily Scorecard** (refer to the story **How To Keep Score Of Your Success** in chapter 2), that tracked my contacts, presentations, and orders asked for and gross commissions. Next, I created a sales pipeline of prospects and clients so I knew how many people and how much potential business was possible.

Finally, I tracked daily gross production and knew exactly if I was above or below my goals at any given time. When you make tracking a priority you get excited to achieve more.

A Strong Reward

At the end of my third year I was shocked at the amount of success I had achieved by greatly surpassing my goals. Looking back at it now, it's not about the numbers it's about all of the other things that are obtained when you surpass what you believe you are capable of, confidence, pride, increased self-esteem to name a few.

However, that's not to say that you shouldn't have a strong reward system. In fact, I went from eating ramen noodles the previous year to buying my first house. When you have a strong reward system you have an extra-added incentive to achieve your goals.

Why the Reality of Creating a Record Setting Year Works

By now you might be saying to yourself, *"You can't teach an old dog new tricks."* If so, just know that isn't reality. In fact, in my book **101 Advisor Solutions**: *A Financial Advisors Guide to Strategies that Educate, Motivate and Inspire* I tell a true story about my client Gale Z. who after 25 years was forced to realize that she was barely hitting the corporate minimum production standards at the end of a year.

We applied the strategies and by the end of the first quarter she was the top producer in her region. She exceeded her numbers by reaching 66% of the previous year's production goals.

The reason why the Reality of Creating a Record Setting Year works is because you do not leave anything up to chance. Instead, the brief outline gives you a process for a new level of success.

When you have an unwavering commitment to succeed, the daily discipline of prospecting, a systematic way of selling, a detailed tracking system and a strong reward you can't help, but create a record setting year. So, if you are tired of being stuck on a production plateau use the outline above and break your own personal production record.

Story #105
The Client's Evolution

It's no secret that advisors/agents want to have a client-base made up of loyal clients. However, most advisors/agents don't take the time to fully understand "why" some clients are "one-time customers" while others are "life-time advocates".

Let's take a brief look at what I call The Client's Evolution, an evolution that we all have with our clients to some degree, so that you can better comprehend how you can build client relationships that last a life time.

The Customer

Over thirty years ago, I began building my business by following some simple advice from my branch manager, *"Find a good double tax free municipal bond and tell everyone you can about it."* As an eager rookie I did just that and soon I was opening up new accounts with what I thought would be "forever" clients. Unfortunately, I soon realized that many of those clients were "one-time customers', people who had decided to buy a product.

They were trying to find the best yielding bonds and it didn't matter who they were buying it from. Some of those individuals bought additional bonds, but for the most part I was one of several advisors they were working with and my value was merely a function of how well my product was doing at the time.

If you have several customers working with you and you would like to forge stronger relationships with them, you must find a way to show your value to them. One of the best ways to do this is to stop being a product pusher and start being a problem solver by getting to know them. Once you do, you can find their needs and fill them.

The Client

As my practice grew, I decided to take a different approach and offer prospects a complete plan to help them achieve their financial goals.

I would bring up the subject by explaining, *"There are two types of advisors, the product pusher or the problem solver. Which one would you rather work with?"* Naturally, they would respond, *"The problem solver."* In which I would agree with them by saying, *"I completely agree! In fact, that's what I pride myself on-helping my clients solver their financial problems."*

This opened the door to creating solid connections from the start because I was able to identify specific needs that the prospect had and share with them how my products and services could be their solutions. I was no longer pushing any specific product but rather solving their financial concerns. As a result, these types of people became clients. If you have clients you would like to get to know even better, it's time to get to know them on a more personal level.

The Friend

After a number of years, I noticed that some of my clients had turned into close friends. Just as any friendship evolves with communication and respect so can an advisor/agent/client relationship. Ironically, I never started out to form friendships with my clients, but our friendships occurred naturally over time when I showed genuine interest in their lives.

They were no longer just clients to me, but friends that I wanted to help, not only with their financial goals, but in any way that I could. When this type of relationships was formed I would communicate how I felt by saying, *"We've worked together for a long time now and I wanted to share something that I've realized over the years; strangers become clients and clients become friends. I think of you as a friend."* Typically, I would get the same type of response from most clients by them telling me that they felt the same way-we are friends.

The Advocate

At some point in my career, I realized that a select group of clients whom I had formed friendships with had an interest in my success. I had developed a level of professional and personal trust with them and they were absolutely convinced that I not only was capable of helping with their financial advisory needs, but also that I truly had their best interests at heart.

As a result, I would get phone calls from clients saying, *"I'm thinking about refinancing my house do you know someone I should talk to?"* Or, *"I'm thinking about selling a property that I have do you have a real estate agent that you trust?"* In which case, I would reply, *"The person I would work with is _____ at the _____. Do you want me to make a call and introduce you?"*

That's when I realized that I had what I now called advocates or clients who willingly wanted to help me succeed by introducing me to their friends and family. In addition, some of these people shared their own experiences in business and suggested marketing, staffing and even branding strategies to help me with mine.

Why Client Evolution Works

I'm sure by now you might relate to having clients of every stage that I mentioned. The reason why The Client's Evolution works so well is because it increases your awareness of your relationship with clients at each stage of the evolution. In addition, it helps you to know how to move them along to the next stage. The secret to evolve your client-base is to evolve as an advisor yourself and become involved with your prospects and clients from the very start.

Story #106
Is There Passion In Your Practice?

Recently, a veteran financial advisor was asked a tough question by a colleague during one of our group coaching sessions, *"Why are you in this business anyway?"* The advisor had been discussing his lack of motivation and constant frustration with the industry.

His deflated attitude had become a common one and the rest of the group was weary of hearing it, hence, one brave peer decided to pose the question. Momentarily silenced, the veteran humbly admitted, *"I don't know."*

He hesitated, but then went on to explain what aspects of his practice that he didn't like; plus having just lost his assistant he stated he felt like that was the last straw. Does this scenario sound familiar? Have you ever felt this way? Many financial advisors feel overwhelmed at some point in their careers. When this happens, you need to put passion back into your practice.

Understanding Your Passion

The first step on the road to re-infusing the passion in your practice is to comprehend the reason you got into the business in the first place. You may have always had a passion for investing, or a desire to start your own business or maybe it was your own personal experiences towards money that drove you to wanting to work in financial services. As you seek the answer, you may also find that deep down you enjoy helping people.

Translating Your Passion

Once you make the realization of why you are working in this particular field, it is important to translate that passion into the feelings you have experienced while doing so. Let's use the example of "helping people."

Helping people accomplish their financial goals is rewarding, satisfying, and makes one feel accomplished. This process allows you to identify what emotions are most likely to motivate you. When times are difficult then you remind yourself that the reason you are in this business is to help people and the reason you love helping people is because it makes you feel "X".

Communicating Your Passion

It has been said, *"Communication is the lifeblood of every great relationship."* Healthy relationships with prospects and clients support ongoing and future connection. So, why is communicating your business passion(s) crucial? Once your prospects and clients know how you feel from getting to work with them it provides awareness that you genuinely enjoy what you do. That can only strengthen relationships.

One of the ways to communicate your passion is by using an attitude of gratitude, by taking a moment to offer your appreciation to the clients that give you their business. Then, watch what happens next. Clients will immediately feel more connected to you because you have opened up and explained the passion behind your practice.

The ripple effect of the conversation is that you are more likely to hear what they (your clients) are passionate about. This allows for a complete circle of communication. So be sure to ask yourself *"Is there passion in my practice"?* If the passion exists, be sure to keep the embers burning brightly. If the passion has waned, it is time to re-ignite it before your business burns itself out.

Why Putting Passion into Your Practice Works

As you may have guessed putting passion into your practice is better than not doing so. Why? It is because advisors/agents that know what motivates them and why, are more likely to succeed than those who don't. The reason why understanding, translating and communicating your passion works so well is because it gives you a system for staying motivated. Without it you may find yourself (like the advisor above did) feeling burned out.

Story #107
Watching Where You Step

Success or failure is a choice; albeit a conscious or unconscious one, but a choice nonetheless. The ironic thing about success and failure in your business is that you are constantly stepping towards one or the other, as change is constant.

Abraham Maslow, the renowned psychologist, echoed this belief when he said, *"You will either step forward into growth or you will step back into safety."*

Watching which direction you step is to choose each step wisely. Choosing to step forward towards pursuing your goals could bring with it the fear of the unknown. Choosing to step backward towards complacency could bring with it the comfort of familiarity. But, you must ask yourself this, is it better to boldly succeed or is it better to safely fail?

Understanding Your Daily Direction

Most advisors start each day without any thought of what direction their business is going in. Granted, some may have, what I refer to as, pro-active activities, which are scheduled such as prospecting appointments, but the majority of advisors/agents spend their day on re-active activities, which are those things that interrupt any scheduled ones, such as putting out client fires.

At the end of the day, many may feel like it was productive or unproductive based on their perception of the amount of pro-active or re-active tasks they have accomplished.

One example of this is an advisor who would be feeling accomplished because they opened a new account; thus, growing their business. On the other side, would be an agent who felt they were productive returning/taking calls, thus keeping clients satisfied.

The real question is which advisor/agent moved towards accomplishing their goals? Let's explore the answer below by looking at three choices and how it may pertain to you and your business.

Choice #1: Stepping Backwards

Stepping backwards in your business is a slippery slope that seems to be paved with good intentions. While "putting out fires" is important, your client-base will never consistently grow unless you incorporate daily prospecting. An advisor/agent who only works with their current client-base is in fact taking a step backwards by doing so because over time the client-base decreases due to client attrition. The solution is to schedule time to prospect daily, so you can fill up the pipeline and grow your business.

Choice #2: Staying Stationary

Staying stationary in your business is a misnomer because a business is either growing or shrinking. However, many advisors/agents who are on a production plateau feel comfortable because their business is not trending downward. That is until they experience a bad market and quickly realize that their assets under management are spiraling south. It is oftentimes at this crossroad where any unhappy clients leave as well.

Again, the solution here is to prospect daily. The reason why growing a client-base is more important than just the returns on investment growth is because the more qualified clients you have the less dependency you have on any one client.

Choice #3: Stepping Forward

Stepping forward with your business takes dedication and discipline to integrate the activities that are needed to grow in addition to maintaining and servicing your existing client-base. It's done by ensuring structure to the day and having a method to prioritize and/or delegate interruptions. In also requires that you work smarter by getting more effective at everything you do and not just by working harder by doing more of what you have been doing. Look for areas of your business that you believe need improvement and find ways to make those areas stronger.

Why Watching Where You Step Works

Before we explored these three choices, I asked you the question regarding, which advisor/agent took a step forward towards accomplishing their goals? The answer is…neither, because each advisor/agent focused on only one aspect of the business. To find your path to success you need to create a balance between all facets of running a business by evaluating and implementing best practices.

Story #108
The Advisor's Guide to Perseverance

Advisors come to me for coaching as they find themselves working harder and harder focusing on what they want their outcomes to be only to find that at some point they inevitably are not living up to their own expectations. When this happens, they are feeling frustration and disappointment and end up exhibiting anxiety. Successful advisors know that they must dedicate themselves to working smarter by figuring out what is working for them and leading them down the path to greater success and what activities are time wasters and are better off retired. The mantra needs to be "never give up on reaching your goals, just find innovative ways to persevere."

William Feather said, *"Success seems to be largely a matter of hanging on after others have let go."* To keep "hanging on" you must have defined your purpose, be continuously evaluating your activities and let your progress guide you to your destination.

Let's take a deeper look at some best practices for working smarter and how they have helped one advisor:

Know Your Purpose

If you want to see any great endeavor through to completion you have to find a great reason to keep going and the best reason of all is knowing your purpose. The most important thing to do initially is to define "why" you want to accomplish your goals not necessarily "how" as that is secondary.

Todd D., a fifteen-year veteran financial advisor was frustrated at being on a production plateau when I first started coaching him. He asked me how he could work smarter and not just harder. Before getting into the details of what to do, I first needed to know his "why". He confided that his mission was to help as many people as he could to be setup for experiencing a comfortable retirement.

Evaluate Your Activities and Actions

Once you landed on your purpose it's important to understand what's working (or not). In other words, you must evaluate your activities and action steps to analyze if what you are doing is leading you in the right direction.

In Todd's case, it didn't take long to determine that he was working hard because he was using the wrong tools. Look at it this way, if your goal is to chop down a tree and you use a baseball bat it's going to take you a long time (if at all). All Todd needed to do was understand what prospecting tools were best for him, learn how to use them and establish a systematic way to evaluate the results. Over time, we did just that and he started to move people into and through the pipeline.

Let Your Progress Guide You

When you know your purpose and you sharpen your skill sets you will no doubt increase the likelihood of successful outcomes. If you are struggling, it is so important to remember that *"Nothing succeeds like success"* and to continue moving forward by using your recent milestones as stepping stones to reach new levels.

Todd saw the fruits of his labors and was excited because he was helping more people and with much less effort than he had ever done before. In addition, he was no longer frustrated because he was off the production plateau that had prompted him to want to be coached. As a result, I explained that if he wanted to keep helping more people he had to regularly reinforce his purpose and fine tune his skill sets.

Why The Advisor's Guide to Perseverance Works

The reason why this way of thinking works is because you have a tangible process for motivating persistence. In tough times when you feel like giving up it is important to have a proven technique for creating tenacity.

Story #109
It Is All About Perception

Years ago a rookie financial advisor (me) new to the area asked a veteran colleague and friend, *"What is the wealthiest street address in the city of Milwaukee? Well, that's easy. It is Lake Shore Drive because that is where all of the money and mansions are. However, I would not prospect them. They all already have an advisor,"* stated his peer.

Many weeks later, the veteran stopped the rookie as he rushed by him on the way out the door. "Where are you going in such a hurry?" the veteran asked. "I'm going to see my client at his home on Lake Shore Drive" I replied.

T.S. Eliot said, *"Only those who will risk going too far can possibly find out how far one can go."*

Risk has many definitions. To my co-worker it implied taking time to prospect an affluent niche that he believed would most certainly reject him. To me, the rookie, the risk was in not attempting to prospect them, since no attempt at all would absolutely result in failure.

My point today is that the reality of business risk is really about how our perceptions dictate what we believe is possible. The lesson learned should be, don't limit yourself.

The following is a brief outline of how you can live beyond any business limitations you might have set up for yourself.

Identify Your Business Risk

It was a simple thought, *"I'm not going to get rejected by people who don't have money,"* that led me down a path of forming my belief system around who I was going to prospect. In other words, I didn't care about rejection; I cared about wasting time with unqualified prospects.

Unfortunately, it took some time to realize that although I was closing these new wealthy clients, they were only willing to invest a small portion of their assets with me; thus, my updated business risk was in not being confident enough to put together comprehensive financial plans, but merely pushing a product.

Model the Masters

Once you've identified any challenge, it is important to look for the solutions. In this case, my solution came in the form of a conversation with my then branch manager who said, *"You've got 500 accounts. You don't need 500 more with the same average asset per account, what you need is a minimum account size. I recommend from this day forward that you never take an account under $100K."*

He was a former top producer turned branch manager and to me he walked on water. So, it didn't take long before I picked up the phone and cold called business owners inserting the phrase into my introduction, *"I tend to work with business owners who have $100K or more in investable assets."*

Create a New Reality

Change can be a scary thing until you realize that not changing will cause you more risk. Take for instance what happened just thirty minutes after I started using the phrase mentioned above. The thirty-year veteran business owner that I was speaking to replied, *"I know what you mean, I don't have time for small accounts either."*

And, just like that everything changed for me! I was no longer afraid to position myself as an advisor with a minimum account size. In fact, I embraced and was proud of it.

Become the Mentor

Now, as a business consultant/coach I've had the pleasure to help others break though the realities of their own business risk. Take Sandra P. a thirty-year veteran client of mine who agreed to set her account minimums at $500K, then at $1M and later at $3M. It wasn't until she gathered $10M of new assets in one month that she realized how limited her thinking had previously been.

Why Acknowledging Your Perception Works

The reason why acknowledging your perception works is because it helps you to become aware of what those business risks are, then by modeling your mentors it supports a paradigm shift of what is truly possible. Then becoming a mentor yourself brings another level of satisfaction knowing that you helped someone else who had the same limiting belief that you once had. So, the next time you are faced with a challenge ask yourself how changing your perception of it could in fact be the first step towards the solution.

Story #110
To Give is To Get

The saying "To Give is to Get" should be attributable to many aspects of one's life and it rings true no matter what industry you work in. Giving of your time, energy, integrity, empathy, expertise and advice are just a handful of ways in which we also receive.

Martin Luther King, Jr. said, *"Life's most urgent question is, what are you doing for others?"* So ask yourself, am I giving enough? Am I giving my all to prospects and clients and truly ensuring I'm making a difference in their lives? Or, am I coasting through my days, weeks, months and even years doing just enough to get by?

One way to determine your answer is to consider what you are getting from your business. Are you satisfied with the type of business you have? At the end of a day do you feel like you have gone above and beyond to assist your prospects and clients? If you are not getting enough from your business and you cannot answer "yes" then it is time to evaluate and find a way to give more to your business and to those you can affect each day.

Let's take a look at ways advisors/agents can offer value to client and prospects, in a manner you might not have previously thought about.

Give of Your Time

Time is a precious commodity and the best way to give of your time is be in control of it by creating structure to your activities and ensure you have tools to manage interruptions. If you don't incorporate these items you will end up being reactive every day rather than productive.

Chuck R., a financial advisory client of mine who after only five years felt burned out because he was constantly putting out fires. After learning about two of my time management coaching tools, the **Bottom Line List** (refer to the story **Bottom Line List** in chapter 2), which is a framework for building structure and the **Time Matrix**

To-Do List, which allows you to prioritize tasks and handle interruptions, he was able to double the business he did in only one year and then doubled it again the following year. By being responsible with his time, an outcome was that it gave him more time each day for communication and outreach with his clients. A win, win.

Give of Your Energy

Energy can be a hard thing to offer up sometimes. There is much research that has found that if you can keep the energy flowing, you will experience greater satisfaction in your endeavors. Sandra P., a veteran financial advisor client of mine decided years ago to open her own charity to help under privileged girls in Africa.

Each year she puts on an auction called "The Power of the Purse," which auctions off purses that are owned by celebrities with last year's event raising $40,000! By finding energy to volunteer, assist in your community, mentor a student or a new colleague or by donating your energy for a worthwhile cause, you will feel fulfilled.

Give of Your Integrity

Integrity is a must as a character trait, but even more so when you are entrusted with someone else's money/finances. Telling the truth even when it lends itself to a challenging conversation, explaining every detail, benefit and risk of a product or recommendation and educating prospects/clients are all key foundational facets for our industry.

Tom C. a coaching client never wanted to mix friendship with business so he had never offered his friends or even his acquaintances an opinion on their investments. That is, until we discussed why! As a result, Tom has now done countless reviews for those he knows for free and has shared his insight that their portfolios were spot on for them. Conversely, he made the realization that several of his friend's plans were taking way too much risk. His expertise has value and yet giving of that expertise for those he cares about regarding their financial health is a "give" that has a return that cannot be measured.

Why Giving Works

It may go without saying on why giving works but it really comes down to this, it's because it offers our lives purpose and it feels good. Whether it is giving of your time, energy or integrity you are doing it out of the goodness of your heart. And, that is priceless. Conversely, if you are sensing that something is missing in your life, look for ways to give to others, you may be surprised at what you get in return.

Story #111
Learning From the Lessons of Failure

Let's face it, we all fail from time to time. In fact, if you didn't fail it would most likely be because you were not even trying. The problem is that most advisors/agents tend to view failure negatively. And, here in lies the paradox, trying and failing can create an avoidance atmosphere, which lends itself to failure because the very items that were necessary to result in some form of success, were never attempted. Does this cycle sound familiar?

Let's view this topic from a different perspective: Every failure is a lesson to learn from.

Malcolm Forbes said, *"Failure is success if we learn from it."* If we could take away from each of our failures some wisdom we would likely be more effective in the future. It would also mean that the act of trying, failing, learning and not repeating the same action would itself be a win.

As I coach advisors/agents each week, I'm looking for the lessons to be learned from the failures that they have experienced. Then, I help them articulate and identify those lessons. You can learn a lot from your failures if you are open to doing so.

The following lessons are a handful of the more common ones that I see.

Lesson 1: Learning From Experience

Failure can teach you what not to do next time. Experience can be a great teacher, but you must be willing to be a great student. You have to choose not to repeat things that caused you previous failure. If you don't, you in fact did not learn your lessons.

One example is the common challenge of overcoming objections. I was a financial advisor for thirteen years and it took me over a decade before I realized that hearing objections such as, *"I'm busy.*

Or "I handle my own investing." Or, *"I already have an advisor"* were merely objections that I could overcome.

Initially when I came up against those objections, I had thanked them for their time and hung up the phone. In other words, for many years I didn't learn from my experiences. That is until the day that I was in a training seminar.

Lesson 2: Learning Information

Failure can help you gain insights that you would have never known otherwise.

During a training seminar I attended, the instructor explained two ways to overcome a core objection (the real objection). The methodologies were the **Objection Resolution Model** (refer to the story **Beyond the Gatekeeper** in chapter 2) and the **Feel, Felt, Found** techniques. Once I honed these techniques, I actually applied them and realized that although they weren't fool proof they did work much better than not doing them at all and as a result this built resilience for me.

Lesson 3: Learning Resilience

Failure can build resilience as long as you don't quit. You must make course corrections along the way and continuously keep at it.

Over the course of a few months of using these tools, I noticed that sometimes I could not overcome an objection. I realized that it was typically when the prospect was not fully being transparent with their core objection. I gave this scenario a name referring to them as a "screen". Instead of giving up, I created my own process called **The Smoke Screen Technique** to unearth a core objection so I could then overcome it.

Lesson 4: Learning to Succeed

Failure inevitably leads to success if you learn from any failures and keep reaching for your goals.

My success at overcoming objections didn't happen overnight, but with patience, practice and persistence it became second nature. When I teach my clients to do the same their success increases. In fact, one client makes a game out of seeing how many objections he can get and overcome in a day.

Why Learning From Failure Works

The lessons above are just a few of the possible things that you can take away from adversity with every obstacle an opportunity for growth. The reason why learning from failure works is because when you learn from failing it actually changes your perception of failure; the learning what not to do next time is in fact a win. In other words, failure is never truly failing if you learned a less from it, be it something you do not want to repeat or a new behavior pattern you want to enforce.

Story #112
The Picasso Factor

As a business coach, I am constantly looking for ways to assist my clients as they map out their goals. While doing some research on what motivates people, I stumbled across an interesting story about knowing your own value. I've coined the phrase, "The Picasso Factor" and use it as part of my coaching curriculum.

Here is the story:

Many years ago, a woman was sitting in a restaurant having dinner when she noticed a man sitting at a neighboring table. She quickly realized that he resembled one of her favorite artists, Pablo Picasso. Apparently, he was drawing on a cocktail napkin and after he finished she approached him, introduced herself and asked if she could have the drawing.

He politely said "no," but offered to let her buy it for $20,000. She said, *"But I watched you draw this and it only took a few minutes."* He paused studying his work, and in calm voice said, *"What you haven't seen is that it took me a lifetime to be able to draw like that, that quickly."*

This story clearly illustrates that Picasso understood his own value and he wasn't willing to compromise the price of his work just because it took a few minutes to create it.

The Picasso Factor is about knowing your own value by recognizing all of the time it took you to become an expert in your chosen field. In addition, it is also about the growing body of knowledge that you have acquired along the way.

Understanding Your Picasso Factor

After reading the story, I pondered over the 25,000+ hours of coaching sessions I have acquired over almost the past two decade and previous to that when I had been a financial advisor. It is helpful to think about the following things as you fully comprehend what makes you unique and valuable:

Take Stock of Your Experience

Oftentimes, it can be easy to overlook how far we have come when all we are doing is thinking about how far we have yet to go. Does this sound familiar? If so, take a minute and reflect on the time and energy that it took you to get to where you are in your career. Nobody did it for you. It was you who decided take this journey and it was you who has continued every step of the way.

Take Stock of Your Knowledge

Maybe you don't have years of experience under your belt, but I'm sure you weren't just handed everything on a silver platter. No, you had to acquire knowledge in your chosen field.

Did you need an industry specific license? Did you need an advanced degree? No matter how long you have been in your career, your clients and customers are paying you for your knowledge. And, if you are still taking the time to continue to learn, then you are continuing to increase your value.

Take Stock of Your Character

One of the most important things that you do not want to overlook when determining your value is your character. Sure, there are probably plenty of people in your line of work that have knowledge and expertise, but if you were to ask those who do business with you why they do so, they would probably say that they trust you. Your character is something that defines who you are and a person with more integrity and honesty will outshine the competition.

Why Knowing Your Value Works

It's been said, *"Price is what you pay, but value is what you get."* These words are very true and when you realize your value, you shouldn't compromise on your price.

One of the reasons why knowing your value benefits you, is because you now understand that you don't have to work with everyone if they don't recognize or respect your value.

In fact, you can be selective with what type of clients and customers you want to work with. It is my hope that after reading this brief article you see your own value from a different perspective and realize that you are your own masterpiece.

Story #113
Beyond "Yeah But..." and "What If..."

For years, we have been inundated with Nike ads that tell us to, ***"Just do it!"*** Their hope is that we put our hesitations and excuses aside and get out there and exercise while buying their shoes so that we can...just do it. While Nike's motives are obviously like any business, to increase sales, you can't deny that if you want to get into better shape you have to take action.

Your business building activities are no different. For you to reach the next level in the financial services industry as an advisor, you need to ***"Just do it"***-whether that means cold calling, creating seminars, asking for referrals and/or whatever other tasks that will help you get out there and accomplish your business goals.

Now, you might be thinking to yourself that this motto of ***"Just do it"*** is fine as a line for a commercial to sell shoes or for a business coach to use to motivate financial advisors, but this statement just does not work for me. Why?

The Struggle Between Persistence and Procrastination

The reason why many financial advisors have a natural hesitation to take action is because often times it is easier not to do something our excuses masking the real and rational explanations of why we are not taking action. This is done almost unconsciously by tossing out the "yeah but..." or the "what if..." whenever we are faced with a decision about having to take action.

For example, take Jenny-a 29-year veteran financial advisor. During a 1-on-1 coaching session she admitted to me that she was not doing the activities that she had committed to doing just a week before. In fact, she went on to say that when she was filling out her pre-session questions (questions designed for my clients to identify specific challenges for that week that they wanted coaching on) she stumbled across a pre-session questionnaire that she had filled out three months ago.

Much to her surprise, she had not taken action that week either. While this did not happen every week, she was realizing that this was a cyclical pattern and she wanted a way to get past her tendency towards inactivity and go beyond the "yeah but…" and "what if…" statements that she commonly leaned on as a crutch. To break this behavioral pattern, I knew that she needed a way to question the validity of her excuses.

Realizing What Excuses Really Are

Excuses are often used as an instinctual defense mechanism. An excuse is oftentimes a way for us to avoid some type of pain. One example of this would be a financial advisor who is thinking about prospecting,

Coach: *"You need to prospect to grow your business!"*

Advisor: *"Yeah, but I don't have time to prospect in a volatile market because I need to talk to my clients more often. I can't neglect my client base!"*

So, what is the real pain that this financial advisor is avoiding? Maybe it is the perceived pain that he/she will lose their client base or maybe it is the perceived pain of getting rejected while prospecting. The point is that they are avoiding some type of perceived pain and as a result, they will continue not to prospect.

After Jenny and I discussed some of her perceived pains, she realized that to get past her procrastination and for her to take action she needed a strategy to help her get past her own perception of what was and was not painful to her. So, what does it take for you to take action?

Pushing Past the Pain to Make Lasting Change

The following are some things to consider that can help you understand why you may be using "Yeah But…" and "What If…"?

Get Real with Yourself

If you absolutely know that you need to do something, but are not doing it then take a minute to get real with yourself-admit that you are avoiding taking action. Identifying the pattern is the beginning of understanding and breaking it. I hear financial advisors say *"I know what I need to do. I just need to do it!"* but ultimately (and unfortunately) "it" just never gets done.

Call Yourself Out

At this point, you need to be completely honest with yourself by calling yourself out-ask yourself a simple, but difficult question to determine if procrastination is helping or hurting you, *"Is avoiding this activity moving my business forward or backward?"* If you are completely honest with yourself you already know the answer.

Get Leverage on Yourself

The simplest and most powerful inquiry you can ask yourself at this point is... *"Why?"* By asking this question, you are required to search for the answer to why you are hurting yourself and/or business; thereby increasing the perceived pain of the procrastination.

Find Your Target

Getting crystal clear on what needs to happen is vitally important for taking action. In other words, you can't hit a target you can't see; thus you need to map out the list of activities that you need to do. Your mind will start focusing on all the steps to accomplishing this goal/outcome. This is where you will either get caught up in your anxiety loop (the "Yeah But" or "What If") or you break it.

Prove Yourself Right

Proving yourself right means knowing what you need to do...and doing it. Success is subjective; some people feel that success is only achieved if your goals are accomplished, while others feel that taking action (in-and-of-itself) is success! Regardless of what you believe one thing is absolutely true, there can be no success without first taking action.

So, what happened to Jenny? She realized that the pain of procrastinating was going to cause her much more pain in the long run both financially and emotionally than actually taking action and completing tasks. She also clearly and quickly identified what things she needed to do and did them.

Why Beyond "Yeah But…" and "What If…" Works

Now that you understand why you use excuses to rationalize your lack of action and the real long-term pain of this process, you must also understand that excuses have never and will never help you succeed.

The reason why getting beyond "Yeah But…" and "What If…" works well is because it's a stepwise approach for eliminating procrastination. When you follow these steps you are in fact changing your mindset, focus and direction. You are now moving forward towards accomplishing your goals instead of staying stagnant.

Story #114
Maintaining the Momentum

Success-we all strive to obtain it, but how many times have we maintained the momentum that got us there? And, should we expect to keep that momentum up indefinitely?

Let's take a look at Linda P. who became a client of mine late last summer. She was struggling with her business in all facets. She needed guidance to help get her back on track, someone to hold her accountable and a plan to evaluate her progress. I worked with Linda as a group coaching client on a weekly basis to assist her in putting some of my tools and techniques to use.

Over several months she began to see a steady rise in her production, she gained traction with her motivation and felt her confidence level rising. In only a few short months, Linda had achieved the goals she had set earlier in the year that she was concerned about hitting.

As the first 6 months of this year passed, Linda was up 120% year to date for her numbers, had been designated as a top producer by her firm and was reveling in such a successful year. The resources I had given her 10 months ago that she never thought she could implement were now ingrained in her everyday activities.

The Moment You Realize You Have Run Out of Momentum

Last month, Linda and I met for our first of two bi-monthly 1-on-1 coaching sessions and I could tell that she was not herself. I probed a bit and she shared with me that she was feeling burnt out.

The success she had accomplished was fantastic, but what had been working for her over the past months no longer seemed to have their punch. During the previous two weeks, she had not been hitting her numbers, she was avoiding making calls and she felt that she had hit the proverbial wall.

I asked Linda if she would ever consider taking a two-week vacation. She responded with *"absolutely not, there is too much to do and I am behind already."* I inquired what her pipeline looked like and surprisingly she answered, *"Well, actually I have quite a lot going on, I've just been procrastinating."*

Then, I had her tally up the pipeline to discuss the potential business that she could close this month. She was even more surprised to realize that it could become her second best month ever.

I replied *"Terrific...so you know what I think is going on with you?"*

There was a pause as she quietly said *"No, what are you thinking."* I said *"You needed to take a break, but you were not listening to your mind/body, so your subconscious decided to take a vacation for you. During the past two weeks you feel like you lost your momentum and spent your energy trying to look busy and feeling guilty that less was getting accomplished. But, in reality you subconsciously told yourself you needed a break. It is like riding a bike, sometimes if you are pedaling fast, you get tired and you have to coast to give yourself time to regroup, then when you are ready, you can pedal fast again."*

There was an exhale from her as if a burden had just been lifted from her shoulders. *"Wow, Dan that makes perfect sense...I think I'm ready to start pedaling again!!"* Two weeks later, when Linda and I met for a coaching session, the first thing she shared with me was *"I'm back...I hung up with you and realized that I had just needed to get back on the bike and sure enough as soon as I did, it was like I picked up where I left off before my "vacation."*

Scheduling Strategic Breaks Into Your Business

Taking a vacation from doing a high level of day-to-day activities is a great way to recharge. We naturally take a break when our body tells us enough-is-enough and that it is time to sleep. So why not give yourself permission to take a scheduled break from your business?

Some may say that this is a recipe for disaster-advocating a decrease in activities, which results in a decrease, is success.

However, if you have scheduled your business break, determined the time horizon of how long you will take that break (be it a one week vacation or a fifteen-minute "vacation" from making the next call) and what you will do once you get back to the business then really it is truly a recipe for success because you will be energized and ready to maintain your momentum!

Unlike unconsciously sabotaging success (for fear of not feeling worthy of being successful) by decreasing activities once you have reached the level of success that you desire-taking a scheduled break from the business is a conscious action and one where you are fully aware of what you will do once you do go back to work. The following is an example of the difference:

Conscious Business Breaks vs. Unconsciously Sabotaging Success

Having a "fear of success" would be hitting your monthly goals half way through the month and then discontinuing the daily activities that got you there; only to then find you fell way short of your goals the following month versus hitting your goals half way through the month.

Knowing that accomplishing your goals early would result in a scheduled four-day weekend as a reward, is the recipe to rest and recharge. The former is an unconscious reaction to the "fear of success" and the latter is the conscious decision to reward yourself for a job well done.

Understanding and applying the latter is the psychology behind maintaining momentum and ultimately sustaining success

Why Maintaining the Momentum Works

The difference between having a fear of success and maintaining momentum comes down to having an unconscious reaction versus making a conscious decision. The reason why maintaining the momentum works well is because you are consciously deciding to rest and recharge when you have accomplished your goals so that when you start up again you are ready to accomplish your next goal.

This is how some successful advisors are able to have four-day work weeks and still have record years!

So, the next time you find yourself feeling the fear of hitting a record month stop yourself and instead map out your "maintaining the momentum" strategy, then accomplish your goals and reward yourself for a job well done. When you do this, your fear of success will dissipate.

CHAPTER 5
Putting the Last Puzzle Piece into Place
Summary

At the beginning of this book I had said that living the life of an advisor is not an easy one. And, that is why I decided to write this book-to make your life just a little bit easier, if I could. By now I'm sure that you understand how important it is to have the right tools, techniques and transformational moments. Without them you most certainly will be stuck in mediocrity making a living, but not really enjoying the best life you can, **The Advisor Life.**

As you may know, since 2006 I have created numerous group coaching courses and facilitated more groups than I can count. Literally, thousands of people with titles such as financial advisor, insurance agent, wholesaler, portfolio manager, branch manager and agency manager have also held the title of… being my client.

What you don't know, is that although the group coaching courses, course content, client titles and people have changed over the years, one thing has remained the same for every group in every group coaching session, which is the question I ask each-and-every one of them before they go, *"What's your single take away?"*

It never ceases to amaze me, that the responses are too numerous to remember. However, each response only really fits into two categories. First, some clients say that getting a more in-depth look at the course material gives them insights that they never would have gotten had they simply tried to figure it out on their own.

Second, other clients say that it wasn't the course material so much as it was the ancillary learning that they received from one specific group member who had shared their story of having had the same challenge we were discussing in the group coaching session that day, but who had already learned the solution and applied the tool or technique to get a transformational moment.

No matter what each person's "single take away" is one thing is for sure, that in that moment they are most likely putting the last puzzle piece into place regarding that topic. In other words, when they began the group coaching session something was not working regarding the topic at hand. However, somewhere during the group coaching session they had an epiphany that helped to define the challenge as well as the solution.

As we are now approaching the end of our journey together in this book, I'd like to ask you the same question as well, *"What's your single take away?"* Unfortunately, time and distance is most likely between us and I may never know your answer to that question. But, I'd like to summarize what I hope you have gleamed from this book or at least add an additional nugget of wisdom should we never meet.

I have mentioned numerous times that your business is like a puzzle. And, each day that you are working "IN" your business and not working "ON" your business is like having one half-done puzzle taking up space on your table. That is why it is so important to spend time daily identifying your unique challenges so that you can find the solutions and your business (puzzle) can be complete.

Tools are like the corner pieces of the puzzle, which create the architecture for taking your business to the next level. **The Tools Section** has given you plenty of insight into what tools work for your peers. To find the right tool for you, identify a current challenge, the desired solution and then go back through the Tools Section to find the appropriate tool.

Also, it is important to note that tools are only as good as the person who is using them. In-and-of-themselves they will do nothing to help you unless you put them into daily practice and eventually using them becomes a habit.

Techniques are like the non-corner pieces of the puzzle or in this case the heart of the business that makes up the details of what to do and how to do it. As you have noticed, each technique was made up of a step-by-step process that will help you to make effortless connections with prospects and clients alike.

The Techniques Section has given you plenty of insight into not only what a successful business could look like, but also about developing not only business skillsets, but personal skillsets as well. Like Tools, Techniques in-and-of-themselves will do nothing to help you unless you also put them into daily practice and eventually apply them enough becomes a habit!

Transformational Moments are moments that transform your business. Remember, the more you apply the Tools and Techniques to become habits the more you will have Transformational Moments. Once you do this you will find that **Transformational Moments** are commonplace.

Unlike the previous picture of your business before applying **Tools** and **Techniques**, which may have seemed like a chaotic mess (much like a pile of puzzle pieces sitting on your table) you soon realize that your business has taken shape and it's starting to look like your business vision (aka a completed puzzle). **The Transformational Moments Section** has given you plenty of insight into what a successful business could look like when this happens. When you do this you will find that success becomes a habit.

In addition, this book was to be read over time. Hopefully, you had taken your time to digest each tool, then each technique and lastly each transformational moment. And, since you have made it this far I suggest that you take the next step that I had mentioned at the beginning of the book, which is to use this book as a reference guide.

Hopefully, you took my suggestion of grabbing a highlighter, magic marker or red pen and circled what stood out to you. Then, you started to apply what you learned. Now it's time to go back and re-read what you had highlighted and apply what you haven't yet, but know you need to. As I've said before, I've seen too many people get information, but then don't want to do what it takes to make lasting transformation. You don't want to be that person.

Also, this book was intended to take you into the lives of ordinary people who have done extraordinary things by turning obstacles into opportunities to build a better business…one solution at a time.

The final step is for you to reach out to me at **Advisor Solutions** so I can help you put the pieces of your business puzzle together so you too can live **The Advisor Life!**

Afterword
Leaving The Advisor's Legacy

At the beginning of this book, I shared my story of how nearly seamlessly I went from an unemployed twenty-six-year old looking for a job to finding my career, my own advisor's journey. I shared my humble beginnings of feeling lost and alone looking for direction while focusing more on surviving than ever considering the possibility of thriving.

And, somewhere along my journey thirty years slipped by.

As we come to end of this book, you might believe that our journey together is over. However, you would be quite wrong. In fact, the journey continues. That is, if you want it to.

I mentioned in the introduction of this book that I have found that most people read a book in one of two ways: either cover to cover or as a reference guide, seeking out specific topics found in the table of contents and going to the appropriate pages and reading only those passages. This book was/is designed to help you do both.

I recommended that you first read it cover to cover. Take your time…digest each tool, then each technique and lastly each transformational moment. The reason is because this is not meant to be devoured in one sitting. Rather, read ten stories or so and absorb the concepts before you move on to your next helping. Hopefully, you did just that.

I also recommended that as you read, ask yourself this question—*"Is this something that I have gone through, am going through or could possibly go through?"* Finally, I mentioned that I'm a big believer in you getting the most out of this book by grabbing a highlighter, magic marker or red pen and make notes about what stands out most to you. Then take your newfound knowledge and apply it. Hopefully, you will do that too!

I'm a former financial advisor and current business coach who can understand what you are going through because I've experienced the same challenges. So, as you read this book did you take my advice? Is your book full of dog-eared pages, circled solutions with notes in the margin to remind yourself to just go do it, whatever solution "it" is?

In addition, it was never my intent to just give you information. Instead, it was my intent to give you the tools and techniques to create real transformation in your business.

In the following section **About Advisor Solutions** you will be introduced to the next step in our journey together. It is your choice whether to take that step or not. In that section, I have briefly described several of the coaching programs that we offer: *one-on-one coaching* and *group coaching*.

Throughout this book, I mentioned a number of my clients—financial advisors who were once just like you looking for solutions. As you know, they did in fact experience success by applying the tools and techniques to get "real" transformational moments. But, what you may not know (or not have even considered) is at one time each one of them was either staying on a production plateau or their business was in a decline. And, each one of those advisors had once considered whether or not they wanted to take a leap of faith and invest in themselves in order for them to succeed. Luckily, they made the right choice and for many of them their journey still continues with me to this day.

Also, it's important for you to keep in mind that someday, it will be your last day in the business. You will wake up and realize that ten, twenty, thirty or even forty years have passed. On that day you will be leaving a legacy.

How do you want to be remembered? Do you want to be known for someone who was stuck in complacency doing only the bare minimum to get by? Or, do you want to be known for hitting the pinnacle of success and someone who lived a life full of honesty, integrity and who gave exceptional advice?

My parting words to you is something that I mentioned at the beginning of this book, but I hope you can commit them to memory and take them to heart if you are a rookie financial advisor or a multi-million dollar producer, all financial advisors go through the same or similar challenges so it is important to know that there is always a solution. Also, that you are not alone on this journey. You CAN build a better business…one solution at a time. This book offers you a whole lot of them.

P.S. I would love to hear how this book's Tools, Techniques and Transformational Moments work for you. Please email me at dan@advisorsolutionsinc.com and share your success stories!

Acknowledgements

As I begin to reflect on the magnitude of this book's journey, I am quickly reminded of the sage advice that was given to me over twenty-five years ago by a top producer in the office when she said, *"Building a business is a marathon...not a sprint."*

Little did I know at the time, how true her words were. Building my business has been a marathon event, one which helped me move from my grand illusion of believing that it would be easy into the harsh reality of discovering challenges, which I never knew existed. These realizations quickly turned to a fascination for finding solutions, which eventually led to a fork in the road.

In one direction, the familiar path of growing my investment advisory business as a financial advisor and in the other direction, taking an uncharted path of growing a business development consulting and coaching service as a coach helping others enjoy their journey. I ultimately chose the path less traveled, and I have found that it has made all the difference, both for myself as well as for my financial advisor clients, many of who I am honored to also call friends.

Like building my business, writing this book was a marathon, not a sprint. This book's journey began thirty-years ago—the day I opened the want ads and read, *"Investment Advisor Wanted"*— not because I began writing this book at that time, but it was then that I began to have the experiences that would eventually contribute to the material in this book.

Ironically, it is not the "starting gun" event, which initially needs acknowledgement, but rather the "finish line" moment, which should be acknowledged first...

To Melissa Denham, my editor, colleague and friend— your natural ability to "wordsmith" my rough drafts have been THE #1 SOLUTION in making this book a reality. Without you this would be an unedited, typo-filled manuscript in a three ring binder collecting dust at the side of my desk. Instead, this is a book that we both can be proud of. The thanks and praise I give to you for clarifying my written words, while maintaining my voice could fill this page. I am now and will always be ever grateful.

I am also grateful that you followed your own path to create your business, The Word Muse. I truly believe that you are correct, in that your wheelhouse is in the ability to translate other's thoughts, perspectives or point-of-views into crafty, original and captivating copy. If you are looking for the wordsmith to help you turn your dream of writing a book into a reality then she is your gal! Check her out on the web at www.thewordmuse.com.

Professionally, let me begin by saying thank you to the three principal partners at Portz, Knackers and Grant Inc.—a registered investment advisory firm in Milwaukee, WI, Tom Portz, Tom Knackers and Chris Grant, who not only placed the ad in the paper many years ago, but who gave me the opportunity to enter into this business, I am indebted to each of you as without each of you, who knows what path I would have taken.

To many of my former branch managers in the financial services industry, each playing a pivotal role in my business development— your mentoring has had a rippling effect on hundreds of other financial advisors whom you will never know.

To Steve Cramer-my former branch manager at A.G. Edwards who was kind enough to give me a place that I could call home—my office in Milwaukee. Your genuine support and willingness to help me go from surviving to thriving is a debt I can never repay. Thank you for supporting my decision to move back to the Twin Cities.

I wish to also thank Mike McCarty-my former branch manager at A.G. Edwards in Minneapolis, whose support and encouragement gave me the strength to move my business 350 miles so I could be closer to family. You were always a pillar of strength. May you rest in peace.

Thank you to John Eckman—my former branch manager at A.G. Edwards who encouraged me to create "stretch" goals—I will never forget and will always appreciate your response to the top producer you recruited who wanted my office when you said, *"I can't kick him out, he was the number one producer this month!"*

To David Gibb—my former branch manager at Wells Fargo Investments, who not only recruited me, but gave me one of the best bank branches in the most affluent suburbs in the Twin Cities. I appreciate the opportunity to be a part of the bank brokerage culture. It has helped me understand the challenges and solutions that my bank financial advisors go through.

Finally, to Steve Kruchten, my former branch manager at Wells Fargo Investments, who for being only two years older than me seems to have decades more of insight into this business. Thank you for being a great mentor!

To my friends and former colleagues (from my early years in the industry)—Tom Dornoff and Michael Shannon, who took it upon themselves to become my mentors as well as surrogate big brothers— thank you for your genuine willingness to help a brand new rookie learn from your mistakes. I am now and will forever be grateful. I truly am proud to call you both my friends (and I always knew you would become top producers).

To my close friends who met me after my journey as a financial advisor began—David Wolf, Brian Keenen, Todd London and Fred Lawrence.

David, your continued encouragement, support and friendship for the past twenty-eight years has been a true blessing. If there were ever a medal for having a positive outlook on life, you would receive it. I sincerely appreciate all of your help and look forward to your continued success.

Brian, your continued interest, encouragement and motivation on this project as well as countless others business and personal things "going on" in my life have always been the nudge I've need when I've felt that I didn't want to take the next step. I am truly grateful for your friendship.

Todd, thank you for your continued support and enthusiasm as I have kept you updated on the progress of this book, as well as my business. Our Saturday morning breakfasts have been one of the biggest highlights of my weeks! I am proud to call you one of my good friends.

Fred, thank you for your interest, input and inspiration on this journey called life. I am truly honored to be your friend and the godfather of your daughter.

A special thank you goes out to a man who will not be able to read the words, but hopefully will indeed hear the message and know that I appreciated his constant and never-ending encouragement—Gene Lawrence. Although it's been sixteen years since your passing your words are still as true today as they were then when you said, *"Anything can happen..."*

To those who knew me well before my journey as a financial advisor, business coach or author ever began—Jim Shortreed, Dick Howe, Rod Balliette, Gary Malinowski, Brady Halverson, Joe Wachtler and Todd Cook. Thank you for your genuine enthusiasm as I continuously updated you on the progress of this book; my standard phrase *"We are getting close to being finished"* was never questioned. I cherish my band of brothers!

To my siblings—Tim Finley, Jim "Buck" Finley, Mindi Tronnier and Lisa Finley-Hofmann—thank you for keeping me grounded as well as loved. I appreciate your never-ending patience and support as I attempted to explain the inner workings of this book; your spouses Tina Finley, Mary Jo Finley, Matt Tronnier and Tim Hofmann as well as your collective thirteen children, eight grandchildren (and one on the way) have enriched my life beyond words. I am proud of all that you have accomplished and I'm grateful to be your brother, brother-in-law, as well as your children's uncle and great-uncle.

To my aunts—Marlene Meier, Sandy Richardson and Mary Ann Cavender—thank you for your continued interest in my business as well as the progress of this book as well as your confidence in my ability to write it. I will never forget your reply Aunt Mary Ann, when at age fourteen I announced my dream of one day writing a book; you confidently replied, *"I believe you can."*

And lastly, to my father and mother—David and Kathy Finley, who have always given me a wealth of unconditional love and support; it is hard to imagine even attempting to write this book, much less become a financial advisor as well as a business consultant/coach without both of you. As I said in the dedication, it's amazing how a parent's love can fuel a child's dream; thus, my tank is forever full.

Mom, if there were an award for love and encouragement, you would receive it every year. Thank you for your unconditional love, encouragement and compassion! Dad, you lived a life of faith, unconditional love for family, friends and even strangers and you left that love as your legacy for all that had the gift of having you in their lives. My wish (as it is the wish of all that love you) is that you were still alive today. As I said at your recent funeral, *"Thank you for being MY dad."* And, as you said in the midst of your physical pain, *"God is good, all the time!"*

References

Allen, D. (2015). *Getting Things Done: The Art of Stress-Free Productivity* (2nd ed.). Penguin Books.

Canfield, J., & Hansen, M. (2013). *Chicken Soup for the Soul.* (20th Ed.) Amy Newmark Publishing.

Covey, S. (2020). *The 7 Habits of Highly Effective People* (30th ed.). Simon & Schuster.

Dickens. C. (1843). *A Christmas Carol.* Chapman & Hall.

Finley, D. (2011). *101 Advisor Solutions: A Financial Advisor's Guide to Strategies that Educate, Motivate and Inspire.* Lulu Publishing.

Hill, N. (2016). *Think and Grow Rich.* Sound Wisdom Publishing

Warren, R. (2004). *The Purpose Driven Life: What on Earth Am I Here For.* Zondervan Publishing.

About Advisor Solutions

Advisor Solutions is a financial advisor business development consulting & coaching service run by experienced, successful financial advisors. We have designed a proven system that will help any advisor build a better business.

Whether you are a brand new advisor or a seasoned veteran wanting to create the business you have always dreamed about, **Advisor Solutions** can help guide YOU to build a better business!

Our mission at **Advisor Solutions** is to give you successful tools, techniques, camaraderie and ancillary learning to succeed in each of the eight most important facets of your business; *time management, prospecting, sales, relationship building, client servicing, marketing, product and financial market knowledge* as well as *portfolio management.*

Advisor Solutions has a number of coaching programs to help you reach your goals. They are as follows:

Advisor Solutions Financial Advisor One-on-One Coaching is a unique blend of three types of coaching modalities: *Fundamental Coaching,* which is designed to focus on fundamental tools that **Advisor Solutions** has created, *Topic Coaching,* which is designed to address any one of 24 different topics, and *Situational Coaching,* which is designed to focus on specific business opportunities within an advisor's pipeline.

Each 45-minute coaching session may focus on one or all three of these types of modalities. This is not a cookie-cutter coaching approach, but rather a highly specialized coaching service tailored to each financial advisor's specific challenges and solutions.

Advisor Solutions Master Class Group Coaching Program is a monthly group coaching program that accelerates the advisor/agent's ability to turn what they have learned into a habit; thus, mastering each month's topic! Just like anything in life, having a strategy is a must for increasing the probability of success.

This group coaching program is designed to create an intense amount of understanding around a specific topic and to help the advisor/agent apply that knowledge first in a group coaching setting and then each week in the real world to further hone those new habits.

The Advisor Life Group Coaching Program is the perfect complement to the book **Advisor Life:** *A Business Coach's Collection of Short Stories with Tools, Techniques and Transformational Moments.* Each group coaching session is designed to focus on one tool, technique or transformational moment in the book.

The group members read the story, discuss the concept, and share their answers from that week's questionnaire on how the concept pertains to their business and then applies the weekly action step. This group coaching program is designed to take the concepts in the book to the next level by creating additional awareness of how they pertain to the advisor or agent, action steps to apply what is learned and accountability to share the results, so the advisor or agent creates new habits and works smarter instead of just harder.

The Advisor Solutions Team Coaching Program is a groundbreaking, unique blend of Group, Team, Mastermind and Individual Coaching, which will help you and your team members build a better financial services business. It is designed for million dollar and multi-million dollar teams. To fully understand how team coaching can help you and your team, you must first understand the Team Coaching Process.

Advisor Solutions believes that to have truly effective teams, each team member needs to understand the vision of the team, team goals, team expectations, individual roles within the team as well as be able to quantify each team members expectations of the others in the team. This is a six-month group coaching program that will change your business.

Advisor Solutions' Mastermind Group Coaching Program assists advisors specifically on facets of their business that they need to improve upon in order to get to the next level. The ***Mastermind Group Coaching Program*** is about actively applying the information an advisor learned in individual and/or other group coaching program course material; as a result, each group member is required to be in a group coaching before entering the ***Mastermind Group Coaching Program***.

This program has two unique characteristics about it; **The Advisor Solutions** *Mastermind Action Guide*—a 240 page action guide, which compliments the previous group coaching course material, and *The Solutions Journal*—a 24 week journal to record the advisor's progress. Both features complement each other to ensure sustainability of the overall material as well as focus on specific challenges and solutions for building a better business. It's not enough just to learn "what" to do, but rather "how" to actively do it.

In addition, **Advisor Solutions** offers a number of business building products and services:

- **Building Your Business Blueprint:** *A Financial Advisor's Guide to Accomplishing Your Goals*
- **The Solutions Series:** Turning Obstacles into Opportunities
- **The Advisor Solutions Toolbox** Audio Book
- **The 25 Most Common Ways to Conquer Rejection**

To receive an overview on any of our coaching programs or to sign up for **Advisor Solutions** e-newsletters and podcast, email dan@advisorsolutionsinc.com.

About the Author

Daniel C. Finley is the President and Co-Founder of **Advisor Solutions**—the Premier Financial Advisors Business Consulting and Coaching Service dedicated to helping Financial Advisors Build a Better Business.

His 30-year financial services career began in 1993 and includes 13 years as a successful financial advisor. Dan has acquired over 25,000 hours of individual and group sessions coaching financial advisors and insurance agents since 2004. His financial advisory and consulting experience includes all three major channels of distribution: wire house, bank and independent. He has personally experienced and coached successful strategies in all types of business environments so he truly understands the financial advisory business. He has held licenses with the NASD, (Series 7, 63, 65) life, health and annuity.

He is the creator of the Advisor Solution *S.M.A.R.T. Start Financial Advisor Coaching Program*, which stands for **"Systematically Managing Activities Requires Training"**. **Advisor Solutions** *S.M.A.R.T Start Financial Advisor Coaching Program* is a dynamic experience that takes an individual along a path of business awareness, action and accountability by focusing on over 400 pages of course material covering 24-Weeks of group coaching.

Dan also has several advanced tiers of coaching programs including *Pipeline and Sales 1.0 and 2.0 Group Coaching, Advisor's Edge Group Coaching* and *Master Class Coaching*. In addition, he is launching his *The Advisor Life Group Coaching Program* based on the tools, techniques and transformational moments from this book.

He has facilitated one hour, two hour, half day and full day in house training workshops for financial advisory associations, independent broker/dealers as well as national insurance and financial advisory firms in the United States. Dan has also worked remotely with over 100 financial advisors in Canada at a time.

Dan has published numerous articles for the *Financial Planning Association (F.P.A), Advisor Max, National Association of Insurance and Financial Advisors (NAIFA), Horsesmouth, Association of Financial Counseling, Planning and Education (AFCPE)* and *Annuity Selling Guide*. Dan is actively engaged in discussion boards, expert panels and webinars for many of those same affiliates.

Dan is also the host of **The Advisor Solutions Podcast**, a weekly podcast designed to give real world solutions to financial advisors and insurance agents. This program is heard in eighteen countries around the world each week!

He published his first book, **101 Advisor Solutions:** *A Financial Advisor's Guide to Strategies that Educate, Motivate and Inspire* in December 2011.

Made in the USA
Columbia, SC
03 December 2023

9b5d6150-e35d-4b85-8c29-1ca1fa381a66R02